Megatrends Asia

The Eight Asian Megatrends that are Changing the World

John Naisbitt

NICHOLAS BREALEY
PUBLISHING

LONDON

This paperback edition first published in 1997 by
Nicholas Brealey Publishing Limited
36 John Street
London WC1N 2AT
Tel: +44 (0)171 430 0224
Fax: +44 (0)171 404 8311

First published in Asia in 1995 and in Great Britain in 1996
Reprinted 1995, 1996 (with corrections)

ISBN 1-85788-144-3

British Library Cataloguing in Publication Data
A catalogue record for this book is available from the British
Library.

Printed in the UK by Biddles Ltd.

Contents

For my grandchildren:
Rory, Lily, Jake, Abe, Sophie, Eli, Eric, Paul,
and Hannah Rose,
who will know a lot more about Asia than we do

Acknowledgements

Any acknowledgements for contributions to this book, and there are many, must begin with my debt to Foong Wai Fong who has been my partner since the beginning. Not only could I not have finished *Megatrends Asia* without her; I would never have taken it on without her. Wai Fong is an outstanding representative of that new Asian phenomenon — young entrepreneurial women. She is the founder and Managing Director of the Transforma Group of Companies, based in Kuala Lumpur, Malaysia. Wai Fong has been my collaborator from conception through research, the dialogues, writing and editing. Her extensive knowledge of Asia and her extraordinary intelligence have instructed the creation of this book every step of the way. While the final judgements are mine, I could not have made them without her. My advice to almost everyone who wants to do business in Asia is to get an Overseas Chinese partner. I could not have chosen a better one.

My second large debt is to my long-time researcher, Joy Van Elderen. I doubt that there is a better researcher in the book world than Joy, who performed superbly again this time around. My heartfelt thanks and gratitude go to Patricia Aburdene who edited the entire manuscript, and whose support of my work on this project will always be cherished. My thanks also go to Corinne Kuypers-Denlinger, researcher and writer, who was there yet again as she has been on project after project for the last 15 years. My old friend Steve Rhinesmith read the manuscript and, as always, had valuable advice and comments. To Linda McLean Harned my grateful thanks for managing my office, my itinerary, and thousands of complicated details and arrangements, and for reading and commenting on the manuscript.

I must give special thanks to my German-language publisher, Doris Dinklage, of Signum Verlag in Vienna. Her entrepreneurial verve and attention to getting the job done resulted in *Megatrends Asia* being published first in German, and thereby helped me make the deadline for the other editions as well. Nick Brealey, founder of Nicholas Brealey Publishing in the UK, was an early supporter and, as always, very helpful on the editorial side as well. Fred Hills, my editor at Simon & Schuster, New York, is a joy to work with, a true professional, always on top of his game. My agent Bill Leigh orchestrated the business side with these and other publishers and also provided invaluable editorial advice and counsel, for which I am very grateful.

My grateful thanks go to Gordon Crovitz, the brilliant young editor and publisher of the *Far Eastern Economic Review*, who offered early support and convened a wonderful dialogue meeting in Hong Kong. Under his stewardship the Review is today by far the most important source of information and intelligence about Asia (as the many references in this book attest).

I send very special thanks to Dr Noordin Sopiee, the Director General of the Institute of Strategic and International Studies (ISIS) Malaysia in Kuala Lumpur, the head of the Asian institution where I serve as an International Fellow, for his steadfast and generous support throughout this project.

Lastly, my thanks to all the participants in the dialogues that were held throughout the region, and especially to the conveners of these extremely fruitful sessions: Ambassador Tommy Koh (Singapore); Jusuf Wanandi, Chairman, Supervisory Board of Center for Strategic & International Studies (Jakarta); Gloria L Tan Climaco, Chairman and Managing Director of Sycip Gorres Velayo (SGV) & Co (Manila); Prof Charas Suwanwela, MD, President of Chulalongkorn University (Nangkok); George Fields, whose books in both Japanese and English have served us all so well (Tokyo); Dianne Ying, Editor of *Commonwealth* (Taipei); Gordon Crovitz, Editor and Publisher, *Far Eastern Economic Review* (Hong Kong); Dr Cha Dong-Se, President of Korea Development Institute (Seoul); and Prakash Hebalkar, President, Profitech (Bombay).

Introduction

The Asian Renaissance

Since publishing the hardcover edition of *Megatrends Asia* a year ago, a backlash has set in — a backlash that derides the great economic game of the countries of Asia, usually under the banner of "The myth of the Asian economic miracle" or "Growth in Asia will soon level off" or "Asian growth rates are not sustainable".

The "Asian miracle" is a set-up. It comes from the West, and belittles the East. The hard-working Asian entrepreneurs do not identify with their efforts being called a "miracle". It was the West — not knowing much about the East — who called it a "miracle". And now some in the West — again without knowing much about it — are calling the "miracle" a "myth".

So here is the riddle: "It is not a miracle, and the miracle is not a myth".

A backlash to globalization has also begun, the same globalization that has served Asia so well. Globalization is now being demonized — mostly by the political left in the West — as a sinister plot against workers and the poor, led, of course, by the United States. Two anti-globalization conferences were held last spring in Washington and New York.

For example, a young Dutch television producer told me during an interview in London that McDonald's, Time Warner and Disney — among others — had created globalization to dominate the world and hold down the masses.

The reality is that in today's globalization, almost everyone stands to gain. It is the best thing that has happened to developing countries. Hundreds of millions of people have been lifted out of poverty. Standards of living are rising all over the world. Now the same people who tend to rail against third world poverty are fiercely attacking the very process that is finally making these countries rich, moving them towards affluence.

Globalization is not an ideological belief. It is a phenomenon, like the Industrial Revolution, and in my view just as inevitable and beneficial.

In lecturing about Asia all over the world during the last year, I have come to believe that there are six considerations about Asia today that are not emphasized enough.

The first is **entrepreneurship**. The new economies of Asia have been created by millions of entrepreneurs from the bottom up. Governments have increasingly moved out of the way. The billionaire entrepreneurs like Li Ka-shing and Robert Kuok have almost rockstar status in Asia. But they are only the tip of the iceberg, standing on the shoulders of Asia's millions of entrepreneurs, especially the Chinese overseas.

The second consideration is the **reverse brain drain**. As I say in this book, the best thing to happen to Asia in the 1960s, 1970s and 1980s was the millions of young people it sent to the West to be trained and educated. Now this enormous resource of talent is returning to Asia, including Nobel Prize winner Dr Lee Yuen Tseh who left the faculty of the University of California, Berkeley, gave up his US citizenship and returned to Taiwan to become President of the Academia Sinica. Dr Lee has become something of a symbol of the reverse brain drain.

At an open lecture I recently gave at Nanjing University, the Chinese students cheered when I said that the main reason for the reverse brain drain was that the opportunities in Asia today are far greater than those in the West. Now young Westerners are going to Asia to check out these opportunities.

The third consideration is the **importance of the Chinese overseas** in Asia's great economic development. I am deliberately calling the overseas Chinese the Chinese overseas, because about 90 percent of these Chinese are citizens of the countries in which they reside. "Overseas Chinese" suggests that they are still part of China. This subject is covered at some length in the book, where I now use the terms "Chinese overseas" and "ethnic Chinese".

The fourth is that these are **young countries**, just getting underway. For the countries of Southeast Asia the West's Cold War was the post-colonization period. They got their independence (except for Thailand which was never colonized) only in the 1940s and 1950s.

The fifth is the unappreciated **level of sophistication** of Asia's great urban centers. Many in the West who have never been to Asia, or who have not been there for a long time, have the mindset that Asia is a fairly primitive place when, for example, Asia's best hotels and best airlines are better than those in the West. The just completed Patronas Towers — the tallest structures in the world — in Kuala Lumpur (who would have guessed?) symbolize the modernization of Asia's cities.

The sixth consideration is what we might call the **Easternization of the West**. There has been a widespread concern in Asia that the modernization of Asia would mean the Westernization of Asia. This has led to a high level of consciousness about modernizing Asia in the "Asian way". Asia's influence on the West is less discussed. As Asian countries become increasingly economically successful, attention is being called to their emphasis on the primacy of families taking care of themselves, compared to the perceived deterioration of the family in the West, especially in the United States. Eastern art is undergoing a dramatic renaissance which will have a great impact on the West. An early harbinger of the East's influence has been the West's extraordinary interest in Eastern religions. Buddhism is one of the fastest growing religions in the West. And Hong Kong's Gordon Wu giving Princeton University

$100 million was a dramatic example of the East helping the West. Taiwan successfully staged its first democratic presidential election, although the institutions and culture necessary for Western-style democracy to operate effectively are not yet established. Almost all media attention was focused on China's military posturing during the run-up to the election. But the big story remains the integration of the economies of Taiwan and the mainland. Officially, Taiwan has invested $27 billion in projects and joint ventures in China. Some people put the figure at closer to $50 billion. There are tens of thousands of Taiwanese/Chinese joint ventures on the mainland. On a visit to Shanghai during the spring military manoeuvers I met with some of a dozen Chinese entrepreneurs who had been in Taiwan making joint venture deals when the missiles were being shot in the Straits. Business as usual. The integration of the economies is the important story, the end of which will in my view be some kind of face-saving arrangement in which Taiwan will be said to be part of China while continuing its independent ways.

The question I am asked most often in the West has to do with Hong Kong and 1997. This is partly because people in the West know so little about Asia, and Hong Kong's return to China is one of the few things they read about in the Western press. My answer is that not much will happen at all. It will be quite a smooth turn of the wheel. China needs Hong Kong (as it is) a great deal more than Hong Kong needs China. Although it could be said that as part of China Hong Kong will be more important in the world as a financial center. I always end my comments about Hong Kong with what for me is a rhetorical question: in the year 2010, do you think Hong Kong will look more like China, or will China look more like Hong Kong?

In the 1990s Asia came of age. As we move toward the year 2000, Asia will become the dominant region of the world: economically, politically, and culturally. We are on the threshold of the Asian Renaissance. If you have any doubts about the speed with which that megashift is occurring, I believe they will be erased, one by one, as you read this book. This is not a change the rest of the world will readily accept. Yet it is time for all of us to face reality. And to devise a strategy for change. This book will help you do just that. It will provide the data, trend analysis, regional and cultural patterns that will empower you to seize the moment and profit from the cutting edge of change. If you are a small to midsize producer of consumer goods, for example, why should you consider Thailand, let's say over South Korea, as your next market?

Given the extraordinary changes in the works, it is high time for the West to try to see the world from Asia's perspective.

In Asia, for example, it is widely believed that the West is losing moral standing internationally, as shown in its lack of leadership in the crisis in Bosnia-Herzegovina (there are more than 500 million Muslims in Asia). Given this perception, Asians are increasingly irritated by the West's lecturing and hectoring on freedom and human rights.

America's moralizing may come back to haunt it. Down the road imagine a big, economically powerful China threatening to withhold Most Favored Nation status from the US unless it did something about the slums in its big urban centers (or improved those SAT scores!).

A new network of nations based on economic symbiosis is emerging: the Asian network. A spirit of working together for mutual economic gain, a new Asian collaboration, is emerging in Asia for the first time. The catalyst is the free market.

The old Asia was divided by culture, language, political ideology, religious philosophies and geography. The new Asia, forged by economic integration, technology, especially telecommunications, travel and mobility of people, will increasingly look like one coherent region. My Telluride neighbor and friend, John Lifton, an Englishman, remembers that in the 1960s young people in Europe began for the first time to call themselves Europeans, rather than English, French, or

German, just as many young people throughout Asia are beginning to call themselves Asians.

Reflecting this, *Megatrends Asia* is not a country-by-country inventory, but descriptions and predictions about subject areas that cut across Asia. It is a story about Asia as the continent it is and will become.

All the more than 30 countries in Asia are dealt with to one degree or other in this book, but the principal emphasis will be on China, Hong Kong, India, Indonesia, Japan, South Korea, Malaysia, the Philippines, Singapore, Taiwan, Thailand, and Vietnam. These are where the main dynamic of growth and change is located. I have visited and worked in all of these countries, some of them many times. During the process of writing this book and with the help of my Asian friends, I engaged in a series of dialogues with key government, business, academic and community leaders in Singapore, Kuala Lumpur, Jakarta, Manila, Bangkok, Bombay, Hong Kong, Taipei, Tokyo, Seoul and Nanjing, in order to gather Asian voices and insights (their names are all listed at the end of the book). In addition, my staff in Kuala Lumpur, conversant in many Asian languages, did a content analysis of the region's leading newspapers and periodicals.

Up until the 1990s everything revolved around the West. The West set the rules. Japan was run by those rules during its economic emergence. But now Asians — the rest of Asia — are creating their own rules and will soon determine the game as well. Even Japan will be left behind as the countries of Southeast Asia, led by the ethnic Chinese and China, increasingly hold economic sway.

As far as Hong Kong is concerned, it sometimes seems as if Westerners think China is stealing a little European outpost. Hong Kong is China.

Peking changed its name to Beijing; Saigon became Ho Chi Ming City; Burma became Myanmar. Just recently, Bombay was renamed Mumbai. How many people in the West took notice? These are symbolic changes, and we will have more of them.

When Macau returns to China at the end of this decade, the final chapter of Western dominance will have been written. For the first time in 400 years, every inch of Asian soil will be controlled and managed by Asians.

As I pointed out earlier, the modernization of Asia must not be thought of as the *Westernization* of Asia, but the modernization of Asia in the "Asian Way".

At the same time as Asia is modernizing, the Asian conscience is rising. It is very much the Asianization of Asia.

The West needs the East a lot more than the East needs the West.

The Asian continent, from India to Japan, from below the old Soviet Union down to Indonesia, now accounts for more than half of the world's population. Within five years or less, more than half of these Asian households will be able to buy an array of consumer goods — refrigerators, television sets, washing machines, computers, cosmetics, etc. And as many as half a billion will be what the West understands as middle class. That market is roughly the size of the US and Europe combined. As the widely placed Hongkong Bank advert says, "There are 3 billion people in Asia. Half of them are under 25. Consider it a growing market." This is a consumer miracle holding vast economic consequences.

Many Asians have told me that they believe in the long run they will best the West competitively because they do not have and will not have a social security system, or any of the other manifestations of the welfare state. Yet this is an economic factor most Westerners have completely closed their eyes to. What does it mean, particularly in economic terms?

In Asia families take care of themselves, above all else, and personal responsibility is emphasized. For Asians, the very idea of a central government being involved in family life is culturally unthinkable, horrifying. The concept of taking care of family first is why the savings rate in Asia is 30 percent or more in almost every country. Asia lives out family values and self-sufficiency.

Not only do Asians believe the cost of the welfare state is a heavy burden on competitiveness, they also contend that it undermines the importance of family and leads to out-of-wedlock children (in the US 30 percent of children are born out of wedlock, while in Malaysia it is 2 percent), high divorce rates, crime, loss of self-reliance, and lower academic achievement.

This raises central questions for the West, especially for the US and Europe. Are our welfare states now burdening our global competitiveness to a point where we must make some changes? Have they undermined the self-reliance of our citizens? Has our noble experiment failed? It is, I think, important to notice that today every country in the West, including the United States, is trying to cut back on welfare state excesses.

What can Asia teach the West and its young people? Buried under the collapsed department store in Seoul for 10 days, 20-year-old Korean Choi Myong Sok became a youth hero in his country. Businesses were eager to cash in on his image of courage with lucrative media offers. But Choi would have none of it. "They don't understand my pain," he said. "They just want to make money. I don't believe in that." Can Asia's philosophy and teachings help to spark off a global moral renaissance, led by Asians?

In the West the least understood Asian phenomenon is the role of the ethnic Chinese who live outside the mainland of China, not only in Taiwan, Hong Kong, and Singapore, but also those in Indonesia, the Philippines, Malaysia, Thailand — and in Vancouver and Los Angeles and London. The most successful entrepreneurs in the world, they are the force that will catapult Asia to economic dominance.

Paradoxes abound. BMW is now assembling cars in Vietnam, paying its auto workers $1 a day, while the hotels of Asia's cities (including Saigon and Hanoi) are among the most expensive in the world.

Fifty years from now, it will be clear that the most momentous global development of the 1990s and the early part of the twenty-first century was the modernization of Asia. The chapters of this book describe the eight major shifts taking place in Asia today:

⊕ **From Nation States → Networks.** Japan's economic dominance has reached its apex, and its relative economic position in Asia and the world is on a long downward slide. The power of Japan as a nation-state is giving way to the dynamic collaboration of the Chinese network. Considerations about China and the ethnic Chinese now drive decision making in Asia as China becomes central to the total Pacific region. But it is the ethnic Chinese network that will dominate the region — not China.

⊕ **From Export-led → Consumer-driven.** Built on exports, Asian economies will increasingly be fueled by consumer spending and, with it, the emerging middle class. By the year 2000, Asia will have almost half a billion people who are what we generally understand as middle class.

⊕ **From Western Influence → the Asian Way.** The most significant development of the 1990s and the following few decades will be Asia's modernization. In economic competition, the West is handicapped by the heavy burden of the welfare state, which the East will not adopt, but new options in all aspects of life are now open to Asians.

⊕ **From Government-driven → Market-driven.** Central government control and direction of the economies of the region have shifted to market economies, fueling an explosion of economic growth and opportunities. This has been accompanied by unprecedented economic cooperation and coordination among the countries of Asia.

From Villages → Supercities. Migration from rural areas of Asia to its cities is taking place at an astounding pace. This urban shift is transforming Asia, moving it to the next era of development, away from agricultural societies to those where telecommunications and the information age dominate.

From Labor-intensive → High Technology. We are witnessing a dramatic shift from labor-intensive agriculture and manufacturing to state-of-the-art technology in manufacturing and services, most pronounced in the rush to computers and telecommunications.

From Male Dominance → Emergence of Women. The shift from male dominance is most apparent in the increase of women entrepreneurs throughout Asia. In China, women make up 25 percent of all entrepreneurs. Women are participating in all aspects of Asian life in unprecedented ways, as voters, consumers and members of the workforce.

From West → East. The world used to mean the Western world. Today, global trends are forcing us to confront a reality: the rise of the East. It is becoming apparent to those in the East and to some in the West that we are moving towards the Asianization of the world. The global axis of influence has shifted from West to East. **Asia was once the center of the world, and now the center is again returning to Asia.**

These are eight Asian megatrends that are reshaping the world. For the Chinese, eight is a very lucky number. Some people in Hong Kong pay hundreds of dollars to get an 8 on their license plate or in their phone number.

Also for the Chinese, the year 2000 is the year of the dragon, the year that will usher in the Dragon Century.

1

From Nation-states

$\longrightarrow$ *Networks*

"The Japanese are coming." For so many years it appeared the Japanese were going to dominate the world economically. But now the shift is to the global network of Chinese entrepreneurs. In the new global economy nation-states are becoming irrelevant; networks will dominate.

Japanese economic power has reached its peak and begun to recede as the Chinese prepare for the Dragon Century.

There are some people in Asia who already have a sense of the real importance of the events occurring today. In the West, preoccupied with its own well-being, almost no one has the faintest idea that what is going on in Asia today will radically change the world. The economic resurgence of Asia, driven by an aggressive global network of Chinese entrepreneurs and off-shore money, is moving in the direction of eclipsing the West. Unless the US and Europe start to participate in the new Asian game, they will end up playing very second fiddle to the new global leaders in Asia by as early as the beginning of the next decade.

The US's gaze (especially in the media-thick northeast) continues to be toward Europe. And while what has happened in the old Soviet Union and Eastern Europe will in time greatly affect the rest of the world, it will not compare with the impact the changes in Asia will have.

The modernization of Asia — economically, politically, and culturally — is by far the most important event taking place in the world today.

China, the Great Dragon, is flexing its economic and political muscle. Asia sees China as a major market, now and in the future. In the context of the region's rapid growth, companies that do not have at least a third of their revenues coming from Asia cannot hope to remain substantial global players.

- About 1,000 Hong Kong companies are already controlled by Chinese state-owned companies, up from just 400 in 1992.
- In China, three million Chinese are employed in 25,000 factories owned by Hong Kong companies — six times the number of employees the companies have in Hong Kong.
- By the end of 1995, annual two-way trade between Taiwan and China had already reached more than $25 billion.
- China's foreign trade in 1995 totaled $280 billion, an increase of 18.3 percent over 1994.
- China is also becoming an important investor in the region: 134 Chinese companies have invested more than $200 million in Malaysia.
- China's economy has doubled in just six years.

The Chinese are coming. But China's potential, as it usurps Japan's economic leadership, is not simply as a nation-state. The true force that the world must promptly come to reckon with is more dynamic. The force at work is a secretive, sophisticated network — invisible to most — that will catapult China and the Chinese to being the world's dominant economy. It is decentralized, pan-Asian, increasingly global, and family and education oriented. And most of all, fabulously rich. It is the phenomenon of the ethnic Chinese. There are 57 million of them, 53 million in Asia alone.

The ethnic Chinese: the new great economic power

This phenomenon has been around for centuries. But only now is the world becoming aware of its extraordinary presence.

The dynamics of Asia's extraordinary growth cannot be understood without a thorough examination of the ethnic Chinese who live outside the mainland, the greatest entrepreneurs in the world. According to an assortment of estimates, Chinese around the world hold between $2 trillion and $3 trillion in assets — many believe the real figure is higher.

In 1994, Chinese language *Forbes Zibenjia*, the franchised edition of *Forbes* magazine published in Hong Kong, analysed the top 1,000 companies (with the highest market capitalization) from 10 Asian stock markets — Seoul, Taipei, Shanghai, Shenzhen, Hong Kong, Bangkok, Kuala Lumpur, Singapore, Jakarta and Manila. Their combined assets total $1,138 billion, or 89 percent of total market capitalization. Of the top 1,000 companies, 517 had an ethnic Chinese as the single largest stockholder. So Chinese overseas controlled $541 billion, some 42 percent of the total in these 10 markets. Quite a bit more than the $200 to $300 billion cited above.

Fujitsu Research in Tokyo looked at the listed companies in just six key Asian countries. As the findings below illustrate, the overwhelming majority were owned by ethnic Chinese.

Ethnic Chinese companies as percent of listed companies			
Thailand	81	Malaysia	62
Singapore	81	Philippines	50
Indonesia	73		

This astonishing revelation of the tremendous economic power of the Chinese is confined to public listed companies. What about the less glamorous small and midsize enterprises which together make up 96 percent of all companies in the APEC (Asia Pacific Economic Cooperation) realm? According to Bustanil Ariffin, the former Indonesian minister who co-chaired the Pacific Business Forum, it is believed that small and midsized companies employ half of the workforce in most Asian countries. Chinese own 90 percent of these small and midsize companies.

The economy of the borderless ethnic Chinese is the third largest economy in the world.

In the thriving new countries of Asia, ethnic Chinese control a huge chunk of the wealth — far more than their numbers might suggest. In Malaysia, they represent almost 30 percent of the population and account for 61 percent of the economy. The numbers elsewhere are even more remarkable:

- Indonesia — 3.5 percent, account for 73 percent of the economy
- Thailand — 10 percent and 81 percent
- the Philippines — 2 percent and 50–60 percent

Some historians go so far as to say that the economies in Southeast Asia were in a sense leased to the ethnic Chinese, while the natives concentrated on government.

The ethnic Chinese are not a nation-state, and the vocabulary and concepts used to think about nation-states will not help us understand the phenomenon.

The science historian Thomas Kuhn pointed out that we simply cannot understand a new paradigm by using the vocabulary of the old paradigm.

Centuries ago, when scientists decided the earth was round, the flat-earth vocabulary and formulations were of no use in understanding a round globe, the new paradigm.

Today, the Cold War is over and market economics prevail,

but we are still thinking with the same vocabulary and concepts. Unless we adapt and create a new vocabulary and new concepts for the new circumstances, we will never know what is going on. The new economy of the world today is dominated by inter-company trade and person-to-person communications. Countries don't trade; people and businesses do. Networks are at the core of the new global economy.

The Chinese overseas are a network of networks. That is a new paradigm, a new formulation within the framework of the world's economy.

- If we counted the economic activity of the ethnic Chinese as a country by itself, it would be outranked only by the US and Japan.
- Ethnic Chinese dominate trade and investment in every East Asian country except Korea and Japan.
- Chinese in Hong Kong, Taiwan and Singapore supply more capital and foreign investment for the region than Japan.
- Ethnic Chinese — not the Japanese — are the largest cross-border investors in Thailand, Malaysia, Indonesia, the Philippines and Vietnam.
- The ethnic Chinese account for 80 percent of all foreign investment in China, in the motherland.
- In 1995 estimates put the number of people in China employed by ethnic Chinese businesses at 20 million.

All the key players among the ethnic Chinese know each other. Their businesses stay singularly apart, but they work together when necessary. They are intensely competitive among themselves, and exclude outsiders, especially those not of the same family, village or clan. When a crisis arises or a great opportunity presents itself, they will close ranks and cooperate. Chinese business boils down to people and contacts. As one Hong Kong banker puts it, "If you are being considered for a new partnership, a personal reference from a respected member of the Chinese business community is worth more than any amount of money you could throw on the table."

The family businesses of the Chinese overseas are networks, of companies and other enterprises, of clans and villages. These networks are in turn woven together to constitute a huge global Chinese network of networks. The Internet is the model for understanding. Just as the Internet is a network of thousands of networks, the ethnic Chinese have tens of thousands of networks together.

The number of networks and individuals on the Internet is not limited because the Internet is totally decentralized. There are now more than 60 million individuals on the Internet. That number could reach 1 billion by the year 2000.

It is decentralized right down to the individual; only the individual can access the Internet. Because of this complete decentralization the Internet can have as many members as want to join. And the ethnic Chinese network can get as big as it needs to be to transform Asia's economy.

The other general characteristic of both the Internet and the ethnic Chinese network is that no one is in charge, or the marketplace is in charge. With the Internet, it is the marketplace of ideas and information, although, more recently, the commercial marketplace as well. With the ethnic Chinese network, market mechanisms are the deciding factor. Motherland or not, economic decisions involving China are driven purely by dictates of the market, guided strictly by rates of return.

Individual ethnic Chinese networks of companies are completely decentralized from the whole; they are extraordinarily efficient parts.

In *Global Paradox*, I posited that the bigger the system, the more efficient must be the parts — to function as a successful system. And because autonomous parts are the most efficient, we could say that the bigger the system, the more autonomous must be the parts. That clearly describes the ethnic Chinese network of networks. The Chinese function efficiently as individuals, in contrast to the Japanese who excel and misbehave collectively. This mode of operation makes the Chinese, and their enterprises, immensely nimble in the competitive global economy. They react speedily to changing conditions, especially to political vagaries.

All powerful networks have one thing in common: each of the parts functions as if it were the center of the network. When I am on the Internet in my home in Telluride, Colorado, sending and receiving messages to others all over the world, I experience being in the center, just as each person does when they are on the Internet. That is very powerful.

Chinese overseas experience the same thing. As each individual deals with other people in their network in various parts of the world, each experiences being in the center of the network. The individualistic Chinese want to have control of their own destiny. The Chinese proverb has it that "there is no prospect working for others". Everyone wants to be at the center and be their own boss. This inner entrepreneurial drive makes them very proactive, risk taking and enterprising.

Joining the global network

Now the entrepreneurs on mainland China are joining the ethnic Chinese network. It is not that the ethnic Chinese are joining China.

The ethnic Chinese form a very self-aware network. Yoji Hamawaki, who is famous in Tokyo for his spectacular success in the introduction of the BMW to Japan and is now with Digital, told me of his discussions with a group of ethnic Chinese who wanted to computerize their network. He told them that the project would cost more than "one billion US dollars". "That will not be a problem," he was told, and got an on-the-spot commitment. The Singapore Chinese Chamber of Commerce is committed to launching a computer network called the World Chinese Business Network, which will link Chinese Chambers of Commerce worldwide. This high-tech link in cyberspace will facilitate the flow of information for all

Chinese entrepreneurs. A Chinese CNN based in Hong Kong, called Chinese Television Network, was launched in December 1994 to provide coverage of events in the worldwide Chinese communities.

To the world it is China. But it is more than China. It is the Chinese network.

It is not who will become part of China. It is who will join the Chinese network, which parts of China, which entrepreneurs in China. Together they will drive the economic transformation of Asia — and the world.

I am more and more convinced, as I said in *Global Paradox*, that the Chinese network is the organizational model for the twenty-first century.

The world is moving from a collection of nation-states to a collection of networks.

Who are the new billionaires?

The world's 57 million ethnic Chinese are dispersed among 60 countries all over the world. But about 85 percent reside in Southeast Asia. There are about 5.5 million Chinese in Malaysia, 6.1 million in Thailand, 6.5 million in Indonesia. More than 1 million Chinese live in Singapore, Philippines, Vietnam. There are more than 1 million Chinese in California, the largest community outside Asia. More than 90 percent are now naturalized citizens; only about 2 million people have kept their Chinese nationality.

The Chinese overseas dominate in general trading and the service industry, and many big players are involved in banking and property. In the last 20 years, expansion in banking and property development activities has become increasingly global. For example, Chinese-owned Bangkok Bank, Thailand's largest bank, is expanding regionally. Asian Chinese banks and property companies are taking up similar interests in North America and other parts of the world. Even the Bank of China, Beijing's main international bank, has a branch in the Cayman islands.

Many of us already think of Taiwan and Hong Kong as part of China. Now we must extend the boundaries of "greater China" to include ethnic Chinese in countries like Singapore, Malaysia, Indonesia.

At the top of the network — or perhaps we should say at the core — are a remarkable number of self-made billionaires. Among them are:

Liem Sioe Liong (net worth $4.5 billion). Liem left the south of China in the 1930s, moving to **Indonesia** where he created a rural trading network. He began to supply the rebels fighting the ruling Dutch, and met a young lieutenant colonel named Suharto. They were partners when Suharto overthrew Sukarno in 1965. This connection helped Liem build his Salim Group with 1994 sales of $9 billion, accounting for 5 percent of Indonesia's GDP. Liem's personal holding company has evolved into a seamless network of enterprises with interests in banking and property.

Robert Kuok (net worth $5.7 billion). Kuok's father came to **Malaysia** from China in 1911 and opened a grocery store. Son Robert went into the commodities trading business in the 1950s, establishing the Malayan Sugar Manufacturing Co. By the 1970s he handled some 10 percent of the world's sugar trade (he was known widely as "The Sugar King"). Kuok now owns the Shangri La chain of luxury hotels. In 1984 he built the China World Trade Center in Beijing. His joint venture with Coca-Cola includes ten factories in China.

Nina Wang (net worth $3.3 billion). In 1998 there will be a grand opening of the $1.3 billion, 1,594-feet high Nina Tower in **Hong Kong**, which will then be, at 108 stories, the world's tallest building. She is Asia's richest woman, and is borrowing no money to finance the construction. "We have always relied on our own resources to finance our projects," says Wang, who took over Chinachem Group when her husband, Teddy Wang, was kidnapped and killed in 1990. She owns all, or some of, 200 buildings in Hong Kong.

Dhanin Chearavanont (net worth $4.2 billion). His family, from Guangdong province in China, moved to **Thailand** in the 1920s, where Dhanin eventually took his Thai name. In the 1950s he set up a new company, Charoen Pokphand (CP), a chicken-feed mill. Today CP is highly diversified with 49 of its more than 200 companies in China. TelecomAsia, a joint venture between CP Group and the US's Nynex Inc., was recently listed on the Bangkok stock exchange.

Li Ka-shing (net worth $10.6 billion). Li's father, a teacher, moved his family to **Hong Kong** in 1940. He died two years later when Li was only 13. After some hard work in factories, Li struck out on his own at 24, starting a plastic flowers business. In 1951, he began buying property. In 1972 Li took his main company, Cheung Kong, public. Today he controls publicly traded companies which account for more than 10 percent of Hong Kong's total stock market value. He is building China's Foreign Ministry offices in Hong Kong, for free according to some sources.

Kwek Leng Beng (net worth $5.7 billion). Kwek runs City Developments in **Singapore**, a property development company. The group made news in the US recently when it was involved in the purchase from Donald Trump of the Plaza Hotel in New York City. He is the eldest son of the late Singapore property tycoon Kwek Hong Png.

Chao Kwan Yuen, a professor of forestry at the University of Beijing, was on vacation in Bangkok with his wife when the Communists took over China in 1949. They choose to stay in **Thailand**. Eventually Chao built the first sugar refinery in Thailand, and the first oil refinery. By the end of the 1960s, he personally accounted for 10 percent of the taxes paid to the government. (In the late 1960s I spent a year apprenticing with Mr Chao in Bangkok. After each of an interminable series of business meetings, he would tell me, "Slowly, slowly; in the end we catch a big fish.")

These are just some of the visible bigwigs. Ethnic Chinese dominated *Forbes* magazine's 1996 list of East Asian billion-

aires, outside of Japan and Korea. Many of the Chinese overseas are rich and some are super rich. It can now be said that
the ethnic Chinese are running things economically in China —
as well as in Southeast Asia.

What has recently become clear to most non-Chinese Asians
is that what is good for the Chinese of Southeast Asia is even
better for the indigenous people and cultures. In a world where
capital and talent know no national allegiance, it will work in
the host country's interest to have players within their midst
who can access a network of capital, ideas, markets and talent.

The Cold War is over and the Chinese won.

Chinese global power

The great Yangtze River in China divided the Chinese people
into two occupational orientations. The northerners preferred
the glory and glamor of the Imperial court, while the southerners sought wealth and money in commerce and trade. The
seats of Chinese governments were almost always north of the
great river; Beijing literally means the northern capital. For centuries, a feud existed between the merchant class and those who
governed. The southern Chinese have always had a refugee-
type, siege mentality. They are forever hiding their wealth,
keeping a low profile so as to be invisible to the governing class
in order to be protected from extortion by corrupt court officials. The merchant class southerners were wary of the government. They stayed away from the centre and sought patronage
with money and gifts so that they could be left alone to make
their fortunes.

For centuries they were used to this mode of operation. They
developed and operated commercial enterprises along the
coastal areas, content to secure the economic well-being of their
families. When conditions at home grew worse due to famines
and natural calamities, they ventured out. They brought this distinct commercial ethic with them to their new homes.

The exodus to the south grew in size and momentum in the nineteenth century. These brave young men set out from China to the South Seas to seek their fortune. China was overcrowded, the backward farmlands could not support its huge populations. Natural calamities and disasters destroyed homes and lives. The Chinese mind is full of vivid images of instability and chaos.

Yet the Chinese are also egocentric: they think of themselves as the children of the dragon, call their country the Middle Kingdom (suggesting the center of the universe), and take great pride in their civilization. But reality and hardship drove some of them to venture afar, hoping to bring back a fortune to enrich their motherland. Large-scale migration started in the years between the Opium War (1830–1842) and the Second World War.

The Han Chinese living along the coastal cities formed the dominant group. Today 85 percent of ethnic Chinese outside mainland China are from southern provinces — Guangdong, Fukien, Hainan, Guangxi — where among other dialects Cantonese is spoken. Cantonese is a broad term used to describe the people living in the Pearl River delta, and they form the major group of ethnic Chinese. That's why most of the world's Chinese restaurants are Cantonese. Much of the world equates Chinese food with Cantonese food, a great distortion since China has a great variety of cuisines.

In the early days, apart from the wandering merchants, what is now the world's wealthiest network was little more than a slave trade. Families received a token sum from contractors and their husbands and sons were shipped off to become laborers in foreign lands. They only hoped that they would return some day with wealth.

Clan networks

As the system evolved, the migrants took care of each other and sheltered each other. They still worked at back-breaking jobs, but the clan associations they formed eased the burden with lodgings, contacts and communal support, helping newcomers settle in their new homelands.

Today there are an estimated 6,000 clan networks in Southeast Asia, which used to serve as contact points for employment, news and exchange, and provided psychological support to newcomers. The clan networks take on different roles today, confining themselves to cultural and community activities, although some ambitious ones are transforming themselves into cooperative and investment holding companies.

No mainframe: just networked PCs. And like all powerful networks, each of the Chinese entrepreneurs experiences being in the center of the network. This works well for the highly individualistic Chinese.

This vast network of clan associations is now serving as a ready platform to help China attract the ethnic Chinese to invest in the mainland. For example, the International Hainanese Association recently convened a meeting of more than 1,000 delegates from 20 countries in Haikow, a southern city in the province of Hainan. To date, the ethnic Hainanese have invested about $250 million in various projects in China.

Integrating locally

In the past, one characteristic of ethnic Chinese enterprises was avoiding long-term investments or businesses with long gestation periods. This was part of the "sojourning" mentality, the desire to return to the homeland after making enough money. Interest in their temporary home was purely economic.

This attitude is changing today. Chinese overseas are tending to invest long term in their adopted homelands. They have been involved in manufacturing, property and finance since the 1960s.

In time, ethnic Chinese assimilate into the local community and contribute to their adopted land.

Contrast Japanese businesses and people who remain Japanese wherever they go. They live in closed Japanese communities and have less occasion to speak English. The Chinese, especially in Southeast Asia, have a working knowledge of many native languages and speak English well, even among themselves. They retain the ability to read and speak Mandarin and Cantonese. The Chinese take on local cultural habits, dress and food. The younger ethnic Chinese generation's command of the language of the new country is indistinguishable from that of the native. Many no longer carry a Chinese name or speak Chinese, though they may still practice distinct Chinese ways and retain many cultural traditions (Chinese food, Chinese celebrations and festivals, Chinese customs, and Confucian values).

Many government officials in Southeast Asia are of Chinese descent, including, for example, the just past Prime Minister of Thailand, Chuan Leekpai, and the current Prime Minister Banharn Silpa-archa. Former President Corazon Aquino of the Philippines is another example. Chinese in Europe, North America and Japan are not as well to do as Asian Chinese, so their influence in politics and government is not as strong. However, in recent years many have become mayors, senators, state governors. Some Chinese in South America are government ministers. (Oddly, the President of Peru, Alberto Fujimore, who is Japanese, is called Chinese and is affectionately known to the people as "Chino".)

Hard work and thrift

One of Asia's most successful ethnic Chinese, Robert Kuok of Malaysia, says:

"As children we learned about moral values — mainly Confucian. Terms such as 'business integrity,' 'honor,' 'your word is your bond,' were often used by the elders and sank into our minds. We would hear from our womenfolk constant urging to remain humble and never practice ostentation. One other interesting thing I learned from my mother was a phrase which literally translates as 'morality of the mouth.' We were not to speak bad of others."

Robert Kuok is known for adhering to these early lessons.

Hard work and thrift are the hallmarks of the Chinese. They work long hours and rarely rest, except for a break during the lunar new year festival. Making money and more money is their preoccupation. Giving their children a good education is a universal Chinese obsession.

Professor Wang Gungwu, Vice Chancellor of Hong Kong University and a noted authority on the study of ethnic Chinese, himself a Chinese born in Indonesia, says, "I believe that these Chinese attitudes towards wealth and culture are still with us."

Wang points out that the Chinese have been trading overseas for more than 1,000 years without the support of their government in China. "They depended instead on their own daring, their skills and, most of all, their entrepreneurship." With no political power themselves, they would link up with those in power in order to achieve their commercial goals. "To achieve wealth while other people held the power was to accept that wealth could not be followed by power in the hands of the merchants themselves." They knew from Chinese history that wealth was safer when the wealthy showed no desire or ambition for political power.

Four roads to travel

These entrepreneurs entertained four possible strategies after they made their fortunes, says Professor Wang. I have recast them somewhat as four archetypes:

- **Returnees**. Accept that living abroad is untenable and therefore take their wealth and return to China.
- **Assimilators/Connectors**. Recognize that total assimilation to the local culture is unavoidable and that to protect

their wealth, they must be connected to those with local
power.

● **Sojourners**. Cultivate entrepreneurial activities in more
than one country, ready to move wealth between various
Chinese communities.

● **Leaders**. Use wealth to achieve extensive influence as leaders in their adopted communities, remaining culturally
Chinese while being loyal citizens of their adopted country.

Successful Chinese entrepreneurs in reality care deeply about
maintaining cultural values in their local community and
strengthening cultural links with China. A good illustration is
how the five million Chinese in Malaysia kept their Chinese
education system alive, entirely through private funding.
Malaysia's Chinese community supports a thriving media of
more than 30 newspapers and magazines in the vernacular
Chinese language.

The *first option*, returning to China, has almost universally
been ruled out. Even with today's openness — and ethnic
Chinese investments are welcomed back with open arms — it is
still easier for most Chinese to make a fortune in Taiwan, Hong
Kong, Malaysia and other parts of Southeast Asia than in China
itself. The system of rule of law introduced by Western colonial
powers in Southeast Asia has created an environment conducive
to Chinese enterprise. Without central authority looking over
their shoulder, and not having to put up with the unpredictability and vagaries of the "rule of man", the ethnic Chinese
flourish in a much more secure environment than they had in
the past.

Chinese overseas do extensive business with mainland entrepreneurs and send a considerable amount of wealth back to
China to build schools and clan temples, and to support rela-
tives. But most ethnic Chinese want to stay abroad to ensure
their security and profitability.

The *second option* — assimilation in the adopted country —
has been widely adopted. Most Chinese who settle abroad

become citizens of their new countries. Some intermarry. But they guard against total assimilation. They continue to hold on to Chinese values regarding business practices, education in the Chinese language, customs and social practices. For younger, well-educated Chinese, assimilation is no longer an issue. After all, the world is becoming a global village. While one can still harbor pride for one's cultural heritage, there is a growing tendency for young people to develop a global mindset.

The *third option* — remaining a sojourner — holds little attraction today. Wang Gungwu defines the sojourning mentality as "that cultural trait or habit of mind among the Chinese that treats every place outside China they may live in as but a temporary home."

Ethnic Chinese entrepreneurs, however, sometimes act like sojourners, doing business from country to country, some commuting between Vancouver and Taipei, between Los Angeles and Singapore. With the gains in air transport and telecommunications, distance isn't what it used to be.

The very idea of the sojourner suggests the Chinese overseas have a very strong attachment to their homeland and its more than 5,000 years of history. And they do. But today it is more of a cultural attachment than a physical one, although going back to visit your home village or that of your ancestors is still a journey that most want to make.

The strategy of maintaining culture while affirming political loyalty to the country of residence — the *fourth option* — is the one most have adopted. While that loyalty is at times questioned, ethnic Chinese the world over affirm their identification with their country of adoption, but without turning their backs on their Chinese cultural roots.

Ethnic Chinese loyalty to Chinese culture is not political. They want to remain ethnically Chinese, but do not want to be citizens of the People's Republic of China.

Chinese overseas tend to keep their heads down, observing the wisdom of the Chinese saying, "The big tree catches the wind."

Nationalist leaders in Southeast Asia have at times been suspicious of the ethnic Chinese. In Indonesia in 1965 anti-Chinese riots killed tens of thousands of ethnic Chinese. At the Second World Chinese Entrepreneur Conference held in Hong Kong at the the end of 1993, Singapore's Senior Minister Lee Kuan Yew felt the need to voice a strong assurance to the governments and people of the host countries of many ethnic Chinese:

> "Ethnic Chinese who come from such 'sensitive' countries, should take care that their investments in their own countries do not diminish as the result of their China investments. And they would do well to use their 'guanxi' to increase China's trade with and investment in their home countries. We are ethnic Chinese. We share certain characteristics through a common ancestry and culture. We can build up trust and rapport easily between ourselves. But we must be honest and recognize the fact that at the end of the day, our fundamental loyalties are to our home, not ancestral, countries. After two or three generations away from China, we have become rooted in the country of our birth. Our stakes are in our home countries, not China where our ancestors came from. The Chinese-Thai is a Thai and in the end he wants Thailand to prosper so that his assets in Thailand can be secure. So too Chinese Singaporeans, Chinese-Malaysians and Chinese-Filipinos. They may invest and visit China frequently, but few want to make China their home."

"Wealth will not last through three generations"

"The father makes the money," goes the Cantonese proverb, "while the son spends it." Deceased Malaysian tycoon Tai Chik Sen, whose family controls the big Soon Seng group, kept a humble lifestyle even after accumulating huge wealth. When local reporters asked about his modest lifestyle in comparison with his sons who are breezing around Kuala Lumpur in flashy BMWs, he replied, "My sons have rich father; I don't."

The rise and fall of family fortunes gives credence to the saying that wealth will not last three generations. The young man who had not known hardship and pain, or how to make money, will not know how to conserve it.

However, for many prominent families a different adage seems to apply: the father builds the business, the son expands it. Many rising sons of ethnic Chinese business families are not only expanding, corporatizing and consolidating family businesses, they are taking them to new heights, thanks to Western education, aggressiveness and global ambition.

A good example — and the talk and envy of corporate Asia — is **Richard Li Tzar-Kai**, 29, son of Hong Kong's number one tycoon Li Ka Shing. Listed as one of *Time* magazine's Global 100 leaders for the new millennium, Richard Li rose to stardom by founding STAR-TV, the first satellite cable-television network, revolutionizing Asia's electronic media overnight. He sold it to Rupert Murdoch's News Corp in 1993 for what ended up being more than $800 million. Richard Li studied economics and computer engineering at Stanford, and is now ready to take to the skies from his base in Singapore, through his new vehicle, Pacific Century Group. He wants to provide satellite telecommunications services across the region. Businesses will buy a six-foot dish and receiver to get a 24-hour dedicated circuit that bypasses local telephone systems by applying a Very Small Aperture Terminal (VSAT) license, a common service in the West. According to Li, "We want to provide Asians with the same basic access to services that the West now takes for granted." Target markets include China, India, Pakistan, Indonesia, Vietnam and the Philippines.

Y. C. Wang's Formosa Plastic Group is one of Taiwan's largest family conglomerates, with $9 billion in revenues. Wang's son, **Winston**, and his two daughters, **Charleen** and **Sher**, are pushing Formosa to greater heights in petrochemicals and electronics. Their global vision includes mainland China and they just ploughed $1 billion into their Texas plant. Asia is watching to see how this second generation of Wangs carry on with their legendary father's enterprise.

Victor Fung, active in his family business and also Chairman of the Hong Kong Trade Development Council, sees a changing mindset in the ethnic Chinese. At the World Chinese Entrepreneurial Conference, he said:

> "We are less inward-looking and more outward-looking. We may still value the family as the single most important unit of our success, but we are poised to move to the next threshold, whereby our small-to-medium sized family companies acquire a multi-national character and a global presence."

Asia's own name brands

"My dream was to make computers available to everyone," says Stan Shih, chief of Acer, Taiwan's premier computer maker. He started with 11 people and just $25,000. Today, the Acer Group is the world's fourth largest maker of PCs and PC parts, and had sales of $5.8 billion in 1995. "My vision for Acer in the year 2000," says Shih, "is to market Acer products as a global brand to countries all over the world." Acer is already the number one PC producer in several countries, and expects to have 21 listed companies and revenues of $15 billion by 2000.

Stan Shih is in the forefront of promoting Asia's own-randed manufacturing. Chairman of Taiwan's Own Brand Federation, he is helping and educating local manufacturers to create strategies of developing their own brands:

> "We [Chinese] have never had our own brands. We are excellent at contract manufacturing for other brands. With the rise of Asian economies, manufacturers in Singapore, mainland China, Hong Kong and Taiwan must seriously contemplate creating world class indige-

nous brands. This will be the aspiration of businesses in the region in the next century."

Expanding the networking model

The networking of the ethnic Chinese is a powerful phenomenon, and few have thought more about it than Singapore's Lee Kuan Yew:

> "It would be a mistake for Singaporean entrepreneurs not to participate in one of the greatest transformations of our age... And we would be foolish not to use the ethnic Chinese network to increase our reach and our grasps of opportunities."

In fact, Lee sees the ethnic Chinese networking model as a way to extend tiny Singapore's powerful reach into other ethnic communities. He wants Indian, Pakistani and Arab businesspeople to "take up residence" in Singapore and serve, in effect, as Singapore's business ambassadors to their home regions. And, of course, Singapore has the best air links and telecommunications infrastructure in the region. Now Lee invites others to embrace the model.

The Chinese overseas can forge key relationships in international cooperation and between their host country and mainland China. That is appreciated — even by the region's most nationalist leaders.

There is yet another side to this networking model. The education-obsessed Chinese have been sending thousands of their children to the world's best universities and private schools in the West. These offspring kept company with the children of the world's business and political power elites at Eton, MIT, Harvard, Stanford, Oxford and Cambridge. Although not initiated by foresight, but more as a response to contingency planning, the ethnic Chinese have created another powerful worldwide network. I heard talk in Taipei of

Taiwanese parents wanting to send their children to universities
in mainland China, this time to bond with the children of the
Grand Dragon's power elites, anticipating the future.

Japan's long downward slide

Ever since Japan began to spread its economic wings, the rest
of Asia has engaged in a need–hate relationship with it. Asians
like Japanese money and knowhow, but they still fear being
dominated by Japan, partly because of residual hostility arising
from the experience of colonization and war. Asians have
looked to Tokyo, rather than Washington, to play a larger role.
But Japan has been reluctant to assume leadership except economically. Asia's response in turn has been fundamentally
ambiguous. It looks to Asia as if Japan has reservations about
genuinely embracing Asian culture. Today there are also com-
plaints about Japan's reluctance to transfer technology and to
localize management.

Japan is, of course, a powerful force in Asia and the world. Yet
its influence in Asia has largely been confined to trade and investment. Japan is the biggest export market for most ASEAN
(Association of South-East Asian Nations) countries. Beginning
in 1990, Japan exported more goods to Asia than to the US.
Japan is also Asia's most important market and one of the
region's biggest investors. But now even that strength is waning.

There are many signs, described in detail in the following
section, that Japan's economic dominance has reached its apex.
Between 1991 and 1995 the Japanese economy was in a kind
of malaise:

- Japan's Gross Domestic Product suffered five consecutive years of stagnation.
- For the first quarter of 1995, Japan's industrial output was 7 percent below its 1991 peak.
- Excess industrial capacity now stands at more than 30 percent.
- At 3.4 percent, Japan's 1995 unemployment rate is the highest since records began in 1953. Because of notorious over-staffing, this figure is unrealistically low. Among 1994 college graduates it stood at a stunning 17 percent.
- In 1995, Toyota announced it would lay off its first workers since 1951. As Japan's number one automaker, that paved the way for others to follow.
- Production costs in Japan are the highest in the world.
- In March 1995, Nissan's leading factory in Zama, outside of Tokyo, became the first Japanese car factory to be closed since the Second World War.
- There will probably never be another new automobile plant built in Japan.
- Sony, the flagship of Japan's consumer companies, lost $2.5 billion in 1994.
- Japan's most expensive land, in the Ginza shopping district of Tokyo, has lost more than half its value in four years.
- Only about 3 percent of Japan's personal computers are net-worked, compared with an estimated 50 percent in the US. Less than 10 percent of Japanese homes have a computer. Japan has the lowest PC usage among developed countries.

The bubble economy

In Japan everyone talks about the economy "before the bub-ble", "during the bubble", and "after the bubble", as in "After the bubble, I lost everything."

The bubble occurred in the 1980s when industry over-invested, banks and other financial institutions loaned too much both domestically and overseas, particularly to land and stock market speculators. Everyone was loaning and spending too much and prices went sky high — that is until the bubble burst in 1990. Real estate and stock prices took a nose dive. Japan entered a deadly downward spiral of deflation with no end in sight. Today's stock market is 63 percent below its high. It is still overvalued. Property prices are down about 50 percent. (Even so, in this crazy economy, Tokyo residents pay 55 times more than New Yorkers for land for a house, says a 1995 Japanese government survey.)

The big problem in Japan is massive deflation in stocks and real estate and no political will to fix it. Most troubling is the huge overhang of domestic bad debt.

Japanese estimates of bubble bad loans were first made public in June 1995 at $471 billion — or 8.6 percent of the nation's 1994 economic output. That is a bigger burden on Japan's economy than the savings-and-loan disaster was for the US.

Banking analysts in Tokyo immediately said the government's figure was much too low. Highly respected Yukiko Ohara of UBS Securities said that estimates of the entire bad debt load could be as high as $1.21 trillion, or about 25 percent of Japan's annual total economic output.

If so, the Japanese banking system is in danger of collapse.
"Is Japan finished?" asks Edith Terry in *World Business*:

"The Japan of the bubble economy was as unbalanced in its way as the former Soviet Union, forced to devote most of its human and material resources to creating national wealth. Faced with pressure for change, bureaucrats and politicians are falling back on hoary Japanese values, such as collectivism and obedience, rather than taking bold action. If that continues, a nation obsessed with becoming number one will have to settle for a position considerably lower on the list."

The Japanese economy is emerging from five years of recession "as a misshapen monster — a dinosaur's body with the head of an ostrich," says Terry.

Investor's nightmare

In the 1990s an average Japanese investor will soon have lost more than the American investor did in the 1930s.

The Nikkei Index of the 225 leading issues on the Tokyo Stock Exchange peaked at about $460 in December 1989 and plummeted to a six-year low of less than $200 in June 1992. There has only been a modest recovery since. In July 1995, it stood at $170. When the bubble was still expanding, many expected the Nikkei index would hit $1,000 by the mid-1990s. Now some predict it could fall to $120 before reaching bottom.

Since 1991 the number of foreign companies on the Tokyo Exchange dropped from 127 to 93. Daily transactions are one-fortieth of the 1989 peak. Part of the blame goes to the abysmal performance of corporate Japan. Japanese companies quoted on the Tokyo Stock Exchange in the year ending 31 March 1995 earned total net profits equivalent to only 1.9 percent of shareholder equity. In the same period the return on equity of US firms was 17 percent, Britain almost 14 percent, and Germany 10 percent.

Japan was the star performer of the industrial world, but it is now the sick economy of Asia.

The Japanese have lost more than half the domestic value of the money they invested overseas during the past 10 years. (Remember the 1980s hysteria: "The Japanese are buying up America"?)

Japan's GDP growth rate increased during the first quarter of 1996, but it is still questionable if Japan is finally pulling itself out of its worst recession since the 1930s.

Japan and East Asia

East Asia is replacing Japan as the driver of the region's booming economy. Japan is losing market share to Asian neighbors
and to countries of the OECD (Organization for Economic
Cooperation and Development). Japanese exports to OECD
countries fell from 9 percent in 1986 to 7.7 percent in 1994.
In the same period, the 10 emerging Asian economies (China,
India, Taiwan, South Korea, Hong Kong, Indonesia, Malaysia,
the Philippines, Singapore and Thailand) increased their share
of the OECD market from 9.8 to 14.5 percent.

In 1994, Japan accounted for 24 percent of these countries'
imports, a little less than in 1986. During the same period the
group of 10 countries increased their exports to this intra-
regional market from 22 percent to 35 percent.

The economies of most of Japan's Asian neighbors are
growing at between 7 and 10 percent, thereby doubling every
10 to 7 years, respectively. All this is led by China with average
growth rate of more than 10 percent for the last several years.

Since 1990, it has not been Japan or the US but the Asian
Tigers — South Korea, Taiwan, Hong Kong and Singapore —
who have been the big investors in ASEAN countries. The first
tier of Tigers is financing the next.

As much trade is inter-corporate trade, unless Japan wel-
comes direct foreign investment, not much hope exists for
correcting its trade imbalance with the rest of the world. In
contrast, non-Japan Asia is wide open to foreign participation
in its economies. How much longer will the rest of Asia with-
stand one-way traffic in trade as its economies build? Japan has
to rethink its Asian strategies, urgently.

Japan and the US

But, one might argue, isn't Japan simply evolving into a more
mature economy? You cannot expect sky high growth rates
forever.

True enough. But look at these comparisons between the US and Japan:

- Japan's industrial production at the end of 1994 was 5.5 percent below that of 1990. Industrial production in the US was 15 percent higher.
- Japan's rate of growth in aggregate productivity over the past eight years has been close to zero. The US has averaged 1 percent annual gain.
- Japan's labor productivity is 17 percent below that of the US.
- Japan's budget deficit relative to GDP is already as large as the US budget deficit, and there are pulls and tugs to put money in the rebuilding of the earthquake devastation in the Kobe area, and to otherwise spend more government money to stimulate the economy.
- For the first time since 1985 Japan has lost top ranking as the world's most competitive economy. The US was placed first. Singapore was second. Japan is now third.

Japan trails the US in electronics, computers and telecommunications. Its auto industry, confronting price hikes, trade wars and dwindling productivity, faces an uncertain future. Its once admired educational and managerial systems are now questioned in much of the world. And it has a huge identity crisis (about which I published a book in Japan in 1992 — that crisis has only gotten deeper).

There is a growing sense that the Japanese model — an export economy with lifetime employment and tight regulatory control — is no longer working. The government is so paralysed and chaotic it is incapable of taking the measures necessary, that is, liberalizing regulation, to salvage the economy.

Perhaps the harshest judgement about the state of Japan's economy comes from Brian Reading, former economics editor of *The Economist*, who says, "This is no economic superpower bent on world domination. It is a hara-kiri economy set to self-destruct."

Japan's place in the global economy is further handicapped because:

- The post-war generation that made sacrifices to build Japan's world-class economy is phasing out — and what appears to be a generation of "risk-averse" custodians has replaced it.
- Japan is extremely overregulated, which is a tremendous drag on growth. For example, Japan pioneered cellular communications, but then regulated them so heavily the US and Europe soon surpassed it.
- Widespread sexism and ageism still exist.
- As a result of a very low birth rate, people living longer and virtually no immigration, Japan is ageing faster than any other country in the world. By 2020 an extraordinary one-quarter of Japan's population will be 65 or older.
- People at the top are overworked while the average work week is being reduced. In 1993 the average number of hours worked weekly fell below 40 hours for the first time. The middle and bottom layers are working less and less, while at the top people are working until they kill themselves.
- There is overcentralization of money, people and information in Tokyo — at a time when decentralization and efficient parts make systems successful.

There is no sign in any sector of accelerating momentum in Japan's economy.

Japan's social and political chaos

Japan has entered a period of political chaos from which it will not soon recover. Ichiro Ozawa, Japan's most powerful politician, calls Japan a "small-brained dinosaur". Japan's economic woes are only part of it — or perhaps economic disillusionment is being expressed, or played out, in the hearts and minds of Japan's citizens through some bizarre political decisions and a frightening public fascination with a violent, dangerous and apparently seductive cult.

The comedian party won

The political establishment in Japan was humiliated in April 1995 when the huge body of unaffiliated voters elected comedy actors as Governors (mayors) of both Tokyo and Osaka.

In Tokyo, Yukio Aoshima, a male comedian who played a "nasty grandma" on television, beat seven candidates, including a deputy minister who had served seven Prime Ministers. Aoshima had no party backing, nor did he campaign, preferring to stay at home reading. He spent only $2,352. But his familiar stance against political parties and the central government was enough for voters.

The losing candidate, who had been favored to win, Deputy Chief Cabinet Secretary Nobuo Ishihara, had the support of five ruling and opposition parties, and spent an embarrassing $360 million.

Aoshima, whose family ran a *bento* — boxed lunch — shop, is now the Governor of Tokyo, one of the most powerful positions in Japanese politics.

In Osaka, Japan's second city, Nokku (Knock) Yokoyama, a story-telling comedian who in recent years has appeared on late-night television programs with scantily clad women and who entered the election only three days before the campaign started, beat former Science and Technology Agency bureaucrat Takuya Hirano, who had the support of all major parties.

The outcomes in Tokyo and Osaka were stunning rejections of traditional politics and politicians. Never before has a Governor been elected in either city without party support. The number of voters who say they aren't affiliated with any party has doubled in two years, to 57 percent. Both new

Governors, however, had served for years in the quite meaning-less upper house of the Japanese parliament.

"This is a revolution," said Takeshi Nagano, Chairman of the Japan Federation of Employers' Associations.

"For the first time since the Meiji restoration in the late 1880s," said political commentator Minoru Morita, "the Japanese people showed disappointment with the bureaucrats."

"People's anger against existing parties became my victory," said Aoshima, who had vowed that, if elected, he would cancel the 1996 World City Expo Tokyo, seven years in the making at a scheduled cost of $2.4 billion, more than half of which was already spent. It was scheduled to open in the spring of 1996 for a 10-month run. Most opinion polls and editorial views agreed the billion-dollar city fair was far too expensive at a time when Japan is mired in its longest recession in 50 years.

True to his word, just months after the election he called off the Expo, causing widespread bewilderment and dismay among Japan's business and political communities. "The issue here is not money, but the validity of a public pledge," Aoshima said. "Any money lost, or gained, can be made up eventually. The bigger question is whether Aoshima is a man who keeps his promises."

Since the April 1995 elections, Japan's political parties have been recruiting celebrities to run for office. The Liberal Democratic party, the largest member of the ruling coalition, has gone for some sports stars, including an Olympic ice skat-ing medal-winner, a former soccer star, and a professional wrestler.

Castrated country

Remember Shintaro Ishihara? He caused quite a stir as co-author of *The Japan That Can Say "No"* in 1989 with Akio Morita, the former Sony Chairman. A week after the Tokyo–Osaka political earthquake he abruptly resigned the par-liamentary seat he had held for 27 years, saying he despaired of

Japanese politics.

On the occasion of receiving an award for a quarter century of service in parliament, Ishihara surprised everyone by making a resignation speech. He said Japan now seemed like a "castrated country" unable "to express its will as a nation, like a man who is unable to function as a man." Strong stuff. He said that Japanese politics is "despised by the people, and all politicians, myself included, are responsible."

"Although numerous problems threaten to disrupt a future that ought to be promising for Japan, hardly any politician today wants to touch any of these issues," he continued. "All political parties and nearly all politicians act only for the most ignoble forms of egotistic self-preservation."

"I myself am ashamed, so I'm resigning as a Parliament member," he concluded.

Aum Supreme Truth

But few things in the post-war period have shaken the Japanese as much as the bursting into the public consciousness of the mystical cult Aum Shinrikyo or Aum Supreme Truth. After the cult was suspected and subsequently charged with releasing a rare nerve gas in Tokyo's subway system that killed 12 and injured 5,500, it became an obsession with the Japanese.

When the cult's leader, Shoko Asahara, was arrested, all regular television shows were cancelled and replaced with coverage of the cult, its history and activities. Some of Japan's best and brightest young people were members of the cult. Long profiles of the young senior leaders ran in Japan's leading newspapers. TV coverage rivaled or exceeded the US's obsessional coverage of the O.J. Simpson trial.

Ten days after the subway attack, Tokyo's chief of police was seriously wounded — shot in the back by masked gunmen — and Aum's senior scientist was stabbed to death outside one of the sect's buildings in downtown Tokyo.

The cult's headquarters is in a place called Kamikuishiki, a dairy farming community high on the slopes of Mount Fuji. This commune is now a huge tourist destination. Shoko Asahara has become a household name. Even little children know who he is. On the day of his arrest, the major television stations each assigned several hundred people (yes, several hundred each) to the story. More than 50 newspapers printed special editions about the cult and the events now associated with it.

One of the most curious phenomena is teenage girls' obsession with Fumihiro Joyu, who at a very young-looking 32 was the spokesman for Aum Shinrikyo, and who overnight became Japan's No. 1 media star. Young women and girls all over Japan fell in love with this articulate, good-looking graduate of one of the country's best schools, Waseda University, where he earned a degree in engineering. Described in the press as "a doe-eyed monk who says he shuns wine, women and sex", women all over the land sent him love letters, flowers, and cut pictures of him out of all the newspapers and magazines. Joyu at one time headed the cult's office in Moscow and is a fluent English speaker. He received far more TV exposure than the government, especially during the early stages of the police campaign against Aum.

Cult leader Shoko Asahara, a half-blind 40-year-old with very long hair and large unkempt beard, and more than 100 Aum senior leaders were arrested in connection with the subway gas attacks. Asahara is the sixth of seven children of an impoverished *tatami* mat maker. His young aides hold degrees from prestigious Japanese universities (Tokyo, Keio, and Waseda among them). And it was shocking and embarrassing to the Japanese government to discover that 30 Self-Defense Forces soldiers (Japan's army) were members of the Aum Shinrikyo cult.

Deeply disturbing to many was the fact that Asahara attracted many young affluent Japanese to his cult. His message is that with persistent training, members can gain spiritual powers not defined by science.

"In the past people who have joined 'outlaw' organizations

like the *yakuza* or *bosozoku* [motor-cycle gangs] have been education dropouts or people who somehow failed to cash in on the affluent society," says a retired government official. "The truly frightening thing about Aum is that it attracted affluent young people from top universities. The movement looks a protest to our whole way of doing things, not just against the individual's failure to make good in society."

To rule Japan after a vaguely planned coup, Aum established a shadow government, a political structure that mirrors Japan's ministries. In this structure, Shoko Asahara is the "Divine Emperor". There is a Home Affairs Ministry, a Defense Ministry, a Science and Technology Ministry (which is in charge of fortune-telling by the stars and the development of personal computers), Health and Welfare Ministry, and so on, a network of 22 ministries and agencies.

Aum had become a powerful business conglomerate (from noodle shops to personal computer makers) with assets of more than $1 billion. Members lived together in the sect's commune and donated all their possessions to the cult. However, since the bombing about two-thirds of the followers who lived in the Aum compound have quit the cult. Shoko Asahara, on trial for murder, may face the death penalty.

The country that can't say "I'm sorry"

In the spring of 1995, Japan's then Prime Minister Tomiichi Murayama pushed hard for a parliamentary resolution of remorse and apology for Japanese acts before and during the Second World War, as part of the 50th anniversary of the end of that war. But most in the Diet opposed or were lukewarm to the idea of apologizing for Japan's actions.

In the middle of the bickering over whether to apologize, Michio Watanabe, a leader of the powerful Liberal Democratic Party, said at a political rally that Japan's 36-year military rule in Korea was the result of "a treaty of peaceful merger signed under the auspices of international law". In Korea, where anti-

Japanese feeling runs high, the reaction was quick and furious. (During its brutal colonization of Korea the Japanese banned the Korean language — everyone had to learn Japanese — and made all Koreans take Japanese names.)

In the end the Japanese parliament could not bring itself to apologize, and issued a bland, meaningless statement of remorse that there had to have been a war. This was followed by an apology of sorts by the lame duck Prime Minister — who dropped it out of subsequent speeches and which did not in any case satisfy very many Asians. It is not a Japan that can say "no" — it is a Japan that can't say "I'm sorry".

The whole enterprise leaves one judging Japan as a country that has no moral compass or backbone, no real sense of who it is or what it has done.

In a world where economic considerations will increasingly overwhelm political considerations, future success will rest to a great extent on economic performance. But not that alone. With a recession in political power taking place all over the world, a country's moral balance and stability will stand in its place. On both economic and moral grounds, Japan's rise has peaked, not soon to be regained.

There is a serious spiritual gap in Japan. Japan today is a very tender, vulnerable country.

While Japan is one of the world's most successful economies — in many ways, the most successful — it may have reached a stage where new social and political ideas are needed.

At this juncture, for example, Japan does not know if it wants to be identified with the East or the West. Should it rejoin Asia?

Japan really does not need to decide between East and West. But it has already decided. As one of the G-7, Japan is identi-fied with the West. I hear this all over Asia.

Today, Southeast Asia is certainly more important to Japan than the West is.

My suggestion to Japan (which I made in a speech in Tokyo) is: pull out of the G-7. Make the G-7 the G-6. Show you identify with both East and West by ceasing to be a member of the (Western) Group of 7. It would send a strong message to Asia that Japan wants to be part of Asia. The G-7 is irrelevant anyway — although highly symbolic. Pulling out of the G-7 would also demonstrate that Japan can make a decision.

Find a gateway to Asia

Western companies that fail to participate in the great Asian boom will not only lose opportunities, but may undermine the competitiveness of Western corporations. The fact is, the maturing economies of the West *need* external stimulus. Western technologies and sophisticated goods must find wider application and new markets, and it is in Asia that these technologies and goods will find the greatest potential.

Like accessing the Internet, the West must find a gateway to Asia.

That gateway is the ethnic Chinese. Having lived, worked and dealt with the West both from Southeast Asia and in the West — in Canada, the US and Europe — the ethnic Chinese understand the market economy and how to operate in it.

The ethnic Chinese are the most global among all the players, and are paving the way for the emergence of a truly global operating model. Before Westerners appreciated the value of offshore havens, the ethnic Chinese were already there. An enormous amount of the world's money is sheltered in offshore havens, much of it belonging to the Chinese. They seek out the most attractive operating base, and governments looking for foreign investment should court them.

For now, the Chinese are developing Vancouver (where 20 percent of the population is Chinese) as the operating base for the Dragon Century. Many of the really big players in Hong Kong, like Li Ka-shing and Stanley Ho, are already there. British Columbia won favor because it does not tax income earned offshore, which is perfect for the Chinese. After depositing their families in beautiful Vancouver, and serving out an "immigration sentence" — the residence period required to quality for citizenship — they themselves fly back and forth to Asia, or control through cyberspace empires of business enterprises spread all over the Pacific Rim. The Chinese overseas seem to think national identity is only relevant when it comes to tax rates and mobility.

Ethnic Chinese money represents a good source of capital for the West. Chinese entrepreneurs are increasingly making inroads into the economies of the West, providing healthy stimulus to many parts of the world. As you will read later in this book regarding Asian-Americans, the ethnic Chinese are already reshaping the economic and cultural landscape of some parts of the US, especially California.

While the world moves from nation states to networks, the Chinese are creating the first truly global network.

The Indian counterparts to the ethnic Chinese are usually referred to as nonresident Indians. They have been highly successful in Britain, South Africa, Hong Kong and Southeast Asia, and in the US. They number about 10 million, with a combined income of an astonishing $340 billion, equivalent to the whole of the income of India's 940 million people. As economic reforms settle in place these emigrés are working with entrepreneurs in India, much as the ethnic Chinese have done in China, and they will become a powerful force in India's ever so promising economic development. Stay tuned to the Indian network.

Ethnic networks will be only part of the emerging global network of networks. Business sector networks have begun to form: architecture/construction networks; a fashion network of designers, textile providers and clothing manufacturers; automobile, travel, medical and, of course, financial networks are being formed in an endless process as the importance of political nation-states yields to the economics of global networks.

Still trapped in the old paradigm

Meanwhile the political West, and especially the US, continues to be a prisoner of the vocabulary and concepts of the nation-state, Cold War period. The US government, with its bilateralism in trade, lags behind an ever-changing world. The whole planet is moving beyond multilateralism to borderless trade, and the US hasn't even got to multilateralism yet. It says it supports the multinational World Trade Organization, and indeed played a crucial role in its creation, but its actions all reflect the old paradigm.

The US and other Western governments continue to be obsessed with the government of China. Both government and media hype the growing military threat of China at a time when half of China's military is engaged in commerce, with very little interest in performing military duties.

Governments do not trade. Governments do not create the world's added value. People do — entrepreneurs. Economic considerations have long since overwhelmed political considerations. The role of government ought to be to stay out of the way so entrepreneurs and corporations can continue to create the global economy.

Because the ethnic Chinese network is so decentralized, it does not matter what the point of entry is: everything is connected to everything else. So choose a partner who is in the same business or who is directly connected with the part of China, or Malaysia, or Indonesia that interests you.

Many in the West know a lot about Japan and something about China. Now Japan is in decline and not really part of the new Asia. Many ethnic Chinese operate out of the young, dynamic economies of the region. If you are serious about doing business in Asia, you have to know more about the huge countries of India and Indonesia, about the much smaller but dynamic economies of Taiwan, Malaysia, Thailand, South Korea, Singapore, Hong Kong, and, increasingly, Vietnam and the Philippines.

2

From Export-led

➤ *Consumer-driven*

A new middle class, the size of which the world has never before seen, is being created in Asia.

In February 1995, the Gallup Organization released the results of the first ever scientific national poll of China — the world's most populous country. Its conclusion: a billion Chinese want to become rich and buy millions of TVs, washing machines, refrigerators and videocassette recorders. That news might shock some Westerners, but it comes as no surprise to the 84 percent of Chinese households who already own a TV, the 25 percent who spent their hard-earned money on refrigerators or the 35 percent who purchased a washing machine in the last few years.

Some 68 percent of the Chinese polled desired to "work hard and get rich". Just 4 percent subscribed to the philosophy of the late Chairman Mao: "Never think of yourself, give everything in service to society."

"This is a society with strong material aspirations, not all of which are currently being met," said Richard Burkholder, Jr., Gallup Director of Worldwide Operations.

The trick, of course, is to find out where this new urban class will be, and to find out something about its generational composition.

The rise of the middle class is revamping Asia's economic structure. Once dependent on exports for economic expansion, Asia can also rely on domestic demand to fuel growth. In Thailand, for example, consumer spending now contributes 54 percent of its gross domestic product, while exports contribute 30 percent. That means a bigger economic pie and a more sophisticated, well-rounded economic picture.

That said, one caveat must be offered. The gap in wealth between urban and rural is so significant that average nationwide income levels and other demographic data are almost meaningless.

When a businessperson or well-heeled tourist stays in a five-star hotel in Jakarta or Shanghai and shops in the nearby boutiques, it might *feel* as if they are in Chicago or London. That's how extraordinarily sophisticated Asia's urban centers have become. Ten or twenty miles out into the countryside, however, it is clear you are visiting a developing country.

Nevertheless, the fundamental economic shift in Asia today has profound implications for domestic companies and foreign investors alike. Learning to read this new market can result in enormous profits — failing to do so could mean lost opportunity, even bankruptcy.

In unchartered waters, there is no formula for successful market penetration, no sure predictors of consumer response.

From survival to middle class

What is happening in China, as reflected in that Gallup poll, is happening throughout Asia. The average Asian's living standard is bursting out of "survival" into consumption. Incomes are rising dramatically. In the United States, 45–50 percent of household income goes on rent, health, education, and transportation. In China, where the government still subsidizes food and housing, the comparable number is an incredible 5 percent. In time China's cost of living will rise, as subsidies are cut. But income will grow too. Meanwhile Chinese households have money to spend on products that enhance their quality of life.

For 25 years, Asians needed exports to grow. Producing low-cost consumer products for world markets, Asian countries climbed toward economic prosperity. Later, when Japan and then the Four Tigers diversified into telecommunications, computers, financial and professional services, education levels increased, and employment skills improved. That brought higher labor costs. Manufacturers then sought lower-cost alternatives in neighboring countries. Economies grew in a "flying geese" formation with the more developed countries leading the less developed along the path to prosperity.

Trade within Asia then became a more important piece of the region's overall economy. Companies invested in each other, and there has been a dramatic increase in intra-corporate trade. Standards of living throughout the continent increased.

If Asian economies continue their 6 to 10 percent annual expansion of the last decade, their middle classes will double or triple in the next decade. The Asian middle class, not counting Japan, could number between 800 million and 1 billion people by 2010, resulting in a stunning $8 to $10 trillion in spending power. That's in the neighborhood of 50 percent more than today's US economy.

It took Britain's middle class nearly a century to evolve. In Asia today that process is being accomplished in little more than a decade.

A billion consumers

But you don't have to be middle class to *buy* something.

Hong Kong Bank Chairman John Gray estimates there will be "a billion people in Asia with some consumer spending power" by the year 2000.

- Already, 70 percent of South Koreans who describe themselves as "middle class" are home owners, and 60 percent are worth at least $62,200.
- In India between 1990 and 1991, consumer activity increased 14 percent to US $122.6 billion — four times 1981 levels.
- Almost two-thirds of households in Petaling Jaya, near Kuala Lumpur, Malaysia, earn more than $800 a month; more than a third make more than $1,200.
- The number of Bangkok households earning $10,000 a year has jumped from just 160,000 in 1986 to one million today.

Similar rises in income and consumer activity are recorded elsewhere in the region, and will gather momentum over the next five to ten years.

Purchasing power parity

In many ways, household income is a poor gauge of economic status, not only between rural and urban, but among countries as well. A middle-class family in Taipei might well have an annual income of $40,000, while a family in New Delhi could qualify as middle class with an annual income of $7,000. In China families are still subsidized by the government, resulting in their having more spending power than their incomes would lead a Westerner to believe. As I described it in *Global Paradox*:

> "Traditionally, a country's economy is measured by determining a per capita income which is calculated by converting the value of its gross domestic product into US dollars at the official exchange rate. A big problem with this method is that if a country's currency weakens against the dollar, its economy automatically shrinks, which can be very misleading. But that is precisely what happened in the case of China. Between 1978 and 1992, the renminbi (China's currency) fell from 1.7 to the dollar to 5.5 to the dollar. But

to use this traditional measurement effectively negates China's real economic growth during the same period. By this calculation, China's economy is the 10th largest, and its people among the poorest."

Even keepers of the world's ledger know the numbers make no sense. So in 1993 the International Monetary Fund (IMF) tried a new methodology, purchasing power parity (PPP), and came up with dramatically different results. The IMF calculated how much, for example, a loaf of bread, bicycle or soft drink cost in one country's currency. It then figured out how much the same commodities cost in other countries' currencies, and then each country's national output based on PPP. Under this new method, the IMF found that China had produced $1.7 trillion in goods and services in 1992, far greater than the $400 billion previously estimated, and that in 1992 its per capita income was $1,600, not $370.

Using UN data and a different analysis, the IMF calculated that in 1990 China's per capita income was somewhere around $2,600. Other economists insisted it was much higher, even as high as $4,000, a level which historically in other countries had, in effect, opened the flood gates of consumer spending. Exactly what China is experiencing now.

Using China as an example, the arithmetic is straightforward. If China's real per capita income were in fact $4,000, China would have a $4.8 trillion economy (1.2 billion × $4,000). Furthermore, if China continues to grow at about 8 percent annually (China has averaged nearly 10 percent growth for 15 years), then in five years per capita income will be closer to $6,000 and the economy $7.2 trillion, equal to today's US economy. That's a formula for a new economic order.

To no one's surprise, global corporate giants and entrepreneurs alike have gone into overdrive in an effort to capture a share of this very attractive market. Those most likely to be successful are the ones who take the time to understand the unique nature of each Asian market as well as the new collective consciousness emerging in the region.

Asia is a collection of markets

Certainly, what constitutes middle class differs from country to country, and within countries. In some parts of some Asian countries education and social standing can be as important as economic status and achievement. Owning a car or home, or both, often distinguishes people as middle class. Theirs is a kind of hierarchy of ownership that tracks middleclassdom: television sets and refrigerators and air conditioners, succeeded by cars and homes and vacations. Across the board in most parts of Asia, people's disposable incomes are increasing. The fact is, Asians are getting richer day by day. And they are hopeful of the future.

Companies wanting to sell in Asia should not look at Asia city by city. They should look at Asia as market centers, operating and selling to urban Singapore, Hong Kong, Taipei, Seoul, Kuala Lumpur. In approach they should not differ one from another. But selling to urban and rural within the same country can be very different. Marketing should not recognize countries but examine common profiles in different market centers.

Top of the class

Asia's young population is in its consumer spending prime. Each of the Little Dragon nations of Hong Kong, Singapore, Taiwan and South Korea has more than 65 percent of their population between 15 and 65 years of age. The percentages are also high for countries in developing Asia. Thailand, Indonesia, Malaysia, China, India and the Philippines range between 59 to 66 percent. Averaging more than 8 percent of economic growth for each of the last nine years, 59 percent of Malaysia's 20 million people in the above age group are set to launch a retail boom. The country's retail sector expected 30 percent growth in 1995.

Asia's middle classes are changing the economic, social and political landscape of the region. They are better educated, are marrying later and having fewer children. The young, urban middle class of Asia are as sophisticated as any in the world. They lead sophisticated lifestyles and want sophisticated products and services. They are looking for quality as part of a self-conscious search for a quality-of-life lifestyle.

This new middle class represents tremendous purchasing power, which ultimately will result in tremendous political power. We will see the Asianization of democracy as governments become responsive to an increasingly vocal middle class. (In 1992 in Thailand the middle class took to the streets for the first time, and toppled the government, ending military rule.)

In the meantime, however, purveyors of consumer products and personal services, and peddlers of convenience and quality, will profit handsomely if they can read the market and respond appropriately.

"American hucksters are taking this part of the world seriously," says Mike Ferrier, the Hong Kong-based regional director of US advertising giant McCann-Erickson. "It shows that Asia has turned from a production market into a consumption market. Asia used to only manufacture goods for the West. Now the West is sending things here."

This growing new middle class, by and large, is a more sophisticated consumer. Value sells. But, at the top, so does luxury. Joseph Kanoui, chairman and chief executive of Vendome Luxury Group, anticipates that Asia will be the group's largest market by the year 2000. Vendome owns some of the world's leading luxury brands, including Cartier, Dunhill men's clothing, Piaget and Baume & Mercier watches. Asia is already Vendome's second largest market. Sales of Mercedes Benz cars in Asia increased 3.5 times between 1991 and 1994. Sales of BMWs increased almost 50 percent.

Brand consciousness is on the rise. Those with the means, especially young women in Hong Kong, Singapore, or Taipei, would not settle for anything less than their favorite designer labels. Single Asian women who live with their families have large disposable incomes, and are eager to embrace styles of the very best. Many would not blink an eyelash to spend a month's salary on a Chanel bag or a Fendi wristwatch. Even little kids insist on wearing outfits with Mickey Mouse's label. Disney is expecting to reap a bumper harvest in Asia as Mickey becomes a pal to millions of Asia's children.

Just charge it!

Asia, where buying on credit was imprudent at best, shameful at worst, is ushering in a whole new era — the age of the credit card. Asia's middle class is increasingly comfortable buying on credit. Citibank alone has 5 million credit cards in circulation in Asia, and expects 7 million new cardholders by 2000.

In 1994, regional spending with a MasterCard or Visa totaled more than $220 billion, "more than the economic output of Singapore and Hong Kong combined". And yet only around 1 percent of consumer spending in Asia is done on credit cards, compared to 20 percent in the US.

- In Japan there are 215 million credit cards in circulation, two for each citizen over the age of 20.
- MasterCard International recently became the first to issue credit cards in Vietnam. It plans to issue 500,000 cards.
- Citibank, one of the region's biggest issuers, has seen its credit card revenues in the Asia Pacific region increase from $400 million in 1994 to $1 billion in 1996. Revenues of $2 billion are expected by 2000.
- Credit cardholders in India now number 1.75 million.
- In China the number of credit cardholders reached 8.4 million by the end of 1994. The People's Bank of China plans to have 200 million cardholders by the year 2000.
- With 120 different types of plastic, Thailand might hold Asia's title to "the greatest variety of credit card options", yet many card issuers believe the Thai market is not yet saturated.
- In the Philippines, if you have an income of $300 a month, you can get a credit card.

Shopping is Asia's favorite pastime

Having moved from the days when the refrigerator was placed prominently in a corner of the living room as a symbol of affluence to now having the means to furnish an entire living room, Asians are on a buying spree. Coupling that with the lack of recreational facilities in crowded Asian cities, shopping malls and department complexes have become favorite weekend hangouts. Asians delight in strolling, looking at window displays, either on their own after a day at the office, or as a family activity.

Savoring this trend, the world's retailers are wasting no time establishing a foothold in Asia. Asia's version of the Mall of America which opened in August 1994 in Bangkok, caters to affluent urban households. Bangkok's Seacon Square Mall is another good example. It has miles and miles of shops, a 14-screen movie theater and even an amusement park with rollercoasters. Seacon Square is just one of four malls anchored by a department store in the Bangkok area. The Megamall in the Philippines is the largest shopping mall in Asia. The mall's owner is now planning to build the world's largest mall on reclaimed land in Manila Bay. In the meantime:

- Nike's Shanghai store is open daily from 10 a.m. to 10 p.m. Shoppers want only the most expensive shoes. According to the store manager, no one wants the cheaper sneakers because they think they might be fake.
- There were already 258 7-Eleven shops in Thailand in 1993, with growth projected to reach 1,000 by 1997.
- K-Mart is opening a store in Singapore. Wal-Mart is looking at several locations in Asia.
- Orchard Road in Singapore has been called Singapore's equivalent of London's Bond Street. It is really more a mix of Bond, Oxford and Regent Streets, with "going out of business" sales as well as luxury boutiques. It boasts a global array of stores from Marks and Spencer (Britain), Toys

"R" Us (US) to Takashimaya and Istetan (Japan).
- Giant Japanese retailer Yaohan, headquartered in Hong Kong, is planning to build and operate 1,000 stores in major urban centers in China.

Auto industry as metaphor for modernism

First, every emerging economy creates a national airline, which every Asian country now has or will soon have. Now they all want their own car company.

It is easy to see why Asia has attracted the entire global community. Paying closest attention of all are the car makers. Within the world's mature economies, car ownership reached saturation years ago. Worldwide demand for new automobiles has dropped almost 3 percent since 1991. There will be some increase, but demand is expected to stall at 2 percent around the year 2000.

"The developed world just can't carry the load anymore," says Wayne Brooker, Ford's Asia-Pacific Vice President. "The future of the industry will depend on new markets."

Asia offers new markets of extraordinary potential. Not only are increasingly well-off consumers eager to buy — cars are a universal success symbol — but governments seek to bolster their fledgling auto industries, which are metaphors for economic growth and prosperity.

Throughout the developed world, car ownership brings the individual a sense of independence and freedom. At the same time, the existence of an automotive industry suggests that a country has achieved a certain level of industrial development. Supplying citizens with affordable vehicles is a hallmark of economic progress.

That status symbol, however, does not come without sizeable attendant costs such as strain on an already inadequate transportation infrastructure and outpourings of carbon monoxide in smog-congested Asian cities. Countries throughout the

region face a unique set of logistical and environmental challenges. Nevertheless, the pursuit of "progress" through development of an automotive industry continues, and the world's
car makers are queueing up to capture their share of the prize.

The people's car

China is at work developing what it calls "the people's car",
described as "an affordable compact sedan for the masses in the
world's largest untapped car market".

"The car is the focus of an ambitious effort by leaders of
China's Communist Party to double the country's annual production, to 3 million vehicles, half of them automobiles, by the
end of the decade," reports the *International Herald Tribune*.
"The plan calls for the cars to increasingly go to individual consumers; in the past the emphasis had been on larger vehicles
such as minivans that could move groups of people."

What's more, the government intends to provide incentives
to encourage widespread car ownership. "The official *China
Daily* newspaper reported officials responsible for the automotive sector as saying that to 'increase sales the state will introduce incentives to car buyers to boost market demand,'"
reports the *Financial Times*. Although *China Daily* offered no
specifics, it implied bank loans and other financing would be
available.

China invited the world's top car makers to submit their
concept of the Chinese family car. Even Germany's Porsche and
Daimler-Benz, hardly known for their affordability, responded.
The Asian Wall Street Journal reported:

> "Japan's Mitsubishi Motors Corp. offered a so-called X
> concept car, a minivan that doubles as a cargo vehicle, for
> China's entrepreneurial families. Toyota Motor Corp. indi-
> rectly pooh-poohed the whole idea, and asked China to
> consider a larger Toyota model, the two- to three-liter
> Crown, as a first step... General Motors Corp. and Ford

Motor Corp. urged China to anoint one of their current models as the new family car. Ford recommended its Fiesta line and GM pushed its Corsa model, both from their European operations, as the least expensive and most flexible alternative."

"China is such a potentially huge market that if one percent of Chinese people could afford cars, that would be 12 million," says Michael G. Meyerand, a GM spokesman. "That's roughly our market size of Europe."

Meanwhile, Chinese and Western analysts question the wisdom of encouraging automobile transportation when the country's infrastructure is inadequate to support the cars already on the road, and when cities like Beijing are choking on smog.

Says Vaclav Smil, a Canadian scientist studying China's growth:

> "Forty percent of United States energy consumption goes into private cars, and the United States is importing half of its crude oil. If the Chinese try to model themselves on the United States, or Japan or South Korea, there is simply not enough crude oil on the planet for them to import and, of course, it will speed up the arrival of the third oil crisis."

Will China pioneer what the world has so far ignored — energy alternatives? Perhaps the electric car will finally get some serious consideration.

Energy and environmental concerns, in any event, are unlikely to inhibit the growth of China's fledgling auto industry. There is too much at stake. A profitable auto industry signals China's arrival as an industrial power. For its people, it means freedom and status. China's economic boom is expected to continue. Soon car ownership will lie within the grasp of millions. Currently, there are some 7 million to 9 million cars on the roads, depending on which statistic you trust. But China's population exceeds 1 billion. What car manufacturer wouldn't want

a slice of that pie? And what government would spurn economic growth and the creation of 15 million or so new jobs?

World's car makers make themselves at home in Asia

Although China is the most dramatic example, car sales are
booming throughout the region. By 2000 Asians are expected
to buy 16 million cars a year. The *Financial Times* reports:

> "Hardly a week passes without an announcement of plans
> to invest in the manufacture of cars or trucks somewhere in
> Southeast Asia."

Thailand is home to 17 car makers including Honda, Ford,
Mazda, Chrysler and Volvo. There are also 350 parts suppliers
and 12 major assembly plants. General Motors is spending
$750 million to produce the Opel in Thailand.

Meanwhile, it was recently agreed that the Proton,
Malaysia's "national car", would be built at a manufacturing
plant near Manila — the first site outside of Malaysia. At the same
time, Mrs Rafidah Aziz, Malaysia's Minister of Internal Trade
and Industry, was in Brussels for the inauguration of Proton's
first left-hand drive models in Europe. For some, Proton has
become a symbol of the country's recent economic growth.

Proton sees itself as the next Hyundai. The company is committed to playing in the big leagues. That means prosper, perish
or form a partnership. The same goes for any US manufacturer
moving into Asia.

Ford Motor Co., the world's second largest vehicle maker,
announced it would invest $50 million for a 7 percent stake in
the Indian car maker Mahindra & Mahindra. In doing so, Ford
is following in the footsteps of General Motors, Volkswagen,
Daewoo, and Mercedes-Benz, all of which anticipate big profits from India's growing middle class where annual car sales are
expected to double to nearly 500,000 by the year 2000.
Hyundai is building a factory near New Delhi. As with China,

there are many in the rest of Asia today who question whether it should start filling itself with millions of polluting vehicles.

Dr Lee Yuen Tseh, the Nobel Laureate who is President of Academia Sinica in Taipei, says the West should "help us with the technology and knowhow to build subway and train systems, not sell us cars." He has sounded the alarm. The relative merits of the introduction of massive numbers of automobiles are going to be a big debate in Asia in the years ahead.

Travel and tourism get a tail wind

"The seven day getaway was called California Fantasy, and it sold like a dream," reported the *Asian Wall Street Journal Weekly*. "A promotional flier, issued jointly by a Thai travel agency and a credit-card company, invited a group of Bangkok cardholders to sign up for a tour featuring Disneyland, Sea World and other California attractions for the equivalent of $1,200 to $1,500 per person. Within three hours, all 2,000 packages were sold."

The world's newest middle class is eager to see what lies beyond the boundaries of their village, town, or city. They travel by car to neighboring communities, by train to nearby cities, and by plane to distant countries. Travel and tourism, the world's largest industry, will by the year 2005 employ an estimated 338 million workers — one in five of those workers will be in the Asia-Pacific region, and as likely as not serving other Asians. Interregional travel is growing faster than intercontinental travel as individuals traveling on business extend their trip for pleasure, or as families long separated seek one another out.

Suddenly, people in Asia can afford to travel, and exposure to satellite television has piqued their curiosity about faraway places — and not so faraway places. Comments Peter Sutch, Chairman of Cathay Pacific Airlines: "Cathay Pacific used to be an English expat airline. No more. Today, Asians dominate the passenger list on the 795 weekly flights." Adds Managing Director Rod Eddington, "Now 75 percent of our passengers are Asian, compared with less than 70 percent just five years ago — 40 percent are ethnic Chinese."

Taiwan and South Korea have relaxed restrictions on exit permits and currency exchange. Result: a surge in travel activity. Of visitors to the Philippines 50 percent are from Asia; as are 75 percent of those to Indonesia. In 1995 3.3 million Asians traveled to Japan, more than 60 percent of Japan's tourist arrivals.

Vietnam plans to increase earnings from tourism from 3.5 percent of GDP in 1994 to 27 percent in 2010.

At the first annual International Travel Expo '94 — the combination of Hong Kong's eight-year-old InterTour and China's four-year-old National Travel Fair — 51 countries exhibited, including Japan, Malaysia, Singapore and Thailand. Hong Kong promoted itself as the gateway to the Pearl River Delta, Macau and Guangdong. For some time, tourism has ranked as one of Hong Kong's top-earning industries. It is almost certain this trend will continue. Tourism will become the top-earning industry in a growing number of Asian countries.

Throughout the region travel has become a middle-class rite of passage.

Boeing estimates that 40 percent of world passenger growth in the next 15 years will be from the Asia-Pacific region. The International Air Travel Association predicts Asian traffic will grow 7 percent a year from 1991 to 2010. Asia will represent 39.2 percent of world traffic in 2000. By 2010, it will surge to over half.

Airport signals economic arrival

Jay Khosla writes in Singapore's *Business Times*:

"A new airport is more than the sum of its numbers. It can be a catalyst of development. In Osaka and Seoul, the airport complex is accompanied by massive infrastructural undertakings — from business centre, seaport facilities to entire communities supporting the aviation industry. It is also a product of national image building — a manifestation of political clout. It signals that as a nation you've arrived. Kuala Lumpur's new airport, for instance, is scheduled for full capacity of 60 million passengers by 2020 — the target year by which Malaysia aims to achieve developed nation status. The Hongkong project has been a symbol of the political tug-of-war between China and Britain that under-scores their ideological differences."

Whatever the impetus, Asia is abuzz with airport construction, all with the hopes of achieving the same level of excellence as Singapore's Changi Airport — voted "Best in the World" seven years in a row.

"What makes a good airport?" asks the *Singapore Business Times*, which concludes the question must obsess planners all across Asia, given the number of great airports newly opened and planned in Asia. The article lists Osaka's $15 billion Kansai Airport, along with airports planned in Nanjing, Guangzhou, Shanghai, Fuzhou. By 1997, Hong Kong's new Chek Lap Kok airport will replace Kai Tak. Kuala Lumpur, Manila, Macau, Bangkok and Seoul will have spent billions on new facilities by 2000.

In Singapore, Terminal 3 is scheduled to open by 2002 at the cost of $1 billion. There is already talk of a third runway and a fourth terminal at Changi. If airports are a measure of importance and affluence, and I think they are, New Asia has arrived.

Hoteliers trying to meet surge in Asian demand

Everywhere in the region, airports are expanding, upgrading or undergoing construction. Hotel chains are renovating or build-ing anew, while at the same time reassessing their customer base. Everyone, it seems, wants to ride the tail wind of growth in travel and tourism.

Ten years ago, executive-class cabins and lobbies of five-star hotels were the domain of Caucasians on holiday and Western business travelers working for multinationals in Asia. Frugal Asians, who used to fly coach for business and stayed in mid-price hotels, are increasingly taking those executive-class seats and checking into the region's upscale hotels. And hoteliers are upgrading accordingly. The regular Hyatt Regency has been transformed into a chain of Grand Hyatts throughout Asia, while the Holiday Inns are building their upscale range of Crown Plazas.

A new generation of middle-class Asians intent on visiting friends and family is creating an extraordinary opportunity for the midprice hotels. Most growth is from Asians traveling to other Asian countries.

More tourists from China visited Malaysia in 1993 than did tourists from the US.

"I've never seen anything like it," says Brendan Ebbs, Senior Vice President of Choice Hotels of the US, the world's largest midrange chain. 'We're seeing our hotels mushroom in all of these countries. Over the next 10 years, there is virtually unlimited growth for us in Asia."

Hotels in India are operating at full capacity. There are only about 2,000 international-standard budget hotel rooms (fewer than Singapore or Bangkok) in a nation of 940 million. Compare that with 3.5 million midmarket rooms in the US. No wonder the world's hoteliers are flocking to India, despite the bureaucratic red tape. Holiday Inn, a unit of Britain's Bass plc and Choice Hotels International each plan 80 hotels in India.

Accor SA of France intends to build 123 hotels throughout the Asia-Pacific region, including 40 in Australia and 20 in Vietnam. The group's most profitable Asian hotel is Hanoi's Sofitel Metropole. Accor is eyeing five sites in Malaysia and already owns four Ibis hotels in Indonesia.

Already, China boasts 36 five-star, 87 four-star, and more than 400 three-star hotels. The country began to use the "star" designation in 1987, endeavoring to relate its facilities to global standards.

Hilton International will focus primarily on new properties in China, Japan, Korea, Malaysia, Indonesia and the Philippines. It is also considering Vietnam and India.

Gérard Pelisson, Co-Chairman of Accor SA of France, explains the surge in hotel, leisure and travel: "In this part of the world, there are tens of millions of people in the middle class starting to travel for leisure and business. Our objective is to build hotels to tap this clientele."

Slow boat to China

Twenty years ago the average Asian would have rejected the idea of vacationing on a boat. "Boats were uncomfortable vessels only to be endured because they took you somewhere," explains the *Far East Economic Review*. "You only lived on one if you couldn't afford a 'proper home.' And the Asian experience of larger vessels has been limited largely to ferries, those uncomfortable floating platforms inevitably over-burdened with people and lorries."

Not any more. The world's cruise lines have taken an active interest in Asia. Today, local firms are offering services that meet international standards. Western companies with reputations for quality and service are forming joint ventures in Asia to bring the pleasures of cruising to the masses, to adventurous, upscale young Asians eager for new experiences.

The *East King*, a $10 million luxury river cruiser which has "bars, a gymnasium, a sauna and a telephone in each of its 78 rooms", travels down the Yangtze River. It is owned by Hubei Orient Royal Cruise, and run by Holiday Inns.

China's Dalian Marine Transport Group ordered two vessels from a Dutch company to carry 1,000 passengers, plus cars and other items, between China and South Korea.

Singapore's Star Cruise company spent US$250 million on the *Langkapuri Star Aquarius* and the *Star Pisces* during 1994.

Less is more

Wherever there are people with disposable incomes, there will be amusement parks, restaurants and shops to help them spend their money. But that is only part of the story. Not only do Asians have money to spend, they have more time in which to spend it. In Japan, the average work week has shrunk. Japanese workers now work an average of 1,800 hours a year, less than the 2,058 average in the US.

Attitudes toward work and leisure are also changing. In a survey conducted by the *Far Eastern Economic Review*, when working men and women were asked "which of a number of factors would improve their enjoyment of life, 60 percent of respondents opted for more leisure — that is, spending less time at work. Significantly more of those with high incomes — Singaporeans and Hongkong Chinese — chose more time off than those from still developing countries such as the Philippines and Thailand. This could signal a change in Asian values."

Live and play the modern way

According to Hong Kong's Gordon Wu, there is a "hierarchy" of needs that begin to be met, mostly dictated by affordability, as countries move towards prosperity. The first is that people begin to eat out. If the number and variety of fast-food restaurants in Asia is any indication, then Gordon Wu is right. *Nation's Restaurant News* reports:

> "Twenty-three years have passed since the epoch-launching Osaka International Exposition, when Asians were first beguiled by such exotic phenomena as McDonald's and Kentucky Fried Chicken units, a Western-style cafeteria, a newfangled sushi-to-go operation and a host of never-before-seen foreign restaurants. Although numerous U.S.-

based dining concepts went on to glut the now-sluggish Japanese marketplace, Yankee foodservice innovations are still debuting in Asia as American chains tackle start-up or expansion challenges in countries throughout the region."

The path has not been smooth for these purveyors of food for people on the go. In many Asian cities, prime locations are in short supply and, when available, very expensive. Cumbersome distribution channels pose enormous challenges and satisfying Asian palettes is not as simple as putting soy sauce on hamburger meat. But the promise of access to billions of mouths hungry for new taste sensations is enough to motivate any businessperson to find a way to work around the obstacles.

- Kentucky Fried Chicken, a division of PepsiCo, is so certain of the company's future in Asia it plans to open 25 company-owned restaurants in Thailand and Hong Kong. This is a dramatic departure from its traditional foreign expansion plan of joint ventures and limited partnerships.
- There are 107 McDonald's in China, including five of the ten busiest McDonald's in the world. McDonald's opened four restaurants in Beijing in one weekend in August 1995. The city now has 30. The company plans to have 100 outlets in Beijing by 2003 and more than 600 nationwide.
- T.G.I. Friday's is the darling of the Korean dining-out crowd.
- Starbucks Coffee Co plans to have 12 coffee stores in Japan by 1997.
- Baskin-Robbins, now in 49 countries including China, will set up shop in India.
- Kenny Rogers Roasters is expanding throughout Asia.

The Economist reports that Chinese consumers also are "wooed by Cadbury's chocolate, biscuits from United Biscuits, Maxwell House Coffee from Kraft General Foods, and Knorr bouillon from America's CPC. Smokers are tempted by advertisements for Marlboro, Salem and Lucky Strike cigarettes. Drinkers are invited to open a can of beer from Australia's Fosters, Denmark's Carlsberg or the Philippines' San Miguel. Department stores offer Estée Lauder cosmetics, shoes from London's Gieves & Hawkes and Louis Vuitton handbags."

AB Electrolux, the Swedish vacuum cleaner maker, plans to double sales in Asian markets over the next five years. Unilever, the Anglo-Dutch personal hygiene company, is entering China to take on Proctor & Gamble, which "washes more heads of hair in China than any other foreign shampoo maker". Unilever will invest $100 million each year through the year 2000 to increase production.

Just hours after the lifting of Vietnam's trade embargo, Pepsi sent truckloads of its soda into the streets of Ho Chi Minh City. Coke cut its prices from 60 cents to 20 cents, and put two 30-foot Coke bottles in front of the Hanoi Opera House. The cola kingpins are going head to head in China too. Pepsi's investment in China has already hit $600 million, but says it "will invest whatever it takes to build the China market". Although Coca-Cola is the market leader in Asia, Coke and Pepsi are running "neck and neck" in Thailand. Pepsi introduced its Pepsi Max to Thailand with a three-month, $2 million ad campaign there in the race for market share.

Persuading Asians

Fast on the heels of consumer products are the advertising agencies seeing to it that clients' products get their share of consumer attention. The list of agencies with offices in China reads like a who's who in big-ticket advertising: McCann-Erickson, D'Arcy Masius Bention & Bowles, Saatchi & Saatchi Advertising, Bates Worldwide, Ogilvy & Mather, J. Walter Thompson, Grey China Advertising Co., Leo Burnett Inc., Batey Ads Pte Ltd., Dentsu Young & Rubicam Partners, Dentsu Inc., Euro RSCG Ball, DDB Needham Worldwide, BBDO, Lintas, Bozwell Worldwide Inc., Lee Davis Ayer,

Fortune, and Compu-Ad.

Advertising expenditure in 1993 reached $14 billion in nine east Asian countries, including China, reports Zenith Media Worldwide/Saatchi & Saatchi Advertising. Add Japan, and the figure rises to $47 billion. China's advertising market quadrupled to $3 billion between 1993 and 1995 and is expected to increase to $22 billion by 2000. Taiwan and the Philippines have also experienced significant increases.

Sums like that show how the world views Asia, especially China, which will become one of the top advertising markets in the next two decades, predicts the *Asian Wall Street Journal Weekly*. *Advertising Age* already considers China the fastest growing media market in the world. In 1995 advertising expenditure in South Korea increased 18.7 percent to $5.7 billion. South Korea, the world's tenth largest advertising market in 1994, jumped to sixth place in 1995.

This surge in Asian advertising speaks volumes about the changing political environment. Advertising depends on the media. Ten, even five years ago, advertisers were limited to state-owned media, print or broadcast. Closely monitored and carefully censored, procurers of air time or ad space could never be certain if their material would run, or if it did, whether it would bear any resemblance to its original form.

This is changing too. A combination of deteriorating state media monopolies and the advent of commercial television is creating huge opportunities.

Even Kathmandu has cable

In the past few years, Asia has plugged into the worldwide web of television broadcasting. Four hundred million Asian homes have televisions. In Taiwan, South Korea, Singapore and Japan at least 99 percent of households own televisions; in Hong Kong it's 98 percent. India has 50,000 private cable operators. By mid-1995 there were 30 cable channels — and that was

expected to double in 1996. With one million cable sub-
scribers, Shanghai has the highest cable penetration in the
world, says the *International Herald Tribune*.

For $23 a month, South Koreans can tap into 25 cable
channels. Every citizen in Singapore will soon have access to
100 cable stations, and there are 400 cable operators in Taiwan.

Even Kathmandu has cable. At the beginning of 1995,
about 1,000 homes there could choose among 16 different
channels. Prazwol Pradhan, the person who brought cable to
Kathmandu, intends to grow the industry into a satellite broadcasting hub rivaling Hong Kong and Singapore.

"Every household in Thailand now has a receiver for home
entertainment — whether a TV, a radio, VCR, stereo or CD
player," says Thai entertainment entrepreneur Paiboon
Damrongchaitam, founder and majority owner of Grammy
Entertainment Public Co. Ltd., a $400 million entertainment
conglomerate launched in 1983. "Up country everybody has a
radio, a cassette player and a water buffalo."

Print media are also proliferating as governments relax their
stranglehold on all information. India offers 369 daily newspapers in 18 different languages. Indonesians can choose from
247 newspapers and 117 magazines. There, as elsewhere, the
potential for a crackdown still exists. So "safe-style" reporting
is generally the guiding principle.

Nonetheless, Asians have access to more information than at
any other time in their history, and the media daily push the
envelope of government restrictions. Jimmy Lai's Hong Kong
magazine *Next* described China's Premier Li Peng as the "son
of a turtle's egg with a zero IQ".

A recent article in Malaysia's *Men's Review* carried the sub-
heading "Booze, bars and babes". Other lead stories included
"Sex on your first date". "We are testing new ground," says
founder and publisher Faridah Stephens. "We are writing for a
younger set — many of whom are used to reading magazines
from abroad...people are becoming more liberal."

Straight talk is on the air

Estimates put the number of talk radio fans in Shanghai at one million. Listeners to the call-in show *Citizens and Society* question city officials about infrastructure problems, like why aren't the phones working? *No Appointments Tonight* is devoted to relationships, love and marriage. "The people have needs, and the time has come to let the authorities know what these needs are," says Yuan Hu of Radio Shanghai. "That's the primary purpose of the talk shows."

"Taiwan is seeing a radio revolution," reports the *Far Eastern Economic Review*. "Despite periodic crackdowns by the government, underground stations have mushroomed." In 1994, Taiwan witnessed the growth of 20 new pirate radio stations, whose topics range from literature and homework advice to sex and drugs. "Never before have so many people in Taiwan listened to radio as now," says Chen Cheng-teh, manager of Voice of Taiwan in Taipei. "For more than 40 years we haven't had a voice of the people like this. For only NT$1 [4 cents, the cost of a local telephone call] everyone can express their opinions in public."

Regularly raided by the government, Taiwan's pirate stations are usually back on the air in hours. People are hungry for information and increasingly bold about free speech. When Voice of Taiwan was raided in 1994, riots erupted in Taipei. Having sampled the information explosion, people are unwilling to return to the silent days of government-controlled media.

Furthermore, the economy of Asia can't afford to return to those bygone days. Advertising — particularly in print, but increasingly on television and radio — is already a multibillion dollar business. What government is going to turn its back on that kind of revenue?

Access to worldwide satellite broadcasting, movies, print and radio gives the emerging middle class a clear picture of "the international good life" — albeit a somewhat skewed one if it's *Dynasty* and *Dallas* that are shaping their vision. In any event, the closer it comes to being within their reach, the more eager they are to grasp it.

An explosion in broadcast and print media brings Asia more and better entertainment choices. In 1990, StarTV became the first pan-Asian satellite television network. Reaching more than half the world's population, StarTV sparked a cultural revolution. Australia's media mogul Rupert Murdoch's News Corp. bought control of StarTV to capture the hearts, minds and pocketbooks of Asian consumers. StarTV's joint venture, Phoenix Satellite Television, hopes to enter China's market.

For the past year or so, global media moguls have been engaged in a power struggle to determine who would dominate the Asian market. Cable News Network (CNN), National Broadcasting Corp. (NBC), British Broadcasting Co. (BBC), StarTV and Hong Kong's Television Broadcasts (TVB) were all scrambling for a toehold. Not one has made a profit — or broken even. What is becoming apparent is the likelihood of two or three alliances among the major players, with CNN as a "wild card".

Media moguls have learned one important lesson: as much as Asians initially are drawn to all things Western, in the final analysis they want to be entertained in their own language. Part of the joy of being a couch potato is expending no energy whatsoever. Struggling to interpret English language programming just isn't fun.

Entertaining Asia's middle class

Middle-class economic status opens the door to the big world of entertainment.

Jurassic Park was the first major Hollywood movie to be dubbed into Hindi since *Gandhi*. In April 1994 the movie opened in 110 Indian theaters. Chinafilm just recently started importing 10 "outstanding" movies a year. Before only outdated, cheap foreign films were bought.

B.B. King performed at the Hard Rock Café's opening in

Beijing. The 16,000 square foot restaurant is almost exactly like the one in Dallas. There are also Hard Rock franchises in Singapore, Bangkok, Bali, Taipei, Jakarta and Kuala Lumpur. Planet Hollywood has the rights for restaurants in 16 Asian countries.

Phantom of the Opera, *Les Misérables* and even Pavarotti performed to an audience of Asia's glitterati. Michael Jackson's Dangerous Tour was a sell-out in Singapore.

T. Ananda Krishnan — Asia's answer to Rupert Murdoch

Not content to let Western media moguls walk off with the prize, Asian entrepreneurs and established business tycoons are vying for the lion's share of the market. Malaysian businessman T. Ananda Krishnan fully expects to convince the governments of Malaysia and Singapore to team up to capture the regional media market. He very likely will achieve that goal. Involved in everything from oil trading to property development — including the sky-scraping Kuala Lumpur City Centre — Krishnan's passion is media.

With the launching of Malaysia East Asia Satellite (Measat), his next goal is to "become a state-of-the-art provider of multimedia services — the full array from POTS (plain old telephone services) to entertainment by exploiting the synergies in telecommunications, satellites and broadcasting."

Few doubt his ability to become Asia's answer to Rupert Murdoch. He will, in part, because he understands an important paradox: to be truly successful he must appeal to the broadest possible audience within a segmented market, yet without creating one-size-fits-all broadcasting. Somehow one has to do both. It is a lesson that all who hope to market to the new Asian middle class will have to learn. Asia is not a single, homogeneous market, but a collection of countries, a collection of markets.

The theme emphasized again and again in this book has particular application here: although Asians are influenced by Western ideas, styles and attitudes — as seen through international broadcasts — Asians are not becoming Western as such. **They are modernizing in the Asian Way.**

Cultural norms and consumer markets

Part of that modernization is the changing construct of Asian households: with mom, dad and two children, they are beginning to look more like Western households. Grandma and grandpa live elsewhere. More Asian children are now being cared for by nannies, housekeepers, and au pairs from other Asian countries. "In Singapore, Hong Kong, Malaysia and other affluent parts of Asia, many mothers are increasingly willing to leave their children in the care of helpers. The domestics — from Philippines, Indonesia, Thailand, Sri Lanka — are often well-educated and hard-working," says *Asiaweek*.

The widespread exodus of women from household to workplace has engendered endless worry about children's mental and developmental well-being. The pursuit of education, always highly valued, is sometimes a status symbol. In India, for example, children as young as three take rigorous entrance exams to get into the "right" pre-schools. A story in the *Washington Post* says:

> "In India, where the world's fastest-growing middle class is undergoing profound changes...toddler stress has become the latest manifestation of the frenetic race to get ahead. Overachieving parents now begin grooming children as young as two and a half for the battery of entrance interviews for admission to the city's most elite private nursery schools. Once in school, the stress only increases."

Similarly, in China and elsewhere in Asia, private kindergartens are springing up in major cities in a mad frenzy to prepare children to live proper middle-class lives.

"Zhu Xiaoying, a village woman in southern China's Guangdong province, wants only the best for her son," reports a *Korea Times* article. For her that means paying $21,350 up front, the equivalent of 25 years of an average worker's wages in nearby Guangzhou, to send her six-year-old son Chen Juhui to the private Guangdong Country Garden School just south of the city.

Why is the new middle class willing to part with extraordinary sums to finance, not university, but early childhood education? Is it in part a reaction to their own sense of loss? For many, the hope of education was all but eradicated by the Cultural Revolution. Its victims are increasingly aware of the deficit that loss has created. Second, it is a function of the "six pocket syndrome". Strict population controls created a generation of single-child households, many of whom have six income-earning adults — two parents, and two sets of grandparents — indulging their every whim.

The children of the middle class are themselves a significant economic force. Singapore's *Business Times* reports:

> "The sheer numbers of these teens are fuelling a global consumer revolution with youth culture as its raison d'être. Demographically, Singapore's teens have yet to overtake the 30-somethings here…but what teens lack in numbers, they make up for by sheer spending power. These teenagers are out there spending close to $250 million a year (or an estimated $100 a month) — and that's just pocket money. Throw in what their indulgent parents buy them and what they earn in part-time jobs to pay for extra luxuries and you have a formidable force in the marketplace."

Marketers are discovering that teenage consumers, heavily influenced by Western television, nonetheless reflect local tastes and conform to some traditions and cultural norms. "If you take a typical Indian teenager in Bombay, Delhi or Calcutta, you would find that tangibly he has moved toward the West," says

Jagdeep Kapoor, director of Parle Agro, a Bombay-based marketer of Frooty, a boxed fruit drink, and Bailley's mineral water. "He'd be wearing a Lacoste shirt, Wrangler jeans, Nike shoes and maybe a pair of Ray-Ban glasses." But he is very much an Indian in his values, says Kapoor. He respects his parents, lives with his family and takes off his Nike shoes and Ray-Bans before entering a place of religion. Alygue Padamsee, well-known Bombay adman, says:

> "This is the land of karma, where everything is worked out for you, your destiny, your kismet. But the new generation feels, 'The hell with waiting for reincarnation!' and they are breaking the karma handcuffs. They're deciding that what they want is a better life, now, and if they have any money, they want to spend it now."

Savings, investment and retirement

Asia has high savings rates, averaging around 30 percent. But with the rise in consumer spending, will the savings rate go down? If it does more investment capital will have to be raised outside the region.

It is reported that urban Chinese have about $200 billion outside the nation's banking system, "in their hands or under their beds". Per capita income in China is $2,500 (using the purchasing power parity method explained earlier). There are more than 80 million Chinese earning between $10,000 and $40,000 a year. We also know that there are more than a million millionaires in China.

To channel savings into productive capital and let money make money for the Asians, tremendous opportunities open up in the field of personal finance. The region's major financial institutions are launching unit trust and mutual funds to mobilize domestic savings and help its citizens hedge against inflation.

"In terms of life insurance, China represents the end of all roads," said Andres Kabel, National Mutual Asia's chief executive of finance. A new era is dawning on the region's life insurance industry, with local players revitalized by the new-found wealth and foreign players keenly eyeing the market. With markets in the West nearing saturation point, US and European insurers are looking to Asia to underwrite their future growth. *Asia Inc.* reported:

> "In 1992, according to Swiss Reinsurance Co, 35 percent of the world's 1.47 trillion insurance business was written in the U.S., 31 percent in Europe and 22 percent in Japan. The rest of Asia represented just 5 percent of the global market so far. But within 10 years, China will be the world's single biggest insurance market, predicts Mick Newmarch, chairman of Prudential Corp. Asia Ltd."

Veteran American player American International Assurance (AIA), a wholly owned subsidiary of American International Group of the US, is already writing new policies at the rate of 55,000 a month. Its Chinese salesforce already numbers 5,400.

It is not only China that has attracted the interest of the world's insurers. Except Japan and South Korea, all other Asian countries have insurance premiums less than 5 percent of their GDP (Japan has 8.6 percent, totaling $320 billion, while South Korea has 12.3 percent, totaling $36 billion a year). Besides China, the wealthy, high net-worth individuals in Singapore, Taiwan, Hong Kong and Malaysia, along with the rising middle class in Indonesia and India, offer great untapped potential.

Art connoisseurs

The next stage of human gratification after material needs are satisfied is the quest for aesthetics and the past. Asia has been a world source of supply of art objects for centuries. The richness of Asian civilizations, its people, culture, religions and a long and sometimes glorious past have produced a steady supply of art to the world's discerning connoisseurs, who until recently were mainly in the West. Collectors and art lovers from Europe and America have long been fascinated with Oriental art and have created the greatest demand, thus setting standards and prices. But the balance of interest and buying power is now shifting to the East.

In an auction held in Singapore in March 1995, Singapore artist Tan Swie Hian sold his *The Sound of Sutra* painting for $90,800, the highest price ever paid for a living local artist.

At a Christie's auction in the same city in the same month, a painting by the famous nineteenth-century Indonesian artist Raden Saleh Bastaman Saleh sold for $640,000, a record high for the artist.

Art appreciation is a function of affluence. The rising economic tide in Asia will lift the fortunes of the Asian art market. From Shanghai to Singapore, Bombay to Bangkok, Hanoi to Hong Kong, Tokyo to Taipei, the art scene is becoming increasingly vibrant and holds great promise. Galleries are opening, cultural promotions are receiving heightened attention from governments, all driven by a growing middle class. The Korean government is expending tremendous energy on a national cultural program it calls "New Renaissance", aimed at reshaping the cultural climate of the country. Demands in the Indian art market are so great that artists sell their works as fast as they are finished.

Renaissance in Asian art

The assertiveness of being Asian is rippling through the world of art. Money has a liberating influence on the soul, and as Asians begin to display greater confidence in themselves, they will focus on and appreciate indigenous culture. Contemporary Asian art is set to flourish. The antique and craft markets are also set to boom as Asians celebrate their success and reassert their pride of the past.

Asians are collecting each other's art. Chinese art has been the most prized and popular. Interest in a wide range of contemporary art is on the rise among the increasingly affluent middle class. The Singapore Art Museum is on a buying spree to put together a collection of the best from the region.

One Japanese, Masanori Fukuoka, the owner of a food processing company and founder of the Glenbarra Art Museum in Himeji, Japan, has a collection of 3,000 works of contemporary Indian art. Fukuoka said of his interest in Indian art, while:

> "European art may be very beautiful, it is less provocative to the modern audience. Given that India, which contains about 15 percent of the world's population, faces daily many problems plaguing much of the world, contemporary Indian artists often address and/or reflect the circumstances of the modern world. To the extent that these issues are global, the art can touch the Japanese mind and can affect a Japanese more profoundly than the older European works, which are of a wholly different time and world than ours today."

Given the dynamics of the region, the world may soon see exciting contemporary creations from Asia.

$39 million for a Van Gogh Sunflower, anyone?

When rich Asians begin to buy art, will they outdo the Japanese and do for the art market what the Japanese did in the 1980s? And who in Asia would have so much interest in Western art as to outbid everyone at all costs? The Chinese, Indians, Indonesians, Thais or Koreans?

The answer is, none of the above. Asians have long traditions and they are very centered in a universe of their own values. Unlike the Japanese, whose culture is largely derivative and highly insular, the Indians and Chinese particularly take great pride in their civilization and greatly value their past. Interest in Western art is not likely to rise.

At the most, the interest will be confined to well-traveled and Western-educated Asians, whose interest may center on Western contemporary and modern art.

A boom in classic Chinese art

While all of Asia is growing, the greatest impact on the art market is expected to come from the Chinese, especially the Chinese overseas. Their wealth is growing dramatically following the region's economic explosion. The implications of this are enormous for the world art market. However, one important point must be noted: the Chinese are very culture bound. The 57 million ethnic Chinese diaspora, wherever they are in the world, remain culturally Chinese. They hold on strongly to cultural identity and manifest it in all aspects of their lives. It is this "Chineseness" that is creating the excitement in the classical Chinese art market. In auctions of Chinese art in and around Asia, the Chinese are the most interested buyers, and they are prepared to outbid each other. For example, in a Christie's auction in 1995 in Hong Kong, an anonymous Chinese buyer — rumored to be from the mainland — paid $1.5 million for a jade bangle. Auction houses dealing with Chinese art in Asia are reporting breathtakingly high prices.

Given its scarcity and the heightened interest in classical objects of art, prices are expected to go through the roof when the Chinese return to reclaim the trophies of their civilization. Collectors and dealers of the art world, fasten your seat belts.

Changing market trends

We are not talking about a few rich individuals buying art. We are talking about millions of middle-class Asians coming to appreciate the finer things of life. When preoccupation with GNP and stock market performance gives way to greater refinements, the middle class will be buying art. A new generation of buyers has emerged and are buying midpriced antiques, preferring them to classic ceramics. Ten years ago, only 5 percent of buyers at Hong Kong's Atfield Galleries were Asians — today the figure has risen to 40 percent.

The demand for art, not just fine art, but everything from architecture and home furnishings to fashion and entertainment, is set to boom.

Eastman Kodak CEO George Fisher likes to say, "Half the people in the world have yet to take their first picture." And most of them are in Asia, where most of the region's 3 billion people have yet to own a wristwatch, a suitcase, sunglasses, a Wonderbra, or a radio, not to mention a computer, motorcycle, refrigerator, microwave oven, television, an apartment or a house, a trip abroad, a Ming Dynasty ceramic... The list just goes on and on. That's Asia.

Catching moving targets

By now, it should be beyond doubt that Asia is the new gold rush for the West, as California was the gold rush for the early Asian migrants to America. But the Asian gold rush is not so easy to mine. It takes great skill and tenacity to find, study and then reap rewards. In marketing to Asians, one has to address the mosaic of varying levels of purchasing power, and of diverse cultures and religious sensitivities, and to persuade in different languages.

The reward is there for those with patience, for those who are looking at Asia as a 20–50-year project.

Today's new urban Asia is just as sophisticated and is more exciting than Western cities. Urban Asian consumers are sophisticated, modern and keen to embrace the global lifestyle. Young Asians have grown up accustomed to many things originated in the West. They have, for example, completely embraced pizza, some even claiming that it is part of their heritage. There is a story about a young Singaporean child who is taken by his father to Rome, where the little boy remarks, "Hey, look Dad, they have pizza here too." On sampling the product he decides it is not as good as the original back home.

Nury Vitachi, who writes for the *South China Post* and *Far Eastern Economic Review*, describes the Asian middle-class phenomenon as follows:

> "Executives in Asia have become rich at warp speed by taking full control of their own lives. They invest a great deal of time in their work, they use strategy to scramble up the corporate ladder, and they demand payment in cash — so that they can make their money work as hard as they do."

Signs of affluence are everywhere, but don't get carried away. Traveling around Asia, no matter how rich the Asians become, signs of their frugal nature are still apparent and Asians are very cost conscious. I am often reminded of the shopkeepers in many Asian cities, most pronounced in Hong Kong, where discounted merchandise means payment in cash instead of plastic.

Most people save the increases in their income, and many prefer to put it into fixed or other income-generating assets. Stock, land and property are their favorites.

Most affluent Asians still regard financial security as the most important form of security, and they are confident that Asia is the place to be to achieve that. While many have begun to savor the good life, they are not letting go of their top priority of education for their children. Education is looked on as the most important contributing factor to success in life. In many of Asia's competitive urban centers, there is a rush to acquire a second degree and other forms of professional qualification to ensure personal competitiveness in the workplace. There are extraordinary opportunities in Asia for education and training, from language to software programming.

Despite the rise in Asian assertiveness, they still look to the US and not so much Europe for ideas and trends. In general Asians, except those in Hong Kong and Japan, are not particularly concerned with being fashionable. For today's Asia, Japan and Hong Kong are the sources of fashion ideas, but as the region becomes more affluent there is a great opportunity to develop an indigenous fashion industry. For example, a huge market potential exists in introducing new materials and simplified but fashionable designs for countries in tropical Asia with a humid and warm climate throughout the year.

The population density and lack of space in urban areas have prohibited Asians from exercising frequently and few have tended to indulge in outdoor activities. This is changing. Most Asians consider themselves in good health. Compared with Americans, few are overweight — largely due to the Asian diet. But now health clubs are becoming popular with younger Asians. There is great potential for indoor exercise equipment. Also it is important to dress for the gym, and they are serious about looking good, complete with make-up, sunbeams, designer exercise shoes and outfits, and a gym bag.

To catch Asia's moving targets, regardless of what you are selling, it is a good idea to stick with market density — not country by country but, mostly, city by city. Asian markets can be a marketer's dream in that densities are among the highest in the world. Java, Indonesia's main island, has 115 million people. On Nanjing Road, Shanghai's busiest street, businesses are open 12 hours a day almost every day of the year. More than 1.5 million people visit its shops each day, and each day they spend more than $50 million.

Someone said that you can only become rich if you sell to the rich. I would add that you can become richer faster if you sell to the new rich. For investors in the West, watch for Western companies that are preparing a big push in Asia. The world has not seen anything like it before, and you can reap handsome dividends if you back those stocks that are going Eastward.

One measure of the incredible spread of consumerism in Asia is the growing celebration of Christmas. In December in downtown Tokyo, Kuala Lumpur, Hong Kong, Singapore and, of course, (Catholic) Manila, there are wall-to-wall Christmas decorations. In Japan, Christmas is a verb: "Christmas your best girl". Retailers all over Asia have adopted Santa Claus as a helper to escalate gift giving. Since Asians are great gift givers it will be a stupendous market.

Another measure is the number of new cars. Sales of new cars in Malaysia in the first half of 1995 were up 50.6 percent over the same period in 1994. In Bangkok 500 new cars a day are added to the absurdly heavy traffic, where speeds average less than 1 mile an hour during peak times. "They come with briefcases full of cash," says Anthony McDonald, who sells Rover cars in Bangkok. Range Rovers sell for about $160,000. Sales increased from 1,206 in 1994 to 2,000 in 1995, and are expected to increase 30 percent in 1996. Sales of new cars in Indonesia increased more than 30 percent in 1995.

Singapore has made it very expensive to put a new car on the road. It imposes very high import duties and taxes, and the new owner must also purchase a certificate before operating a vehicle in the city. Consequently, even a little cheap Proton from Malaysia costs $65,000 to put on the road. A Mercedes can cost $300,000. Even so, sales remain high and waiting lists long. Tommy Ng, a car dealer in the state of Johor in Malaysia who sells luxury imports, says: "The more expensive the car, the longer the waiting list." He adds, "We keep thinking that it is going to slow down, but it never does."

Credit cards are issued by banks in China, but the banks are so outmoded they are the main obstacle to developing a nationwide system. Nonetheless, progress is being made. At the end of 1994, there were about 8.5 million credit cards in use in China, double the year before. As we saw earlier, the People's Bank of China, the central bank, has made a goal of 200 million credit cardholders by the year 2000 — nice round numbers.

In this exploding Asian market it will pay to Asianize Western efforts as much as possible. Do not open branches. A company's operations should take on an Asian identity — and a local identity as well. Asia's leading computer company, Taiwan's Acer, is going all out to become a truly local operation in each Asian country.

In a multipolar world, sharing of ownership and leadership is greatly desired, and it fits well with Asians' need to have individual ownership in the companies they work for. Acer is launching a program that will create local shareholder majorities in each of its key markets. The idea is that in each country the Acer brand would be perceived as domestic. The company is restructuring itself into 21 companies to keep each unit focused and to create an entrepreneurial environment, and each of these company subsidiaries is planning to go public in local stock markets, to allow employees and customers to own a stake in the operation. A very Asian communitarian approach. If one of Asia's most successful companies takes this path, it should be instructive for Western companies who want to do business in Asia.

From Western Influence
the Asian Way

Asia's new-found wealth has provoked major shifts in Asian thinking and attitudes. Economic restructuring, which grabs most of the headlines, has set in motion a profound psychological revolution involving Asia's self-image, culture and heritage. The changes happening today in Asian values are complex and paradoxical, yet it is important to sort them out if you want to be successful in the region.

The most fundamental truth to grasp is that today's revolutionary change is happening against a backdrop of history and heritage dating back thousands of years. Ancient norms and practices, and well laid out hierarchies, meant everything was pre-determined. In tradition-thick Confucian societies, for example, women were subservient to men, not only in rights and status but in their opportunities for self-expression. The ancient iron-clad caste system of Indian societies made upward mobility almost impossible. The same is true for Confucian societies, which rank scholar, farmer, artisan and merchant in that order. Under a Communist regime, the Party determines where and what you do for a living, and when you can marry and have a child. Men or women trapped in unfulfilling marriages might consider themselves unlucky, but were compelled to endure in the interest of honor and family. Strong social stigma awaited any recalcitrant. In the collective memory, social behavior equaled conformity. Period.

Politically, Asian countries were subject to varying degrees of domination. Every country in Asia except Thailand has, at one time or other, been under colonial rule. Communist governments controlled Vietnam, China and North Korea. After being ruled by England, India was for years on a socialist path. Beginning with Japan after the Second World War, however, Asian countries began undergoing various forms of political transformation, from nationalistic movements leading to self-rule and independence; from independence to the establishment of representative government; from dominant one-party rule to participatory democracy. Decades later these gradual transformations were sparked by a rise in people power, markedly in the overthrow of the Marcos dictatorship in the Philippines and the pro-democracy riots of 1992 in Thailand. All these movements heralded the end of domination, and the beginning of new experiments in multiple political options.

Adding to the structural upheaval is the empowerment of the individual through information and technology. Jimmy Lai, founder of *Next*, a pro-democracy, pro-market Chinese magazine in Hong Kong, said, "Information offers choice; choice motivates interaction; and people's interactions form the network of society. This new society...extends far beyond local physical boundaries."

The more Asian values are challenged by change, the more Asians are learning about what those values are and what they mean. In the process **Asia is moving from traditions to options**.

Wealth, political change, technology and the market economy, as well as the enlightenment and empowerment of people through travel and business, are the key factors behind Asia's new multiple options. As Asia expands economically, as Asian societies move towards greater political openness, individuals, companies, institutions will experience more and more options.

New models and structures, new ways of organizing relationships are emerging between women and men, government and
people, employers and employees — the Asian way.

A huge wave of change is rolling across Asia with unprecedented speed. Individuals, societies and governments in Asia
are now confronted with the challenge of managing not just the
changes presented by these options, but also the speed with
which they are taking place. In some places, the radical changes
are creating turmoil and chaos in the social fabric, increasing
stress and producing undesirable consequences. Both the openness and the ills of progress and prosperity are most apparent in
urban Asia, but increasingly felt in rural areas.

Do all these new options offer a better quality of life than
tradition and pre-destination? That is the question Asia is grap-
pling with. One thing is certain. These new options are
available for the first time in the lives of many people. Chen Li,
69-year-old retired editor at large of the *China Daily* in Beijing,
announced euphorically, "for the first time in history, we have
control over our destiny".

How do Eastern values differ from Western values?

The two recent lightning rods that brought the East–West values debate to the forefront were America's linking of the exten-
sion of Most Favored Nation status to China with human
rights, and the caning in Singapore of American teenager
Michael Fay.

Says Singapore's Senior Minister Lee Kuan Yew:

> "The expansion of the right of the individual to behave or
> misbehave...has come at the expense of orderly society. I
> would hazard a guess that it has a lot to do with the erosion
> of the moral underpinnings of a society and the diminution
> of personal responsibility... The fundamental difference

between Western concepts of society and government and East Asian concepts...is that Eastern societies believe the individual exists in the context of his family."

First of all, the big debate currently raging in Asia is not about the relative superiority of the values of East or West. **It is a rebellion against domination; it is Asia standing up to its former masters.**

Whether Asian or American, some values are universal

One of the main conclusions of David I. Hitchcock's *Asian Values and the United States, How Much Conflict?* is that:

> "the common threads developing between East and West across the Pacific are far more significant than the differing values each holds dear... And that most of the strains of development evident in East Asia today stem from modernization, rather than Westernization."

Hitchcock, of the Center for Strategic and International Studies, a thinktank in Washington, DC, interviewed 100 people from different professions in Singapore, Kuala Lumpur, Jakarta, Bangkok, Shanghai, Beijing, Seoul and Tokyo. The majority were academics and most "would be considered quite influential in their own country", he states. He asked these individuals to rank the importance of values, not in each individual's view, but according to what they believed were "critically important" to the people in their country. Interestingly enough, when compared to American responses on values, the values appear to be fairly universal, not specifically Eastern or Western, but they do differ in priority:

Top Asian Personal Values	Top American Personal Values
Hard work	**Self-reliance**
Respect for learning	**Hard work**
Honesty	Achieving success in life
Self-discipline	Personal achievement
Self-reliance	Helping others
	Honesty
Top Asian Societal Values	Top American Societal Values
Orderly society	Freedom of expression
Harmony	Personal freedom
Accountability of public officials	Rights of the individual
Openness to new ideas	Resolve conflicting political views through open debate
Freedom of expression	Thinking for oneself
Respect for authority	**Accountability of public officials**

Asia choosing its own values

Asia has come of age. It seeks to determine its own agenda, to do things in the Asian way. Throughout the continent, the voices of Asia are saying goodbye to Western domination, politically, culturally and economically. Asia will only join the world as an equal partner. It will make its own decisions, decide for itself what role to play on the world stage.

Any policymaker, government or private, who fails to see this fundamental change in mindset will be greatly disadvantaged in their dealings with Asia and Asians. Recognizing and appreciating this change is basic to building a meaningful or successful East–West relationship.

To modernize was to Westernize

Historically, Asia has accorded the West a sort of "superior" status. Because of its advanced material progress, and overpowering military and political might, the West was rarely challenged or questioned. For decades, modernization was almost synonymous with Westernization. In Japan, beginning during the Meiji era (from 1855), modernization has indeed been a process of Westernization. Traditions handed down through the earlier Edo period were systematically expelled, affecting the government's cultural policy, university system, and legal institutions. Banished subjects ranged from Chinese medicine and literature to the study of national classics, and Buddhism. The Western way was the best way. Those subjects that managed to survive did so by being recategorized under the domain of Western disciplines. The society gradually assimilated the essence of Western culture. It should be noted, however, that Japanese society possesses a great ability to "Japanize" all things foreign over the years, possible in part because of its limited usage of English and other foreign languages and its very tight and closed feudal society. So Japan embraced a sort of Japanized Western way.

In English-speaking Southeast and South Asia, however, Western influence has had a later but much greater impact. When colonies, like Malaysia under the British or Vietnam under the French, became independent nations, there was no immediate return to pre-colonial cultures. Things Western were still considered superior and desired. In Southeast Asia, for example, it was considered prestigious to send children to English language schools, rather than to native language schools, to work at the offices of multinational companies, and in some places (e.g. Hong Kong and Malaysia) for women to marry Caucasians. For many years, Chinese-school educated Singaporeans were considered an underclass compared to their English-language educated counterparts.

Asia embraced Western ways unconditionally. The brain drain to the West in the 1960s and 1970s was inspired by the pursuit of possibilities and driven by lack of opportunities at home and abhorrence of repressive, suffocating regimes.

New Asian assertiveness

There is an upsurge in confidence throughout Asia today. As I traveled around, in all my conversations with government people, academics, business leaders and journalists in Singapore, Bombay, Shanghai, Kuala Lumpur, Jakarta, Tokyo, Taipei, Manila, Hong Kong, Bangkok and elsewhere, without fail I found overwhelming self-confidence, even assertiveness. Today a collective consciousness of being Asian is emerging. Malaysia's young Deputy Prime Minister, Anwar Ibrahim, who himself is at the forefront of a movement towards Asian renaissance, described the phenomenon:

> "Since the 19th century, Asian nations have been overawed by the wealth and power of the West. Under the yoke of colonialism, Asian nations had no choice but to examine themselves critically vis-a-vis their masters, not their neighbors. Even after having gained independence they were unable to exorcise the ghost of their erstwhile superiors. Thus all their energies and efforts went towards the quest for parity with the West, brought about by a deep rooted sense of inferiority and the need to restore their self-esteem. This was the fundamental cause of the crisis in the Asian consciousness, manifested by a profound sense of helplessness in the face of Western military and political onslaught."

Now that Asia rivals the West economically, Anwar Ibrahim continues, "the Asian mind has finally broken free from intellectual morass".

That is it. Asians coming to grips with themselves. In Anwar's words, "a more positive attitude towards our own traditions, and a genuine interest in the traditions of our fellow Asians. What we are about to embark on is a voyage of self discovery, a journey through the myriad Asian traditions in order to understand and know each better."

Noordin Sopiee, Director General of one of the most influential thinktanks in Asia, the Institute of Strategic and International Studies (ISIS) in Kuala Lumpur, Malaysia, is another enthusiast for this Asian Renaissance. Dr Noordin is spearheading the Commission for New Asia, a group of eminent intellectuals from all over Asia, coming together to draw up a blueprint for the modernization of the region.

"A great deal of Asia has started to rediscover Asia," he says, "to begin to have faith in Asia, to begin to be proud of being Asian."

This faith in Asia, faith that it can develop its own models, the Asian way, is now shared by many. Dr Chandra Muzaffar, Director of the Just World Trust, a human rights group in Malaysia, says, "We want a more holistic approach to development, one that addresses in totality the various human realms of existence, material and spritual." Professor Sang-Woo Rhee of Sogang University talks about Korea's national vision for the twenty-first century, "that progress is not quantity, but also quality. We want to create harmony in our societies."

East to West: stop lecturing us

The intellectual discourse between East and West has intensified the values debate. When trade issues are linked with human rights, for example, Asia is increasingly impatient with, even aggravated by, what it views as the West's patronizing "big brother" attitude. Kishore Mahbubani, permanent secretary in Singapore's Foreign Ministry, calls for the West to "stop lecturing Asians". He says the West does not have the *moral standing* to tell others what to do. He sees Western societies in great disarray.

Mahbubani, who is also Dean of the Singapore Civil Service College, recently wrote in the *Far Eastern Economic Review* that it is the West's breakdown of the family that is leading to its social decay:

"Since 1960, the U.S. population has grown by 41 percent. In the same period, there has been a 560 percent increase in violent crimes, a 419 percent increase in illegitimate births, a 400 percent increase in divorce rates, a 300 percent increase in children living in single-parent homes, a more than 200 percent increase in teenage suicide rates, and a drop of almost 80 points in Scholastic Aptitude Test Scores."

So what are Asian values?

For many, the term "Asian values" is a rallying call against the perceived evils of Westernization, a desire to reinstate the best of the old ways in the face of rapid, stunning modernization. Changes that transpired over centuries in the West have occurred in the space of a few decades in Asia. The question now is how best to preserve the old culture and traditions while life changes at an incredible speed.

While the West cannot expect to impose its own social order on Asia, the West, at the same time, cannot be blamed for all the problems inherent with modernization. Although it is popular to criticize the West, Asia must come to terms with its own struggle to modernize and accept the responsibility that comes with it. It must figure out how to hang on to cultural traditions while adapting to the modern world, a challenging contradiction for any culture.

The problem is that "Asian values" mean different things to different people. Asia is a region of great diversity, and there is no agreement on the virtues of Asian values, even by Asians themselves.

"If we like it, it's modern; if we don't, it's Western"

This mocking quote is heard often in Asia.

"You will find people unreceptive to the idea that they be Westernized," says Singapore's Lee Kuan Yew. "Modernized, yes, in the sense that they have accepted the inevitability of science and technology and the change in the lifestyles they bring." Lee is a very vocal representative of Asia, yet many Asians dislike the fact that he tries to speak for all Asians. All Asians are not of one mind and one thought.

For three decades Lee has ruled Singapore, most of that time modernizing and, yes, Westernizing this city-state (go there, it's as Western as Kansas City). Once Singapore became a celebrated success story, Senior Minister Lee himself became a celebrated spokesman, much of the time as the only voice of Asia. With the shifts in the tides, Singapore is returning to emphasizing Asian values, and Lee is its — as Asia's — eager spokesperson for the Asian way. The return to Asian values is a strategy to ward off social decay caused by the excesses of Western individualism.

No monolithic values movement in Asia

The collection of countries and cultures that made up Asia did not undergo any systematic integration until recently, when the free market mechanism started to be embraced. The cultural, religious and linguistic diversities of the region made harmonization otherwise impossible. Historically, no movement was in place to blend Asia together, except isolated dealings between traders and political conquests. In the pre-colonial days, strong imperial powers dominated the smaller states, making them subordinate. During the colonial era, Asian nations were divided, and isolated. Since the rise of nationalism, each has been preoccupied with its own struggle to gain sovereignty, and after independence, to strengthen and build its own nation. These national preoccupations have until now prevented solidarity with neighbors and the forging of common systems.

David Hitchcock, whose report on values was mentioned earlier, found that "on no other point was there more unanimity among those interviewed in seven countries than on the question of an 'Asian way' and Asian 'kinship' or affinity. Most respondents found little significant kinship between their own country and their neighbors in the region."

● One response was from a Singaporean researcher saying, "I
  find it difficult to say there is a kinship... Singapore wants to
  be able to rely on China as a heavyweight vis-à-vis the rest
  of the world... 'Asianness' is largely a reaction to the lack of
  Western sensitivity."
● Another scholar said, "Our only common heritage is
  Asian... Some of us are not very Chinese... We are trying to
  define ourselves."
● A journalist from Bangkok stated that while an "Asian way"
  could be seen in business dealings among the country's
  Chinese population, "we do not feel any special affinity for
  other countries in the region".

Asian values reexamined

When Asian societies talk about Asian values, says Dr Chandra
Muzaffar, director of the Just World Trust, "This is a very selec-
tive approach. They pick up the values that suit them as far as
the elites are concerned, that these values will not challenge
them." Dr Muzaffar points specifically at Singapore: "They
talked of Confucian values, they talked about loyalty to the
state, the attribute of hard work, but no one talks about profit
from the Confucian ethical point of view."

Dr Muzaffar is not excited about what he views as "another
grand cycle of capitalism", which, he says, "betrays the fundamental values embodied in the Asian religions. Asian values do
not mean recycling of some values practiced elsewhere. If we are
to produce something new, our notion of Asian values must go
beyond hard work, family, etc., and deal with more fundamental
values." As stated earlier, Muzaffar promotes a holistic approach.

Malaysian Deputy Prime Minister Anwar Ibrahim goes for
balance. "If we in Asia want to speak credibly for Asian values,
we must be prepared to also champion those ideals which are
universal and which belong to humanity as a whole," he says.
He refutes the notion that Confucianism and Asian traditions
advocate suppressing the individual for the benefit of society.

"It is altogether shameful, if ingenious, to cite Asian values as an excuse for autocratic practices and denial of basic rights and civil liberties."

Now what does Reverend Sage Confucius say?

Is it the Confucian way of family and community over individualism that has catapulted Asia into economic success? Some say it is.

Others disagree. Nobel Laureate Dr Lee Yuen Tseh, President of Academia Sineca in Taipei, says, "In fact, Confucianism was never given that much attention in our society, apart from being promoted as a guide to right living. **The success of the East Asian economies has given Confucianism a good name**."

Many in Asia agree that the impetus to Asia's growth witnessed by the world today is a result of the embrace of Western science, technology and management. Korean scholar Kim Kyong-Dong says:

"Confucianism of any version…was not the spiritual or ideological source of inspiration or impetus for…capitalist development in the initial stage of East Asian modernization. It was the impact of Western modernization that provided the impetus for change."

But what is so unique about Confucianism? That it instills the value of hard work? So does the "Protestant ethic". Just what are these Confucian ideals?

Professor Tu Wei-ming, a world authority on Confucianism who teaches at Harvard University, provides the explanation. Confucianism embraces two main streams of philosophy, political Confucianism and personal ethics. He explained, "Political Confucianism legitimates a hierachical political system culminating in the emperor, and what he called the 'Confucian personal ethic' which regulates day to day life." Some Asian governments are employing political Confucianism as an umbrella to legitimize their mode of governance, whereas, as Professor Tu argues, "the more important legacy of traditional Confucianism is not its political teaching but rather the personal ethic that regulates attitudes towards family, work, education and other elements of daily life that are valued in Chinese Society."

Many Westerners do not understand that in the Asian concept of hierarachy, responsibility flows in two directions. Confucianism is not just "listen to thy father" — the father must also be accountable to the son.

"Confucianism is not simply the advocacy of obedience to government but also the accountability of government," says Professor Tu. He adds that student activists and radicals in Taiwan and South Korea are responding to Confucian teachings.

"Under the Confucian tradition, leaders must meet certain minimum conditions in order to claim moral authority, and that is highly problematic for the current leadership in China," says Tu. He goes on to say that **Confucian tradition would prosper more in a democracy that promotes individual rights than a totalitarian atmosphere**. "If they really want to learn from Confucian humanism, they have to open up to more enlightened values, such as freedom of expression, the dignity of the individual and other human rights."

So it is not individualism or liberalism that is the problem when Confucianism is being promoted as incompatible with Western-style democracy. The answer lies in the relationship between individual families and the State. Francis Fukuyama, author of *The End of History and the Last Man*, says:

> "the essence of traditional Chinese Confucianism was never political Confucianism at all, but rather an intense familism that took precedence over all other social relations, including relations with political authorities. That is, Confucianism builds a well-ordered society from the ground up rather than the top down, stressing moral obligations of family life as the

basic building block of society. The bonds within the family take precedence over higher sorts of ties, including obligations to the political authorities."

Traditionally Chinese families are suspicious of the State and avoid dealings with government. Settling disputes through the courts did not guarantee delivery of justice because of corrupt court officials, who represented the government. Ironically, it is the Chinese people's weak deference to authority that has at times created the need for an authoritarian government. Historically they have experienced continuous social and political instability, so much so that their psychics fear chaos (*luàn*). Chaos undermines development and progress, and the Chinese will do anything to preserve stability. Fukuyama suspects that:

> "the emphasis on political authoritarianism in Singapore and other Southeast Asian states is less a reflection of those societies' self discipline — as they would have others believe — than of their rather low levels of spontaneous citizenship and a corresponding fear of coming apart in the absence of coercive political authority."

The resurgence in Confucian values, both on the part of Asian governments and the academic community, represents a campaign to ward off social decay — the weakening of work ethics, hedonistic consumption, excesses of individualism and agitation for participation in government.

"China is looking for something to take the place of failed Marxism," says W. Theodore de Bary, a Confucian scholar at Columbia University in New York City. The state is trying to advance a Confucian socialism to take the place of a Marxist one.

In 1994, China celebrated the 2,545th anniversary of the birth of Confucius. While Mao would be quite disturbed by the State's support of Confucianism, as de Bary suggests it fills the void left by the downfall of Marxism. The celebration also marked the founding of the International Confucian

Association, whose goal is to "spread Confucian studies throughout the world".

De Bary believes East Asian societies are trying to establish a cultural bond against Western decadence as they see it. China hopes its plans to instill Confucian values will inspire people to care about others, not just themselves.

Confucianism is seen as the way to prevent the decline of the family unit in Singapore, the only East Asian country to "explicitly" stress it in values education. Senior Minister Lee is Honorary Chairman of the International Confucian Association, and he said:

> "It is my business to tell people not to foist their system indiscriminately on societies in which it will not work.
>
> "As an East Asian looking at America, I find attractive and unattractive features. I like, for example, the free, easy and open relations between people regardless of social status, ethnicity or religion. And the things that I have always admired about America, as against the communist system, I still do: a certain openness in argument about what is good or bad for society; the accountability of public officials; none of the secrecy and terror that's part and parcel of communist government.
>
> "But as a total system, I find parts of it totally unacceptable: guns, drugs, violent crime, vagrancy, unbecoming behavior in public — in sum the breakdown of civil society... In the East the main object is to have a well-ordered society so that everybody can have maximum enjoyment of his freedoms. This freedom can only exist in an ordered state and not in a natural state of contention and anarchy."

Why I love America

As the East–West values debate got more intense, Tommy Koh, Director of the Institute of Policy Studies in Singapore and a former ambassador to the United States, became a defender of the United States. Writing for the *International Herald Tribune*, Koh said that reports of America's sorry demise may just be a bit exaggerated.

"America's problems are real. But they should be seen in proper perspective. The United States has many strengths and virtues." He went on to compare the many strengths and virtues he experienced in his 19 years in the United States. Among them:

● In Singapore, only about 1 person in 10 does volunteer work. More than 80 million Americans donate to a cause.

● There is a strong tradition in the US of giving money to schools, colleges, universities, hospitals, libraries, churches, museums and to supporting the arts. In 1993 Americans contributed $126.2 billion to educational and charitable institutions, $9.6 billion to artistic, cultural and humanitarian organizations, most from individuals.

● American culture nurtures original thinking and pioneering research. More Nobel prizes are awarded to Americans than to scientists from any other nation. Asian scientists who have won Nobel Prizes have been based in America.

● Since the end of the Vietnam War in 1975, 850,000 refugees from the region have been taken in by America — no nation has welcomed so many immigrants and refugees, and none has assimilated them so well, as the US.

● Today, Asian Americans are the fastest growing community in the US, made possible by the relative absence of racial or class barriers.

● No other nation has been as generous as the US in sharing its technology with others.

The way forward

Most of Asia is not blaming the West's influence for its problems, but acknowledging the West's economic development and better standard of living. Still, Asia's intelligentzia is con-

cerned with what they see as the impending social decay
brought about by Asia's prosperity. Dr Mahathir Mohamad,
Prime Minister of Malaysia, who volunteers friendly advice to
the West from time to time, summed up the debate:

> "We can easily achieve material progress by physical plan-
> ning and development. But the stark truth is that all the
> material wealth that we have accumulated can be complete-
> ly wiped out if we do not have the morally right set of val-
> ues among the people who manage them."

The values debate, echoed in the media, often sounds like this:
West —"You have caning"; East — "Well you have declining
SAT scores!" Perhaps a little caning could help bring up those
SAT scores.

Choosing lifestyles

> "Today, thanks to a thriving world economy, global
> telecommunications, and expanding travel, exchange
> among Europe, North America, and the Pacific Rim is hap-
> pening at an unparalleled pace. In the urban centers of the
> developing world signs of the international youth culture
> are almost everywhere. So enthusiastically are we swapping
> food, music, and fashion that a new universal international
> lifestyle reigns in Osaka, Madrid, and Seattle."

I wrote that in *Megatrends 2000*, published in January 1990,
and it applies now more than ever. Teenagers around the world
often have more in common with each other than they do with
their parents. Right or wrong, it's reality and there's no going
back. It is the globalization of lifestyles.

How strange a mix of global influences is shown in the fact
that some of the Hindu fundamentalists involved in the destruction of a sixteenth-century Muslim mosque in 1992 had "Rama"

razor-cut into their haircuts. They break-danced at the site.

The intelligentzia, in industrialized and urban Asia where problems are most acute, will continue to debate and agonize over remedies. In the meanwhile, the vast majority of common people, especially the young, are adopting Western, mainly American ways. Too bad their ideas of what is American come from the entertainment media. Led by Hollywood and TV, the media is responsible for the distorted image of American life that is spread all over Asia. Asian governments, in turn, are keen to censor negative signals that glorify violence and sexual wantonness.

In Asia today some major shifts in the social and cultural landscape are beginning to take place. And all these have to do with the changing role of the individual within the system, regardless of whether the outcome is positive or negative.

Paradoxically, I think the widely perceived onslaught on Asian values brought about by galloping materialism will strengthen Asian values. The more the threat is experienced, the more Asian intellectuals will be aware of their basic values and the more they will want to shore them up. And the more economically interdependent people become (thereby losing a little of their identity), the more interested they will be in their identity, and the more they will want to defend it. This translates into renewed interest in who they are as expressed by their language, their arts and literature, and their history. The Thais will become more Thai, the Koreans more Korean, and the Malaysians more Malay.

A new family style

Increasing divorce rates are no longer a unique Western attribute. All of urban Asia has them. They're everywhere. Korea's divorce rate is up threefold since 1970. Taiwan's and Singapore's have doubled since the early 1980s. China's has tripled since 1990. In Hong Kong the divorce rate increased tenfold during the 20 years to 1992.

Even in Singapore, where the family is so emphasized, the juvenile crime rate increased 27 percent between 1992 and 1993. Single-parent households are increasing. In an effort to stop the increase in the number of unwed mothers, they will have certain privileges revoked. Legislation was introduced to allow parents to sue their children for support.

In Hong Kong, the number of single-family households is estimated at nearly twice what census figures report. The suicide rate of those under 19 years of age in Hong Kong has increased substantially. Between 1993 and 1994, police figures show an eightfold increase in the number of drug arrests of 16- to 20-year-olds.

"Families in Hong Kong are very geared towards making money; they don't spend enough time together any more and crime is just one part of a youngster's maladjustment," says C.C. Lu, senior clinical psychologist for Hong Kong's Correctional Services.

While some opt to let individual fulfillment prevail, most Asians still prefer to stick with the emphasis on building families. Some successful women in Asia, when asked to choose between family and individual career aspirations, choose family.

Christmas to New Year cakes

In Japan, unmarried women over age 25 are called Christmas cakes. Increasingly, however, Japanese women refuse to get married well beyond 25. They no longer worry about being called a stale Christmas cake or becoming a (much older) New Year cake.

"We are living in a very different culture to that of a decade ago," comments C.C. Lu.

Honor thy father

In Japan "how to" books on caring for senior family members rank on the bestseller lists, including what to look for in a retirement home.

In China the ancient contract that children would support parents is being renegotiated. While 97 percent of Beijingers, surveyed by the China Academy of Social Sciences, say children should take care of their parents, 20 percent said they would put their parents in "old-age homes" to do this. Seventy-five percent said they were "reluctant to live with their parents".

Still, many Asians are highly uncomfortable with the idea of "old age home", says Indonesia's Wahid Supriyadi. "Sending a grandparent to a nursing home is regarded inhuman in most Asian society."

There will not be a total shift from "communitarianism to individualism", says Lam Peng Er of the Department of Political Science, National University of Singapore. The trends, he says, "will co-exist side by side".

"[It] may not necessarily mean that by going towards individualism one is leaving behind communitarianism," says Marzuki Darusman, Vice Chairman of the Human Rights Commission, and a former member of the Indonesian House of Representatives. "It is a question of balance."

Also there new ways of family and economic life. The nursing home, for example, is an innovation for Asia. Modern ones have the pluses of medical facilities and recreational programs for residents.

Sexuality: it's OK to look at me

In Japan, PDA — Public Display of Affection, i.e. kissing in public — has become increasingly common. Some call it "evil behavior from overseas"; others complain the kids have "absolutely no manners". But while some find kissing in public offensive, posters of nude women are plastered all over the newspapers and on TV.

"Nowadays it's perfectly fine to directly project your sexuality," says Japanese psychologist Nobue Nakamura. Why? Because, she explains, the "self-restraint" of the Japanese culture is changing to allow people to become more "individualis-tic". Or to have the option of becoming more individualistic.

Chapter 2 discussed the growth of talk radio in Shanghai and Taiwan. The Chinese cities of Tianjin, Shanghai, Guangzhou and Jilin air call-in shows that discuss dating, sex, sexual diseases, and other questions. *Secret Whispers* airs in Shanghai after midnight. "Sex" and "banking"(!) top the list of caller questions at Shanghai's "information radio line". Magazines and papers feature stories on contraception and sex.

The place to express one's sexuality is at the disco, where an ordinary office girl can shine like a glamorous diva.

"Most OLs (office ladies) have to wear terrible uniforms all day and make copies and serve tea," says Ken Lyle, manager of Juliana's, a British-based company that opened a huge disco in Tokyo a few years ago. "This is their 15 minutes of fame, the chance to wear sexy clothes and say to men, 'I'm a good-looking woman, and now you're looking at me.'"

More than 50,000 women recently flocked to the Tokyo Dome for a contest of "dancing, waving feather fans and boas".

"It's wonderful," says Misao Kawaii, who at age 67 went to Juliana's to see what "dirty dancing" was all about. "My, the young women's legs today are so pretty and well-shaped! So different from our generation. I was really impressed."

But, some wonder, "is it women's liberation or exploita-tion?" At the Ronde Club in Tokyo's Akasaka area women wear feathers, G-strings and other tiny items of clothing on stage.

No yesterdays, no tomorrow

New Delhi sociologist Atiya Singh said of the young, "They work hard, play hard, and think only of themselves. Tradition and ide-alism are out. Casual sex and mobile phones are in vogue." He says, "They call it maximization. The idea is to squeeze the most out of the time without jeopardizing the future."

Yet it is the future that might be in jeopardy. A young Taiwanese remarked to a colleague of mine, "Why save? If I need money, I just go out and earn it."

"There is a sense of craziness here," said one of about 1,500 people crowed into Shanghai's JJ's disco. "That's why so many young people want to come here. After I go home, I think about how coming here costs a lot of money. But then the next day, I want to come again." What was surprising about JJ's is that there seemed to be almost no one over the age of 30, and they had cash. Plenty of it, reports Hong Kong *Advertising and Marketing*. They paid an entrance fee of $9.40. "It is like a Cultural Revolution all over again," quips a visitor from Hong Kong. "Except this time they're not trying to destroy it — they can't get enough of it." JJ's was started by Andy Ma, an American from Taiwan, who formed a venture with China's People's Liberation Army. JJ's was ordered to close by China's Public Security Bureau in 1995, but it will be back.

The mantra for today's Asian youth is "Let's have fun." In some liberal households it is often remarked that suitable parental advice to a teenager has changed from "Come home early" to "Don't forget your condoms."

Asians work hard and save hard. For decades purchases are postponed to enable capital to accumulate, to save for old age, to finance children's education and to support the obligations of the extended family. The forty- and fiftysomethings knew, in a Chinese expression, the hardships of working "no day and no night" (always working), but today's young seem to be practicing another tenet, no yesterdays and no tomorrow.

The new generation of Japanese workers will not work at the jobs their parents did, even more so now as they see their elders end up on the scrapheap.

However, in the face of growing conspicuous consumption and hedonism, it would be erroneous to assume that Asia is playing too much and not working hard. While some choose to smell the roses now, others are working feverishly to build global empires. A glance at the senior managers of Asian companies, entrepreneurs and professionals reveal a stunning story of young aggressive and ambitious thirty- and fortysomethings.

For example, **Chen Cheng-chung**, 40, one of the most successful entrepreneurs in Taiwan. He started working when he was very young and labors tirelessly to expand his empire. His flagship company, with assets worth $173 million, is preparing for a listing on the local stock exchange.

Catherine Yan, 38, heads a 1,000-strong cleaning service company. She decided to stay single so that she can focus on her business.

There are millions of Chens and Yans around Asia.

Confucius will understand the need to make money

Qufu, the birthplace of Confucius, is becoming a giant enterprise to cash in on the legacy of the "First Teacher of Sagely Accomplishments", according to *The Asian Wall Street Journal*. Kong Qingx, a 73rd-generation relative of Confucius, helped found San Kong beer, named for the three most famous Confucian memorials in Qufu. Mr Kong said that "San Kong has the potential to make the Qufu name famous world-wide". Elsewhere in town, near the Confucius temple, "another Confucius inspired" liquor is born. Called the Kong Fu Jia Jiu or Confucius Family Liquor, the company claims that it has become "China's best selling white liquor".

The commercialization of the "brand equity" of Confucius might appear to be in contradiction with the sage's admonition against drunkenness, "wealth and rank can be as insubstantial as floating clouds", but the disciples have the explanation. Professor Luo Chenglie of the Qufu Normal University, the center for the study of Confucian thought, actually encourages the trend. "In the few years since the local government licensed companies to use the name of Confucius in promoting their products, Mr Luo counts 29 drinks and eight foodstuffs" that use Confucius's name. "Confucius was a very broad-minded and understanding man. He would not have been bothered if someone borrowed his spirit to make money," he says. In any event, the companies will doubtlessly respect Confucius's dictum to students: "If you have wine, you must offer some to your parents and teachers."

We need moral bearings

In a fast-changing world, especially in one where the media so influences lifestyles, a moral grounding is required.

"We are all groping towards a destination which we hope will be identifiable with our past," says Lee Kuan Yew. "We have left the past behind and there is an underlying unease that there will be nothing left of us which is part of the old."

There is increasing concern that the next generation is going to hell. Moral education programs in Asia have been around since Confucius; they are now being created to protect Asian values.

- A 1994 Values Education in ASEAN seminar discussed how to insert Asian values into school curriculums — at the beginning of a child's education.
- In Singapore, the one class not taught in English is moral education.
- South Korean children spend two hours a week studying the "26 virtues" dealing with the individual, family and country. A "national ethics" class is taught in secondary school.
- Taiwanese students receive 40 minutes per week of "moral education". During 1995 and 1996 about 1,000 private schools opened in Taiwan to teach the Chinese classics.
- Members of Hong Kong's Community Youth Club are taught to "learn, be concerned and serve".

Choosing governance

With its sleek modern skyscrapers, carefully manicured lawns and gardens, impeccable public housing, ultra-efficient Singapore is in some ways the envy of Asia and the world.

Delegations from developing countries flocked to learn about the Singaporean model. Singapore's carefully designed programs of social engineering seek to manage the conduct of its citizens' lives.

Secretary Jose T. Almonte, Presidential Security Adviser in the Philippines, says Singaporeans joke about their situation: "Everything here in Singapore is 'fine'." It's "fine" all right. *Fine* if you fail to flush the toilet in a public lavatory, *fine* if you throw a cigarette butt on the street, *fine* if you are caught selling chewing gum. While proud of the prosperity they enjoyed, some Singaporeans wished for greater room for self-expression. Liak Teng Kiat, a researcher in a Singapore thinktank, wrote in the *Far Eastern Economic Review*:

> "The second generation leaders have tried to appease younger voters by adopting a more accommodating style than the Old Guard. But the voting record since the 1984 election, when the PAP [People's Action Party] share fell 12.7 points to 62.9 percent, shows that it is not enough — even with the booming economy. Singaporeans seem to want some more fundamental changes in the PAP approach to governance before they will fully return to its ranks."

Senior Minister Lee Kuan Yew still has a dominating, if not dominant, influence in government. When it was suggested that a referendum be held on the government's initiative to peg the salaries of top politicians to private sector wages, the Senior Minister said, "The people at large...are they in a position to judge? Is it within their range of experience?"

In the meantime, the *China Daily*, introducing a new edition of Deng Xiao Ping's selected works, wrote, "The point of departure and ultimate consideration for formulating various goals and policies are whether the people support them, whether they agree with and are happy with them, and whether they have given them the nod." In this case the rhetoric for democracy is stronger from China than from Singapore.

Is democracy incompatible with Asian culture?

The rhetoric between West and East seem to suggest that some believe democracy is foreign to Asian values. Kim Dae Jung, a leading champion of democracy and human rights in Korea, argues that democratic ideas are fundamental to Asian culture.

"Almost two millennia before [John] Locke, Chinese philosopher Meng-tzu preached similar ideas." If a king did not "govern righteously, the people had the right to rise up and overthrow his government in the name of heaven... The ancient Chinese philosophy of Minben Zhengchi, or 'people-based politics,' teaches that 'the will of the people is the will of heaven' and that one should 'respect the people as heaven' itself... There are no ideas more fundamental to democracy than the teachings of Confucianism, Buddhism, and Tonghak (a native religion of Korea). Clearly, Asia has democratic philosophies as profound as those of the West... Confucian scholars were taught that remonstration against an erring monarch was a paramount duty."

Nobel Peace Prize winner Aung San Suu Kyi, released in July 1995 from six years of house arrest in Burma, says:

"The argument that it took many years for the first democratic governments to develop in the West is not a valid excuse for Asian and African countries to drag their feet over democratic reform. History shows that peoples and societies do not have to pass through a fixed series of stages in the course of development... It is often in the name of cultural integrity as well as social stability and national security that democratic reforms based on human rights are resisted by authoritarian governments. It is insinuated that some of the worst ills of Western society are the results of democracy, which is seen as the progenitor of unbridled freedom and selfish individualism. It is claimed that democratic values and human rights run counter to the national culture...[yet] **many of the worst ills of American**

**society are increasingly to be found in other developed
countries. They can be traced not to the democratic
legacy but to the demands of modern materialism.**

"In each country, the democratic system will develop a
character that accords with its social, cultural and economic needs. But the basic requirement of a genuine democracy is that people should be sufficiently empowered to be
able to participate significantly in the governance of their
country."

Democracy vs development?

Senior Minister Lee Kuan Yew, however, sees democracy from
another viewpoint. "I do not believe that democracy necessarily leads to development," he says. "I believe that what a country needs to develop is discipline more than democracy. The
exuberance of democracy leads to indiscipline and disorderly
conduct which are inimical to development."

However, Malaysian Prime Minister Dr Mahathir Mohamad
said, in a speech at Cambridge University:

"When Malaysia became independent in 1957, our per capita income was lower than that of Haiti. Haiti did not take
the path to democracy. We did. Now Haiti is the poorest
country in the Americas. We could not have achieved what
we have achieved without democracy."

Several studies clearly illustrate the economic benefits of
democracy. *The Political Economy of Policy Reform*, edited by
John Williamson of the Institute for International Economics,
considers 13 country case studies. It concludes that democratic countries get "high marks for effectiveness in economic
reform". *The Economist* reports that:

"nearly all of the world's richest countries are free (meaning, among other things, democratic) and nearly all of the

poorest countries are not...it is absurd to conclude from East Asia's success, and from that fact alone, that non-democratic government is best for development... If dictators made countries rich, Africa would be an economic colossus."

Is open debate un-Asian?

Singapore enforces a strict code of conduct for the press. In recent years, *The Economist, Asian Wall Street Journal, Far Eastern Economic Review, International Herald Tribune, Time* and *Asiaweek* have had their local circulation restricted, accused by the government of interfering with domestic politics. An editor and reporter from the Singapore *Business Times* were fined for prematurely reporting a government estimate of Singapore's quarterly GNP growth.

In January 1995, Singapore found five defendants guilty of contempt of court because of an article by Christopher Lingle in the *International Herald Tribune*. The defendants were fined. Lingle had earlier fled the country. The article referred to an unnamed Asian country where the government "bankrupt[ed] opposition parties". The Singaporean government took offense at Lingle's piece and filed a libel suit against the five defendants and the paper. Lee Kuan Yew also sued the *International Herald Tribune* for calling his political grooming of his son an example of "dynastic politics".

If outsiders find it difficult to justify such censorship, the government does not. Prime Minister Goh Chok Tong's press secretary Chan Heng Wing expressed it as follows on the front page of Singapore's newspapers:

"Singapore is not America. It is small and fragile and needs a strong and fair government to survive. If its government is continually criticized, vilified and ridiculed in the media, and pressured by lobbyists as in America, then the government will lose control. The result will not be more freedom, but confusion, and decline... Singapore will expand its political and artistic space pragmatically and gradually, not in accordance with any formula urged upon Singapore by the Western media, which have pushed for and praised American-style democratization in Taiwan and South Korea. In 10 to 20 years, the results in Taiwan, South Korea and Singapore will speak for themselves."

What do other Asians think?

Media censorship is not limited to Singapore. Thailand, Taiwan, Malaysia, Indonesia and China all require the media to comply with government guidelines. But authorities have grown more liberal with the media in recent times. Newspapers, private radio and television stations enjoy greater lattitude reflecting various voices, even though any pronounced deviance from a code of conduct set by the government might cost them their permits or licenses.

The media in Taiwan, the Philippines and Hong Kong voice criticism of their governments and view this freedom of expression as a necessary condition for a democratic system and survival in the marketplace. In a public lecture at Hong Kong University on freedom of the press, Louis Cha, the widely respected founder and former chairman of *Ming Pao*, a leading Chinese newspaper in Hong Kong, said:

"A well-educated and well-informed community will not allow itself to be cheated and maliciously misled for long. That is the essential merit of the open society, and the mass media has a role is helping to create, promote and preserve this quality of openness in a society. In an open society readers have freedom of choice... To survive in this highly competitive market, the media must have the support of their audience... In other words, ethical journalism is dictated in Hong Kong not only by a moral imperative, but by the realities of the market."

Now how do you deal with cyberspace?

"Technology such as Internet will make it increasingly difficult to suppress information," stated Cheong Yip Seng, group editor-in-chief of Singapore's *New Straits Times*. "What one newspaper suppresses will re-emerge in another. The process will be accelerated by economic development and mass education."

There is no stopping the spread of information and cultural exchange. Taiwan plans to spend $114 million on computers for its schools by 1998. South Korean students study in 60 countries. Hong Kong sent 86 percent more students abroad to study in 1990 than in 1985. China sends 40,000 to the US to study, Japan sends 45,000. And getting on the Internet is the latest Asian craze.

The Internet is an important gateway of access to information, ideas, knowledge and networking with the world. It will do society much good if this access is being facilitated, especially in developing countries, to help to expand the infrastructure for learning. The young generation of cybernauts, comfortable with technology and receptive to new ideas, is indeed a strategic asset to society, serving as agents of change.

"One man one vote; some men two votes"

"Never before in Asia have so many people had the right to choose their leaders through the ballot box," reports *Asiaweek*. "For many, voting has become a routine part of life." Elections were held in Malaysia, the Philippines, Japan, and Hong Kong in 1995, in Thailand and Taiwan in 1996. Pakistan recently held its freest and fairest elections in decades.

"Unpredictability is a certainty in the democratic system," says Thailand's former Prime Minister Chuan Leekpai. "You used to ask about coups; now you no longer ask. It means you yourselves have more confidence."

"No single formula [of democracy] has been adhered to by the Western countries, no single model can be

adhered to by the societies of Asia," reports the Commission for a New Asia, a group of 18 intellectuals from 12 Asian countries.

"There is a trend towards greater political openness, younger electorate, greater accountability and transparency," says former Ambassador Tommy Koh. "The process towards democracy is evolving."

There is yet another trend going on. Concerned with stability, Senior Minister Lee proposed the idea of giving Singaporean citizens of a certain age group two votes, instead of one. The argument is based on the fact that people with family responsibilities will make decisions in the interest of stability of society.

The "new economic world order requires guaranteed freedom of information and creativity," says Kim Dae Jung. "These things are possible only in a democratic society. Thus **Asia has no practical alternative to democracy; it is a matter of survival in an age of intensifying global economic cooperation.**"

Choosing your human rights

Although some have tried to label "human rights" as specifically Western — or even a Western ideal being imposed on the East — what is increasingly being acknowledged is that human rights are basic. They apply to everyone.

"Human rights is...not conferred by society or state; rather it is a right by virtue of birth," writes Indonesia's Tommy Thomas in a recent issue of Malaysia's *New Straits Times*. "**It is futile to examine the issue of human rights from an East–West vantage point or in North–South terms. Instead it is far more productive to consider the universality of human rights**." Human rights are "universal in the sense that one either accepts or rejects the whole idea and concepts".

"It is not fair to impose the human-rights concepts of a developed country on a developing country," states Chinese Premier Li Peng. "For a developing country, human rights are, first and foremost, the rights to survival and development... A person must first survive before talking about rights."

To some Asians it is now clear that economic ascendency goes through stages, and human rights is a luxury item on the development priority list. Is it really?

And is development really the issue? In wealthy Singapore, the government believes excessive individual rights lead to social chaos.

Are human rights something the West is forcing on Asia? Not exactly. Buddhism puts forth that "nothing is nobler than self in the whole universe" meaning each person has "certain inalienable rights". Tonghak, a native Korean religion, says "man is heaven", meaning man should be served "as we do heaven". Consider this admonition from Korean scholar-statesman Yi Yul Gok of the 500-year-long Yi dynasty at the end of the fourteenth century: "The rise or fall of a society depends on whether or not a way is open for free speech."

In *Megatrends 2000* I quoted Walter Truett Anderson, a writer with Pacific News Service and author of *Rethinking Liberalism*. His quote is very relevant here:

> "The emerging global culture is not all T-shirts and fast foods, thank God. It is also a widening acceptance of principles of human rights. Such principles are becoming global norms, fragile ones to be sure, often honored in rhetoric and brutalized in practice, but nonetheless, understandable statements of what peoples all over the world can demand for themselves, and can expect to be demanded of them by others."

All members of the United Nations have signed on to uphold article 55 which provides for human rights. In the Asian region only Singapore, Vietnam, China, North Korea and Burma do not have human rights organizations.

US President Bill Clinton has called for a code of human rights principles that American firms overseas would pledge to abide by. Among the voluntary principles are provisions for "a corporate culture that respects free expression consistent with legitimate business concerns". The code also calls for the right for workers to bargain collectively, which is perhaps even more controversial. Some human rights groups call the code "too vague".

"Wages are only a small part of it," says a trade unionist in Jakarta. "What's important is that the workers have their dignity, and they'll only have that if they have the right to organize."

Some Asians complain American companies are trying to impose Western human rights requirements in an attempt to make Asian products less competitive.

"I don't buy it," responds Deborah Leipziger of New York's Council on Economic Priorities. "There are universal standards of human rights."

Choosing a religion

Spiritual vacuum is sometimes a byproduct of material success. The West took centuries to achieve its present state of progress, Asia will leapfrog in just a few decades. The rapid changes are undermining the support system provided by the extended family, and a quest for spirituality is on the rise in Asia. This has given rise to a flourishing of religious faith.

In Asia, Christianity is growing as a somewhat surprising religious option.

David Barrett, editor of the *World Christian Encyclopedia*, estimates that around 8 percent of Asia's population is Christian. Each day some 25,000 Chinese join the Protestant faith. Three new churches open every two days.

Between two and five million people attended Pope John Paul II's mass in Manila in January 1995, considered the largest mass of his papacy. The Philippines, where about 85 percent are Catholic, is Asia's only predominantly Catholic country.

There are as many as 18 million Christians in South Korea, up from 1.2 million in 1957. About 41 percent of South Koreans are Christian. Christianity is just a little less celebrated than Buddhism.

South Korea's Reverend David Yonggi Cho claims 700,000 members at his church in Seoul. He calls it the "largest Christian congregation in the world". Each Sunday seven services are held. Twenty overflow chapels and eighteen satellite churches with television monitors hold those that don't fit in the church.

Japan is witnessing increased interest in New Age spiritualism. Books stores have added New Age sections which include books on reincarnation and channeling. The Cosmo Space New Age Center in Harajuku, Tokyo, rings up sales of $2 million a year. The store's top-selling items include "power stones that are said to help people meditate or regain their stability".

Religion in China

Todd Crowell, a senior writer for *Asiaweek*, and his church in Hong Kong were guests of the Guangdong Christian Council in southern China. They were allowed to visit and worship with a church in China, and were shown the Baiwan village school — the first instance of the state giving a religious school, turned state school, back to the church. The Baiwan church has 350 members.

Open worship is allowed at 12,000 "registered" Protestant and Catholic churches in China, and there are thousands of meeting places where actual buildings have not yet been built. However, most worship in unofficial house churches.

The estimated number of Protestants in China ranges from 20 million to 100 million. However, official estimates put the number of Protestants at just 6 million. The China Patriotic Catholic Association, the state Catholic Church which has no association with the Vatican, counts 4 million members. The number of underground, Vatican-affiliated Roman Catholics is estimated at around 6 million.

The change in China is extraordinary. A country which tried to ban Christianity is now promoting it: China's Bureau of Religious Affairs is said to be "actively helping churches". A church in Qingyuan was rebuilt with state funds.

A seminary in Guangdong, allowed to reopen in 1986, has graduated 200 students, all of whom are greatly needed: the average Protestant minister in China is 75 years old.

Elsewhere in China, Buddhist temples are being rebuilt, followers are allowed to leave food for Taoist monks, and Muslims are allowed to worship in mosques.

Religious tolerance, however, is not freedom of religion. The number of house churches, and the fact that bibles are still smuggled into China, show the government is not totally comfortable with the religious revival.

The marketing of Buddhism

"Buddhism booms," reported the *Far Eastern Economic Review*, "as monks ride the wave of Thai middle-class prosperity." Ninety-five percent of Thailand's population is Buddhist. Donations are so high, the *Review* concluded, religious institutions operate like "corporate concerns".

Luang Poh Koon, who reputedly holds "the supernatural power to make followers rich and healthy…is a superstar among Thai Buddhists… Hordes of believers, including top politicians and military men" have contributed generously to his temple. Exactly how much he collects is unknown, but in 1994 he gave $2,550,000 to charities, according to ledgers kept by the abbot.

In January 1995, he gave almost $3 million to King Bhumibol Adulyadej for use in his charities, and plans to give almost $10 million more to build schools and hospitals. Thailand's 30,000 temples, called *wats*, have prospered with Thailand's increased prosperity, collecting revenues that run to many milllions annually. According to the *Far Eastern Economic Review*, "the wats are, in a sense, among the largest corporate concerns in the kingdom. One temple has even earned a business-school marketing award."

Wat Phra Dhammakaya, a temple in Phathum Thani, which is north of Bangkok, was so successful at attracting followers it received a marketing award from Thammasat University in 1989. The temple uses a "million-name computerized database for direct mail publicity drives. The campaign promoted Buddhism with glossy brochures promising followers wealth and prosperity...personal beauty, radiance...career success, strong health, and long life...[and] forthrightness and stead-fastness in Dharmma practice."

The way to the Dharma has gone high tech as well. Besides innovations in marketing to help devotees embrace the faith, some Buddhist groups use laptop computers to assist in writing and translating the mantras, and record them on videocassettes to be played on karaoke machines. They caught on rapidly and are spreading like wildfire all over Asia.

The behavior of individual monks is more controversial. Some have earned a reputation for conspicuous consumption, traveling in expensive, luxurious cars.

A recent scandal which many dubbed a "crisis of faith" involved a charismatic Thai monk named Yantra Ammaro Bhikku, who "allegedly used credit cards provided by a follower to pay for illicit sex while he was travelling overseas". Yantra was stripped of his status in the monastery; disrobed as it were.

Rising interest in Islam

Interest in Islam is on the rise too. Asia's Islamic countries, Indonesia, Pakistan, Bangladesh and Malaysia, are experiencing heightened religious interest.

The revival of Islam, like the increase in other religions, is in part a reaction to modernization and outside influence. The past 25 years have seen incredible growth in Islamic fundamentalism. While there appears to be a clash between Western Christianity and Islam, a recent special report on Islam in *The Economist* notes that Islam and the West:

"have more in common with each other than either has with the Confucian world or the Hindu world... Both have their origins in religions that believe in a single God... Few westerners believe that God dictated the Koran, and no Muslim believes that Jesus was the son of God. Those are important disagreements, but they sit alongside a large number of shared convictions. A Muslim and a westerner both believe, more clearly than most other people, in the idea of individual responsibility. They can exchange opinions about the nature of good and evil, or property rights, or the preservation of the environment, in something like a spirit of brotherhood."

To say that the West is evil and materialistic in comparison to Islamic belief is incorrect. "Both the Koran and Muhammad himself assumed a system based on individual enterprise and individual reward."

"Islamic movements today are driven more by appalling local social conditions than by some all-pervasive ideology," reports the *Far Eastern Economic Review*. Khalid Ahmed, a Pakistani writer on Islam, goes even further in saying:

"in the Islamic world, by and large, the ruling elites have failed to deliver the goods to the people, and the end of the cold war has only stripped off the veil [that obscured that fact]. The growing gap between rich and poor, runaway inflation, unemployment, massive   corruption, and widespread disillusionment with the mainstream parties and their leaders are the core issues in the Islamic world."

Young people are embracing the religion with greater intensity. The number of people making the Haj, the pilgrimage to Mecca, the holy land, is on the rise. For economic reasons, the Haj could only be performed once in the lifetime of a Muslim, but with increased affluence, many people are making frequent Haj trips.

A derivative of the mainstream religion is being developed too. The Islamic sect of Al alqum attracted more than a million followers, and grew into a sprawling business enterprise. The Malaysian government subsequently banned the movement, closing it down totally.

Choosing family help or help from institutions

In Asia, the family unit was the foundation of society. The family system, instead of the government, provides social, economic and emotional support to the individual and family. Self-reliance and personal responsibility are nurtured within the family. With increased urbanization and industrialization, however, the family is in danger of breaking down. If it is weakened beyond recognition, what social structure could possibly take its place? Will Asia, like the West, turn to the government for help? Most Asians cringe at the very thought.

How much government do Asians want in their lives?

Should the government assume a bigger role? Many think that its role should be confined to providing basic infrastructure to nurture an environment that encourages enterprise.

"When you give half of what you earn to the government, that's a western philosophy," said Mohammed Sadli, a former minister under Indonesia's New Order administration, when commenting on comparative tax rates.

Lee Kuan Yew, not surprisingly, is against the government assuming the responsibility of the individual. The difference between East and West, he argues:

"is that Eastern societies believe that the individual exists in the context of his family... In the West, especially after World War II, the government came to be seen as so successful that it could fulfil all the obligations that in less modern societies are fulfilled by the family. This approach encouraged alternative families, single mothers for instance, believing that government could provide the support to make up for the absent father."

The challenge for Asia is managing the transition to modernization. Can the family be preserved in the process, thus ensuring Asia's competitiveness?

The traditional family system served Asia well in the past. It provided support to the young and cared for the old. Asia's population is young today, but graying rapidly. The World Bank estimates that by 2030, about 22 percent of China's population will be over 60. "By 2030, Hong Kong, Macau, Singapore, South Korea, Taiwan, Sri Lanka and Thailand will all have a greater percentage of people over 60 than the United States had in 1990."

Is there a welfare system in place to provide the safety net? The answer is no. Asia cannot boast of a well-structured social security system. Two schemes, however, are widely practiced. Japan, South Korea and Taiwan have a defined benefit system which guarantees a certain level of pension. In Singapore and Malaysia there is a defined contribution plan where employer and employee contribute towards the fund. At the end of a stipulated period and subject to specific rules, the contributors get back what they paid in, plus investment return. In Singapore, employers contribute 18.5 of salary and employees 21.5 percent. In Malaysia, employers put in 12 percent, employees 10 percent.

The World Bank dislikes both schemes. First, investment decisions are made solely by the governments involved. Second, rates of return are too low. "The authorities claim the returns have been high, but the claims cannot be corroborated, since audited, published data are not available," the 1994 World Bank report, *Averting the Old Age Crisis*, stated. In any case, it adds, "the relatively low interst rate paid to the fund could thus be viewed as a hidden tax on workers to finance government expenditures and reserves."

Jimmy Lai, a great promoter of personal responsibility and self-reliance, believes that the answer lies with the market. Referring to the low tax rate in Hong Kong, he said:

> "If you only give so little to the government, you don't care a damn what they do with that money. The government can facilitate a lot of self-reliance by allowing the market to take over. When the government only takes 9 percent of our income [in taxes], and leaves 91 percent to the market for us to take care of ourselves, we are only allowing the government to intervene in a very small part of our lives."

Sue your son, and farewell my concubine

Lawmakers in Singapore and Hong Kong are trying to legislate solutions to social problems. One prominent example is Singapore's "Sue Your Son" law, which allows parents to sue children for support. The Hong Kong Legislature debated a law that would have forbidden Hong Kong men from taking concubines (it was especially aimed at those commuting to southern China). It was a big issue among women, but the male-dominated legislature did not "get the point" and the legislation did not pass.

Toward shared values: the learning continues

The ethnic and cultural diversities among and within Asian nations present challenges to national unity and cohesiveness. Asian countries are finding solutions to forge national identities. In the quest to build modern nations, the leaders of Singapore and Malaysia sought to "unify" the diverse cultures within their boundaries with the vision of a single national identity. In Singapore, "One People, One Nation, One Singapore" was the theme of the 25th independence anniversary in 1990.

But now, after years of promoting integration, the leadership has abandoned the quest for a singular identity and come to terms with diversity. Officials speak of a mosaic of cultures, a successful blend of immigrant peoples, and "shared values".

Malaysia has come a long way in trying to integrate the major racial groups within its national boundary. Although mainly driven by economics, the country is now more tolerant and accepting of diversity. Commenting on the showing of a multiracial front in the general election of 1995, Dr Noordin Sopiee expressed optimism on the shift: "Some people have gone so far as to celebrate the end of racial politics in Malaysia. I think it is more like the beginning of an end." There has been a clear shift in mindset from "one country, one people" to "one country, shared values".

On the relationship between Taiwan and the mainland, many people are advocating a postponement of closure. As Taiwan legislator Yung Wei puts it, "no solutions", just hang on with one country (China) and multiple systems.

Greater economic integration, cultural exchange through travel and mobility of people, will, however, bring about blending of Asia's diverse culture. This fits the global paradox of the more universal we become, the more tribal we act — the more we become the same in things economic, the more we become different in those things that represent our unique identities, including our language and our cultural history.

Perhaps the frantic alarms sounded by Asian intellectuals on family values can inspire Western societies to reclaim traditional values. As Francis Fukuyama wrote in *The End of History and the Last Man*:

> "Families don't really work if they are based on liberal principles, that is, if their members regard them as they would a joint stock company, formed for their utility rather than being based on ties of duty and love."

Asia is moving into the future in its own way.

4

Government-controlled
→ *Market-driven*

It has been just eight years since Taiwan was a one-party state under martial law. It was a command economy, run by a government which overwhelmingly dominated economic and social decisions. In 1995 Taiwan's 21 million people elected a provincial governor and mayors of its two largest cities. In 1996 Lee Teng-hui became Taiwan's first elected President.

As Asia moves to a market economy, politics grows dramatically less important, almost irrelevant. With a 7 percent growth rate, quipped one journalist, nobody wants revolution. Indeed. And just think: Asian growth rates routinely hit 10 percent. Politics irrelevant? In India, university graduates traditionally entered the civil service. Now they want jobs in private enterprise. In teeming urban centers Asian yuppies, dressed for success, walk with cellular phones glued to their ears and the latest stock quotes clutched in their hands. Revolution? It would not be good for business. It might interrupt the fruits of prosperity. Throughout Asia, there is talk of the Asian Dream: making money, having the "good life". **Throughout Asia ideology is giving way to economic and political reality.**

To ensure their survival, governments are abandoning all but the pretense of maintaining command economies and betting their future on the vagaries of the marketplace. There is fierce competition among countries to attract foreign investment. Asians have tasted economic freedom; any reversal now would bring disastrous political upheaval. Governments must get out of the way and let the marketplace manage growth.

From ideology to pragmatism

This quote from *The Asian Wall Street Journal* makes the case:

> "What China's Communists consider truly threatening is creeping irrelevance. Ironically, that irrelevance is exacerbated by their greatest success: the reforms the Communists themselves unleashed 16 years ago have produced an economic frenzy.
>
> "The economic opportunities since the party unfettered the economy in December 1978 have made money a rival of the party for people's attention. Nowhere does the party's marginalization show up more clearly than with China's youth, especially in booming coastal cities. Top university graduates used to consider party membership a career-gliding rite of passage required for advancement through the ranks. Now, they scorn party recruiters."

All over Asia, economic considerations dominate.

Development in the "Asian way"

Tales of the success of Asia's "Four Tigers" are legendary. The world watched in awe as Hong Kong, Singapore, South Korea, and Taiwan leapfrogged over the industrial stage and pushed full force into the information age. Singapore, for example, has the world's most sophisticated telecommunications infrastructure, and is an operations center for multinational computer firms. Hong Kong's role in global finance equals that of London or New York. South Korea is a world leader in manufacturing sophisticated, high-tech, quality products.

Flush with success, the Four Tigers invested in the region's less-developed countries with unprecedented confidence. By 1995, Asia's newly industrializing economies and Japan contributed 74 percent of Vietnam's total foreign direct investment. The Asia-Pacific region accounted for 80 percent of Vietnam's exports and 75 percent of imports in 1992.

Gearing up to join the big league

On 24 March 1978, the Vietnamese government closed all private businesses. Restrictions remained in place until 1986. But what is happening today in Vietnam's private sector is incredible.

In some ways, the shift to market-driven is most dramatic in Vietnam.

- Between 1989 and 1993 private businesses created 4.7 million new jobs.
- The number of entrepreneurs applying for business licenses increased from 76 in 1993 to 4,403 in January 1995.
- Entrepreneurs are now responsible for 90 percent of agricultural output, 70 percent of domestic trade, and 60 percent of transport services.

In 1994, BMW began assembling cars in Vietnam, which has 73 million people, a 95 percent literacy rate, and a strong work ethic. In Germany BMW pays auto workers $30.00 an hour, 50 percent of which goes to the government to fund welfare programs. In Vietnam, BMW pays workers $1.00 — a day.

"If we wait to gain experience, we won't be able to do anything," says Huynh Thanh Chung, a 28-year-old millionaire who dropped out of college and developed Hai Vuong Co. into a $50 million business with dealings in construction, beer, and clothing. In 1993, he invested in a $3 million seafood processing plant, 70 percent of whose sales are in Japan.

Vietnam's sizzling economy is growing at 9 percent or more a year. Once out of control, inflation is now comfortably under 10 percent. Historically an importer of rice, the country is now a major exporter. Production of rubber, coffee and seafood is increasing. A natural hub between Northeast and Southeast Asia, Vietnam holds an enviable geographic location. Furthermore, it has a well-educated population, a stable currency, a huge domestic market and a government intent on economic reform. Political reform will follow. Lastly, the 2 million overseas Vietnamese — in Europe, North America and Australia — provide a pool of capital and skills for their former homeland.

Although Vietnam struggles with the same infrastructure problems as other Asian nations, and has farther to go than most, there is a long line of foreign companies eager to invest. While the US struggled with the issue of personnel still "missing in action", others walked through the doors just as soon as they were opened. Now that the US government has formally recognized Vietnam, total pledged American investment in the country is $1.1 billion. Involvement is bound to pick up. *Business Week* reports:

> "Caterpillar intends to supply equipment for a $2 billion highway project. Some 50 other U.S. companies, including Morrison Knudsen, plan to submit bids for the first stage. Mobil has teamed up with three Japanese partners to begin drilling offshore. Exxon, Amoco, Conoco, Unocal, and Arco are negotiating production-sharing contracts with Petro Vietnam."

GE, AT&T, Coca-Cola, Citibank, Boeing, Motorola — a who's who of American multinationals are queuing up to invest in, and profit from, improved relationships between the US and Hanoi. Despite the late start, US companies will almost certainly garner their share of the Vietnamese market. For one, many consumer products, such as Coca-Cola, Pepsi, Marlboro cigarettes, Colgate toothpaste, already enjoy widespread brand awareness as a holdover from the Vietnam war. And secondly, having experienced domination by Asian neighbors, Vietnam is keen to maintain a strong US presence to counterbalance the presence in their markets of Japan and Taiwan, particularly.

The World Bank is at a loss to explain Vietnam's recent rise to economic prominence. By most economic yardsticks, Vietnam simply does not measure up:

● incomes are unevenly distributed
● public administration is still ineffective
● the legal framework is unreliable
● the banking business is shaky
● and personal savings levels are considerably lower than those of other Asians

Perhaps most important, Vietnam does not have the infrastructure to support current growth, much less the anticipated acceleration in growth.

But the switch to a market economy is very popular in Vietnam, and given the intelligence, ingenuity and determination of the Vietnam people the country will become an important economic player in the region.

Privatization and the People's Liberation Army

Like many armed forces across the globe, China's People's Liberation Army (PLA) was hit with painful budget cuts. Its response, however, has proved more entrepreneurial than most — especially considering the short recent history of Chinese capitalism.

Since 1984, the PLA has set up more than 20,000 companies with profits of about $5 billion (yes, $5 billion). **That makes the PLA the largest and most profitable commercial empire in China.** By some estimates, as many as half of China's military personnel are engaged in non-military, commercial activities.

Citicorp has invested in a pharmaceutical company that is part of PLA's San Jiu Enterprise Group, one of Shenzhen's fastest-growing companies. Baskin-Robbins works with a military-run firm to sell its ice cream. Other successful PLA businesses include Guangzhou's three-star hotels, the best karaoke bars, the best bus routes between Guangzhou and Shenzhen, and Shenzhen's fastest-growing securities companies. The PLA also has operations in Hong Kong.

The PLA has figured out the concept of strategic market advantage. "Civilian airports aren't everywhere," says Ge Bulei, an executive of China United Airlines, which is owned by the PLA. "Military airports are. We use this special advantage to fly places civilian planes can't." It's as if a bunch of US Air Force officers decided to use some of their military planes to fly civilians around to various parts of the country in order to make a few extra bucks.

The People's Liberation Army is now the largest privatization project in the world.

Vietnam's military is following the PLA's lead: military-run companies in Vietnam had revenues of $360 million in 1995. The military owns 300 major state companies and by mid-1996 was involved in 49 joint ventures with foreigners valued at $445 million.

Privatization

Would that the rest of China's institutions fared as well. Or that the pace of privatization were faster.

About 50 percent of state enterprises are in the red. Although they contribute a decreasing share of industrial output — 40 percent today versus 80 percent in the 1970s — they still employ one in four urban workers. Some 340 million Chinese, dependants included, owe their livelihood to state firms. **No wonder many argue in favor of maintaining state enterprises.** But inefficient state-owned enterprises are in many countries employment programs for the chronically unemployable. In August 1995 China announced it would retain only about 1,000 state companies and leave 99,000 others to sink or swim in the market.

"The color of the cat shouldn't matter, so long as it catches mice"

The *Far Eastern Economic Review* comments:

> "Yuan Mu may not have a prize in economics, but we'll say this for him: He has his fundamentals down. In a recent article in *Economics Daily*, the head of China's most powerful think tank opposed privatization on the grounds that it denies the 'basis of socialism in China.' That, of course, is the very reason to support it. The color of the cat shouldn't matter so long as the cat catches mice, runs Deng Xiaoping's famous aphorism, and the socialist cat hasn't caught any mice lately".

The original idea behind state ownership was not jobs. It was to eliminate "useless competition". These same defenders of state firms fail to realize that the value of privately owned, profit-making companies is not that they create jobs, although they do, but that they are designed with the goal of keeping fixed costs low to earn the highest possible profit. That is what creates efficiencies, which create profits, which make for robust economies. And that's the important lesson being learned in Asia.

The privatization of Malaysia

Arguably, Malaysia has learned that lesson better than the rest. The country now saves about $24 billion annually as a direct result of privatization; savings that are not the result of scaling down development or of raising taxes. Some 73 agencies have been privatized since 1983 and another 52 government bodies are readying themselves to be privatized.

"To say that Malaysia is a model to developing countries is an understatement," says Khoo Eng Choo, the managing partner of Price Waterhouse in Kuala Lumpur. "Compared with the developing countries, privatization in Malaysia is more advanced and more widely applied." Harvard economist Jeffrey Sachs also applauds the country's 12-year-old program. "Malaysia has proved that privatization works."

Since 1983, the government has raised $4.2 billion in one-off payments alone, while also trailblazing "an international path as a privatization consultant; economists and officials of multilateral-lending agencies tout Malaysia's programme as one of the most successful in the world". Furthermore, the government saves $2 billion annually in salaries and pensions.

What's more, the country's drive to turn the reins of state-run enterprises over to the private sector has fueled growth and efficiency and resulted in almost no unemployment. While some complain that Malaysia's privatization drive has enriched some of the Prime Minister's political cronies, no one denies it has upgraded the efficiency of many services now in private hands.

At the Kelang Container Terminal it takes less than three days to clear cargo; it used to take eight. There are wider choices in TV and radio programs, and a huge reduction in power outages means both can be enjoyed. There is a steady telephone service. And the privately built North–South Highway shaved 90 minutes from the six-hour drive from Kuala Lumpur to Singapore.

The architect of Malaysia's privatization program, Prime Minister Mahathir Mohamad, continues to be its most ardent supporter. It was for Malaysia like catapulting across the great divide. Mahathir's predecessors believed that national economic interests, and particularly those of ethnic Malays, could only be properly supervised by the state. Mahathir proved them wrong by folding into his economic strategy an affirmative action plan to ensure that a significant share of the privatization opportunities went to *bumiputras* (indigenous Malays).

Malaysia's privatization schemes differ from most by carving out a continuing role for government as either shareholder or regulator, to protect the interests of the state. Raising capital has never been the goal of Malaysia's privatization program. "It's never been a fund-raising exercise," says Anwar Ibrahim, the Finance Minister. "We let the private sector take the lead and the government acts as a check and balance. If we make some money in the process, that's the bonus."

Mahathir chose to do things not just in the "Asian way", but in the "Malaysian way". Similarly, Philippines President "Steady Eddie" Fidel Ramos is charting his own course in the Philippines.

The "sick man of Asia" is recovering

The Philippines has been famous for its crippling electrical brownouts — but not any more.

More than $1 billion has been spent in the power sector since 1992, and electricity supplies increased 18 percent during 1994. Long regarded as one of the most backward countries in Asia, the Philippines has become a leader in the privatization of its infrastructure.

Much of the credit for this remarkable turnaround is given to the country's President, Fidel Ramos. To maintain momentum, the general-turned-politician continues to press Filipinos to approve reforms to make the country competitive. He paved the way for foreign companies to come in and get the country powered up, removed barriers to foreign investment and broke up monopolies. That forced the Philippines' mostly family-owned megacorporations to retool and reinvest. In 1993, President Ramos opened the telephone industry to competition. Foreign companies are moving in. During the fall of 1994, Nynex signed a memorandum of understanding to buy 25 percent of a local telecom company and spend $175 million over the next four years.

There are many indications that the Philippines is on an economic development fast track. Filipino companies raised some $670 million on international capital markets in 1993, and many companies are expanding. Intel Philippines Manufacturing Inc. plans to invest $200 million over the next five years to increase the capacity of its memory chip and microprocessor plant. Avon now uses the country as its manufacturing hub, while Procter and Gamble expects to build a $100 million detergent plant.

Although the Philippines has a long way to go before being considered a roaring tiger, it is certainly beginning to flex its muscles. Signs of the times are everywhere as glass and steel buildings rise up to fill the capital city's skyline, and as former military installations are turned into a resort and an industrial park.

Clark and Subic Bay

The Philippines government's refusal to extend the life of US military bases has turned into a win–win situation. With the end of the Cold War, the US doesn't need them — and entrepreneurs see them as commercial bonanzas.

"Tourism will be our cash cow," says Jose Antonio Gongzalez, who invested $65 million into developing Clark, the former US air base, into a resort. The Mimosa resort is scheduled to be finished in 1997 and will include a golf course, a theme park, vacation homes, hotels and restaurants, and a retirement community. And, if the government allows it, a casino.

"Clark is going to be Asia's playground," says Gongzalez. "It can be a major tourist attraction."

Just 70 kilometers northeast of Clark is Subic Bay, the former US naval base, which some hope will be "Asia's next economic miracle city".

"It's perfect," says Jeffrey Koo, a Taiwanese billionaire. "The harbor, the airport, the infrastructure — it's all there."

As a result of Koo's lobbying, the Taiwanese government helped form an industrial park on Subic Bay. Reebok, AT&T, Enron and Acer are just a few of the companies that operate at

Subic Bay. FedEx invested $100 million in Subic and uses it as its Asian hub. Subic Bay's airport can handle 18 planes at any one time. Shipments out of Subic Bay have grown from $19 million in 1994 to $182 million in 1995 and $158 million in just the first half of 1996. Subic Bay had already created 22,000 jobs by mid-1996. President Ramos told me that President Bill Clinton made it a point to speak to him personally about the importance of a FedEx hub at Subic Bay. Malaysian billionaire Lim Goh Tong is part of a venture investing in resort facilities.

In 1993, Subic Bay attracted $300 million in foreign direct investment, versus $250 million in 1992 for the country as a whole. By the end of 1995 investment in Subic Bay totaled $1 billion.

Business confidence in the country's prospects for continued growth and stability is apparent in a comment by Thomas J. Leber, Vice President and General Manager of Wyeth Philippines, a US pharmaceutical company: "When Ramos promised no brownouts by December, 1993, most people laughed. In fact, he delivered."

India opens its doors a little wider

Ramos delivers. These days, many of Asia's leaders are delivering. In 1991, India's then prime minister, P.V. Narasimha Rao, faced limited choices. He could open India's doors to foreign trade and capital, or let the Asian miracle pass his country by. He opened the doors. According to Singapore's *Business Times*:

> "Today, despite poverty, financial scandals and political violence, India's growth is accelerating, and it is attracting money from abroad. U.S. companies invested more in India in 1992 and 1993 alone than they had in the previous 40 years. Ford, which now sells no cars in India…[in late] 1994 announced a joint venture with Mahindra & Mahindra and will begin manufacturing soon."

The return on assets of the country's 300 central and 700 state government enterprises had dropped to below 2 percent. More than 40 percent of central government operations are losing money. If not for the lucrative oil and telecom sectors, the public sector would be drowning in red ink. The *Far Eastern Economic Review* reports:

> "In total these public sector enterprises manage about 55 percent of India's capital stock (excluding households) and account for one quarter of non-farm GDP. As a result, their inefficiency means a serious drag on the economy, knocking two or three percentage points off GDP growth."

Although the government recently suffered some political setbacks, slowly but surely India is implementing the necessary reforms that will allow it to engage in activities with the rest of the global economic village. Included in its efforts are some tentative steps towards privatization. Most of the licensing controls that prevented private enterprises from competing with state firms are now gone. Consumers can fly in private airlines or bank with private banks. With additional capacity and more choices, state enterprises like Indian Airlines have had to improve their services. And the government has eliminated those barriers that made companies dependent on indifferent government suppliers for capital goods. In state-run enterprises that play a strategic role in the economy, management has been given greater autonomy and the authority to run the business like a business, not a welfare program.

India is now the third largest economy in Asia. But more important is its potential for further growth. There are 940 million people, 150 million to 200 million of them middle class and well educated. More than 25 million Indians own stock. Importantly, entrepreneurship has a long history.

Robert Lloyd George, a Hong Kong investor, maintains that India is the most promising of the large emerging markets, more promising than China. That belief is based on the matu-

rity of India's stock market — it has been around for more than
a century — and the fact that the rule of law is entrenched, even
if somewhat difficult to navigate. Not so, argues an editorial in
the *Far Eastern Economic Review*, "The problem is that India
has embraced capitalism with only one arm."

Both have missed the point. It isn't either/or. It isn't either
China grows or India grows. This is not a win–lose situation.
It's a win–win, and while no two Asian countries are going
about the business of economic development in quite the same
way, collectively they are creating the world's third great
regional economy.

The new Asia: leveraging for the future

To the world and to Asians, the great landmass stretching from
east of Iran to Japan and from China to Indonesia is a collection of economies and cultures of extreme diversity. No one in
the past could fathom the idea of looking at Asia as one. This
view has now changed. Market forces are reshaping the region's
economic landscape.

There was no grand scheme coming out of lofty government summits. Asian countries are competing with one another
for direct foreign investment, and their primary commodities
and services compete on the world market.

Conditions at home and external competition, potentially
from Latin America and Eastern Europe, are creating the necessary conditions for Asian countries to close ranks. Asian
countries are discarding their nationalistic preoccupations and
reaching out to each other. The Prime Minister of Malaysia, Dr
Mahathir Mohamad, said at the Pacific Dialogue held in
Penang, Malaysia, in November 1994:

"It is time for us all to adopt a prosper-thy-neighbor policy.
I most earnestly believe that we must work together and for
the first time in human history for a single global common-

wealth founded on the principle of cooperative prosperity. We must seek to establish a new world order securely grounded not only in the idea of common prosperity but also in mutual understanding and mutual regard."

Malaysia's Renong group has a proposal to build a 6,000-mile highway network that will wind the length of the Indian subcontinent, linking the major cities. It will also lay fiber optics along the highways. If it materializes, reports *Asia Inc.*, "it will be the single biggest infrastructure project of its kind in the world, at an estimated cost of $35 billion to be built over a 20 year period. The fiber optic will integrate India electronically, an achievement as significant as the railroad network the British built in the 1850s."

A willingness to cooperate and work together in Asia is emerging. A decade ago, alliances and cooperation among governments and businesses were unheard of and unthinkable.

Much of the integration in Asia today happened in the marketplace. It did not happen by design, but as a direct consequence of demand and supply. The governments helped, by not standing in the way.

"The economies in East Asia are integrating faster than anyone had imagined a few years ago," says Andrew Freris, Chief Regional Economist at Salomon Brothers. Already, he says, one-third of East Asia's shipment goes to Asia, and that number will increase to almost one-half by the year 2000. Asian countries make up 70 percent of foreign direct investment in Asia.

John Jennings, Group Managing Director of Royal Dutch/Shell Group of Companies, said:

"In Asia Pacific, one has much more of an impression of business networks, complex and sophisticated, and infinitely flexible in reacting to the needs of their markets."

Trade and investment dominate government-to-government agendas in Asia. Visits of Heads of State are accompanied by a

- Malaysia's Perusahaan Otomobil Nasional, which produces the Proton, opened its first foreign assembly plant in the Philippines. Proton is a car of "Japanese and Malaysian design, capital and technology and Filipino manpower, marketing and management — a marriage unthinkable two decades ago." Proton will also open a plant in Vietnam.

- Mitsubishi Motors has factories located in Malaysia, Philippines and Indonesia so as to sell in each country. With trade liberalization, one factory could serve all the countries.

- While all of Singapore-based Liang Court Holdings' properties were in Singapore in 1993, by 1995 more than half of its hotels and property developments were outside of Singapore — including China, Vietnam, Thailand, Malaysia, Indonesia and Australia.

- Thailand's largest construction company expects to spend $3 billion transforming Clark airbase in the Philippines into an international airport. A mass transit system will link Clark to metro Manila.

- Nissan expects to come out with an "Asian truck" that would be sold throughout Southeast Asia. Toyota has plans for an "Asian Car".

- Japan's NEC and South Korea's Samsung, rivals for many years, have teamed up to produce chips for the European market. "The Korean Japanese alliances are designed to take advantage of each other's strength for their mutual benefit," says Mr Han Il-suk, electronics analyst for BZW Securities in Seoul. "The Japanese are strong in chip design, while the Koreans excel in the production processes."

- A provincial Chinese carrier, Yunan Airlines, agreed in January of 1995 to buy a 60 percent stake in Laos Aviation for $15 million.

- South Korea's Daewoo is the largest foreign investor in Vietnam, with $2 billion in current and planned business ventures.

legion of corporate chieftains eager to seal deals with their local counterparts, and Heads of State give their blessing for these joint ventures.

ASEAN

The Association of South East Asian Nations, the members of which are Indonesia, Thailand, the Philippines, Malaysia, Singapore, Brunei and Vietnam, encompasses a population of 450 million people. Cambodia has applied for observer status, and Laos and Burma are candidates for future membership. Malaysian investment in Indonesia topped $603 million in 1994, more than 10 times the amount invested the year before. Thai companies, led by telecommunications giant Shinawatra, Charoen Pokphand and the government Petroleum Authority, are starting various projects in the Indochina states of Laos, Cambodia and Vietnam.

The go south initiative

Two-way China–Malaysia trade was an estimated $2.5 billion in 1994, 40 percent more than in 1993. Around 134 Chinese companies have invested more than $200 million in Malaysia. Taiwan, one of the largest foreign investors in Malaysia, increased its investment in Malaysia by 215 percent to $1.02 billion in the first 10 months of 1994. There are more than 30,000 Taiwanese alumni in Malaysia. Taiwanese, Hong Kong and Japanese companies were the leading investors in Vietnam before the rest of the world started to pay attention to this emerging market.

Asia to the Japanese

Japan has dominated Asia economically since the 1970s, but integration is slow, if it occurs at all. Asia is becoming more important to Japan than the rest of the world.

Trade

● In 1985 Japan exported a third more to the US than to Asia. Now Asia buys one-third more than the US and almost three times as much as Europe.

● Japanese imports from Asia increased 150 percent between 1985 and 1995. In 1996, Japan's trade with Asia topped its trade with the US and the EU combined.

Investment

● Japan invested $7.7 billion in Asia during the 1993–94 fiscal year. A study by the Export Import Bank estimates during the next few years 75 percent of new Japanese direct investment will be in Asia.

● China is now the primary investment place for Japanese companies. Japanese direct investment in China increased 78 percent in 1995. The country's direct investment in China totaled $349 million in 1990 and is estimated to be 10 times that now.

● Close to half of Japan's offshore direct investment now goes to East Asia, up from 12 percent in 1985.

● Thailand expects new Japanese investment to reach $8 billion between 1995 and 1998. Japan controls 90 percent of Thailand's auto market.

● Matsushita Electric Industrial Company's 15 Malaysian affiliates make up 4 percent of Malaysia's exports, while 5,000 of Aiwa Japan's 8,000 employees live outside Japan, in Singapore, Malaysia, and also in Wales.

"[Japan's] shift to Asia is driven by the higher profits that the region's growth generates," says Kenneth Courtis, an economist at Deutsche Bank Capitals Markets in Tokyo.

People know no borders

Cathay Pacific Airlines, based in Hong Kong, has recently repositioned itself to be the airline at "the heart of Asia". The airline has more than 650 flights a week in and out of Hong Kong.

In four hours or less, Cathay Pacific can fly you from Hong Kong to within reach of one half of humanity.

Each year 1.75 million Taiwanese travel to Hong Kong, most passing through on their way to China. In 1995, Hong Kong residents traveled to China 26.4 million times.

Thailand is now the home to nearly 100,000 people of Indian descent, many of them concentrated in Bangkok's Pahurat, the area known as Bangkok's Indiatown.

Mobility of talent

The rapid economic growth has created an acute shortage of skilled and unskilled labor in urban Asia. In a region known to the West as the largest labor pool in the world, the varying levels of growth of Asia's "terrace economies" (uneven in levels of progress just like the terraces on which rice is grown) have produced a new phenomenon: cross-border movement of labor. While some countries and regions are exporting labor, the rapidly industrializing centers of growth are welcoming them, not always with open arms, but accepting them into their fold eagerly so as to sustain growth. Asian nations are racing to put up and expand existing infrastructures in order to maintain their competitiveness. Roads, airports, ports, power plants and telecommunications infrastructure are being built as soon as possible. As a result, an enormous number of workers of a wide range of skills are needed. In the last five years, there has been very heavy traffic in cross-border labor throughout Asia. In 1995, more than one million workers went to work outside their home countries.

The cross-border movement is not confined to unskilled labor. For the professional and managerial class:

- In Hong Kong, the number of expatriate workers, ranging from domestic help to senior corporate executives, increased by 45,500 in just the first nine months of 1993.
- In Singapore government estimates put the number of foreign employees at between 150,000 and 200,000, some 20 percent of the country's 1.1 million workforce, the second highest proportion of foreign workers to local in Asia, after the Sultanate of Brunei.
- In Indonesia, some 1,000 Malaysian managers and professionals are serving 2–3 year contracts. About 75 percent of the approximately 600 Filipinos in senior managerial positions in Indonesian banks have been in those positions five years or less. There are about 5,000 Indians holding technical and managerial positions in private Indonesian businesses.
- More than 4.3 million Filipinos work in various parts of the world, exporting human resources to earn foreign revenue.

Muscle for the building boom

In most of the sizzling economies of East and Southeast Asia, armies of migrant workers are building the skyscrapers, expressways, airports and transit systems. In Malaysia's capital city, Kuala Lumpur, as many as 30,000 Indonesian and Bangladeshi workers worked day and night to put up the Kuala Lumpur Twin Towers, the tallest building in the world.

Elsewhere the statistics are stunning. Japan has between 160,000 and 200,000, Malaysia 475,000 and Taiwan 270,000 foreign construction workers.

While the home country faces a tremendous shortage of labor and is forced to take in foreigners, the more adventurous are leaving home to find greener lands with higher wages. The talk in Asia is not the shortage of labor, but the shortage of cheap labor, and companies are forced to import. For example, during the recession of 1983–5, some 200,000 skilled workers left Malaysian shores for Japan, Taiwan and Singapore.

Officially Malaysia has about 1 million foreign workers, but other estimates put the number at close to 3 million. Most are from Bangladesh, Burma, Indonesia, Thailand and the Philippines. In 1995, 400,000 workers left Thailand to work on the building sites in Singapore, Hong Kong, Malaysia and Taiwan.

The way to the future: growth triangles

The diversity of Asia and the varying levels of its economies are prompting Asian governments and businesses to explore new ways to cooperate, to create opportunities in employment and investment for the less developed, and maintain competitiveness for the industrially advanced. The way of the future is the creation of growth centers, be they formal or informal. Some areas designated as growth triangles or quadrangles enjoy political commitment from national leaders, while some where border trade flourishes are merely renewing their regional links and exploiting geographical advantages as trade intensifies with the rising prosperity of the region.

For the first time, a new regionalism is emerging. Growth triangles are a convenient solution to cooperation. President Fidel Ramos of the Philippines wrote in the *International Herald Tribune*:

> "The growth triangle has taken hold because it is a controlled experiment in regional cooperation whose adverse effects, if any, can be limited to the triangle, but whose beneficial results can subsequently be applied to the national economy as a whole. It offers the benefits of regional integration without great loss of economic sovereignty."

The growth triangles began as export zones with "the synergy that comes from mixing various corporate cultures and resource endowments. The exchange is straightforward. Investing countries providing capital, technology and management skills.

Receiving countries provide land, other natural resources and labor, both skilled and unskilled", and businesspeople on the ground cement the ties. Some of the informal growth circles are expected to be more successful because they are not driven by politicians nor administered by bureaucrats, but run by the free market.

Growth triangles are win–win propositions. "The greatest benefits necessarily accrue to the most industrially mature partner. But even the poorest partner gains in practical terms as result of job generation, skills development, technology transfer and the infusion of industrial discipline in the local workforce. Radiations from the growth pole catalyze development in other sectors of the larger national economy."

For the industrially advanced, said President Ramos:

"growth triangles are a way of sustaining the competitiveness for their exports despite rising wages and increasing shortages of land and workers. For Indonesia, Thailand and the Philippines, and eventually for Vietnam, they are a means of speeding up development, creating jobs and importing technology. [They are] flexible, low cost, fast track, uncomplicated and well focused. They can be started quickly with little fuss. Formal trading blocs need gestation periods stretching over many years."

The region's businesspeople are excited at the potential, while carefully assessing its risks. *Asia Inc.* magazine and experts in Asia have identified more than 10 such formal and informal growth circles and triangles. While some of these overlap, and are sometimes known by different names, the growth triangles herald the dawning of the first phase of moving towards a borderless Asia. The growth triangles listed by *Asia Inc.* are:

- The "golden quadrangle" which includes southwest China, Burma, Thailand and Laos.
- The Japan Sea Economic zone: Japan, the two Koreas, northeast China and the Russian Far East.
- The Yellow Sea economic zone: maritime China from Zhanjiang in the south to Liaoning province in the north, the Koreas and Japan.
- A Yangtze River-based growth circle: Wuhan and Shanghai in China backed by investment from Taiwan and Hong Kong.
- Taiwan and the neighboring Chinese province of Fujian.
- Hong Kong, Guangdong province and Macau.
- South China, Vietnam, Cambodia, Laos and northeastern Thailand.
- The Straits growth triangle: Singapore, Malaysia's Johor state and Indonesia's Riau province.
- The Northern growth triangle: northern Malaysia, southern Thailand and northern Sumatra in Indonesia.
- A Sulu Sea-based growth circle: the Malaysian and Indonesian-governed parts of Borneo, the southern Philippines and northern Sulawesi.
- A growth circle linking Indonesia's southern Sulawesi province with Australia's Northern Territory.

The growth triangle experiment, a unique Asian way of development, is creating regional integration. Commenting on the market-led integration in Asia, John Jennings, Group Managing Director of Shell, said:

> "Seen from within the European Union, I have to tell you that we greatly admire the success of the Asia Pacific countries and wish we had our own secret formula to replicate it."

While governments are still busy sorting out the legal and regulatory infrastructure, "business will flow according to its own rules — like water," said Noordin Sopiee, Director General of

the Institute of Strategic and International Studies in Kuala
Lumpur.

Building bridges to tomorrow: Asia's infrastructure challenge

The Asian Wall Street Journal reports:

> "It cost a fortune, was way over budget and took far too
> long to build. It didn't meet specifications. And it helped
> bankrupt a dynasty. About the only good thing that could
> be said about the Great Wall of China as an infrastructure
> project is that the Chinese paid for it themselves, sparing
> foreign investors from taking a bath. Nevertheless, the wall
> serves as a cautionary tale for today's planners of grand pub-
> lic works projects. It was one of the largest construction
> projects in history, snaking the length of one twentieth of
> the earth's circumference, according to one estimate, from
> the Yellow Sea to Central Asia. Yet no one even knows for
> certain how much it cost or exactly when it was started."

All the world is titillated by stories of plans gone awry. There is
some bleak satisfaction in knowing that great plans encounter
great obstacles everywhere, not just in one's hometown, country or century. And opportunity for disaster is ripe indeed as
Asia attempts to build an infrastructure for both the industrial
and information eras. If Asia relies on government action alone,
it might end up littered with projects far less successful than the
Great Wall. Instead, infrastructure development is moving forward at breakneck speed, mostly because the private sector is on
the case.

"A billion here, a billion there, pretty soon you're talking
real money." That could be Asia's new motto when it comes to
infrastructure. A sample of the continent's mammoth projects
follows.

In addition to Gordon Wu's billion-dollar, six-lane super-highway from the Hong Kong border to Guangzhou, *Business Week* reports the following infrastructure projects in Asia:

- **China** is putting $6 billion in roads, a port and telecom links for Shanghai's new Pudong district. Three billion dollars is going into the 2,380 km railway linking Beijing to Kowloon. Then of course there is the $20 billion hydroelectric dam at Three Gorges.

- **South Korea** is investing $13.4 billion in a high-speed train link between Seoul and Pusan, another $50 billion will be spent on 30 new power plants, including 7 nuclear plants by the year 2000. Seoul is getting a new $5 billion airport.

- In **Thailand**, TelecomAsia is building more than 2 million telephone lines costing $3 billion. Another $11 billion is going into 3,800 megawatts of electricity projects in 1995. The first phase of Bangkok's second airport will cost $3.3 billion.

- **Malaysia** plans to spend $9.1 billion on infrastructure, **Indonesia** $11.8 billion; and **the Philippines** some $4.5 billion.

Some countries manage the infrastructure challenge better than others. Malaysia has pulled ahead of Indonesia, claims *Business Week*, which credits "the quality of the government's decision-making, combined with a competitive private sector." Taiwan trails Singapore, Hong Kong, and South Korea. Taiwan, it says, "has made such a mess of infrastructure" it attracts much less foreign investment.

Well managed or not, these sums are utterly mind boggling. The Asia Development Bank estimates the region will spend $1 trillion by the year 2000, primarily on energy, telecommunications and transportation.

John Reed, Chairman of Citicorp, insists that China alone needs to spend $55 trillion to build an infrastructure to support a developed economy — three times the world's current annual

GDP and more than 50 times the Asian Development Bank's estimate.

Of course, no one knows really what the final cost will be or exactly where the funds will come from. Historically, Asia's high individual savings rates meant large cash reserves would be available. But some say the 30 percent savings rate is artificial, that real domestic cash reserves are considerably lower. In any event, we are talking $55 trillion here. That's a lot of passbook accounts. Enter Gordon Wu and his pioneering BOT scheme, an exciting but stunningly simple financial model for public/private enterprise and a win–win–win situation for the entrepreneur, the government, and the public.

BOT — the Wu factor

Gordon Wu pioneered the BOTs (build–operate–transfer) project concept through his Hong Kong-based Hopewell Holdings. Basically, it work like this. A private firm agrees to build a highway or power plant. The company then collects tolls (in the case of a highway) or operates the plant for a fixed period of time at a previously agreed price. When the entrepreneur earns back the investment, plus a profit, the project is turned over to the government at no cost.

The country gets the infrastructure at little or no cost. The private firm makes a good return on investment — a very good return if the project is completed early. And the people get a public utility managed like a private enterprise. *Voilà*!

Famous examples are Hopewell Holdings' two 350-megawatt coal-fired power plants for the Shenzhen Special Economic Zone in China's Guangdong province, and its billion-dollar highway from Hong Kong to Guangzhou.

Gordon Wu got into the BOT business in a strange and interesting way. In the 1980s Hopewell Holdings built a 1,200-room hotel, but the project was going nowhere without enough power. So the company offered to develop the Shajiao B Plant on a BOT basis. It designed, constructed, financed and will operate the power station for 10 years. Then it belongs to the province.

Wu's BOT superhighway connects Hong Kong with Shenzhen, Guangzhou, and Zhuhai. Conceived of when the region was basically a rice paddy, the project is now in the heart of China's fastest-growing area. And the highway project has led to similar deals to build power plants.

Mr Wu's other power projects include a $40 million plant in Navotas, outside Manila. Wu's firm is involved in Indonesia, India, Taiwan and Vietnam. Yet infrastructure projects represent less than 10 percent of company earnings. Some projects are under discussion in power-hungry Pakistan and India. He wants to standardize power plant design through buying materials in bulk to cut costs, an age-old strategy. Wu's economies of scale can offer electricity for less than state-owned companies.

BOTs are not risk free or for short-term investors. There are profits to be had, but pitfalls too. The biggest problem is the same force that makes BOT schemes possible and profitable — political pressure. In February 1994, 23 international banks who loaned the Thai government $250 million for a motorway in Bangkok declared they wanted out and demanded full repayment. The problem was, people resisted the toll hike that was supposed to make the project profitable.

Undaunted, the Thai government is seeking private contractors for a BOT project to build an elevated railway in Bangkok. There are plenty of takers. The appeal for many is a steady flow of earnings. Lance Gokongwei, a Senior Vice President at JG Summit Holdings Inc., says the Philippines conglomerate's investments in power-generation projects are "almost like an annuity". Of course, quips *The Asian Wall Street Journal,* that is "if governments never change, consumers never demand rate reductions, monopolies are never broken up, fuel prices never fluctuate and demand forecasts always come true."

Pakistan's $1.6 billion Hub power project, a landmark in private-sector financing in the third world, will add 13 percent to the country's generating capacity by 1997. Britain's National Power invested $100 million for a 25 percent equity stake. The project was negotiated through eight changes of government. Legal documentation, says the *Financial Times*, weighed 28kg a set.

Pitfalls aside, BOTs remain an attractive means to develop projects on time and within budget, and regional and international players can reap handsome profits.

The dam project

Anyone who doubts the efficacy of Wu's BOT model should look at Bangkok, where more than 16 agencies have tried to unsnarl traffic. Or at China's long winding path to the Three Gorges Dam project.

First suggested by Sun Yat-sen in the 1920s, the Chinese have long wanted to dam the Yangtze River in order to manage and control flooding, and at the same time generate power. In the 1940s US engineers from the Bureau of Reclamation worked with the Chinese to design a dam. In the 1950s the Russians took over. The very idea of alternating the path of the river the Chinese call "the Great" evokes strong emotions, and has even sparked almost unheard of public dissent among Party members. Environmentalists oppose it, and no one knows how the government will relocate the 1.2 million people who live in 13 cities and towns that will be flooded by the giant reservoir. No other dam in history has faced such a huge relocation problem.

However, Premier Li Peng is determined to pull it off. Some 18,000 workers toil 24 hours a day clearing the path for the diversion channel, dynamiting canyon-sized grooves in hillsides, and building the massive locks that will carry ships over the mountains toward Central China. But it may be economics, not politics or the environment, that determines the fate of the dam project.

The World Bank is not coming forward with the cash, and so far neither are foreign investors. The government increased electric rates — as much as 25 percent for some residents — to generate revenues. That only renewed opposition. Still the workers keep digging.

Multinationals betting the bottom line on infrastructure boom

Many multinational megafirms are betting their bottom lines on Asia's infrastructure. General Electric and Westinghouse compete with power brokers like Siemens, ABB Asea Brown Boveri, Hitachi, Mitsubishi Heavy and Toshiba. Still others are vying for the opportunity to manage plants that are up and running. For example, Mission Energy of California will run a $2.5 billion coal-fired plant in Java. CMS Energy, a subsidiary of Michigan's Consumer Power, operates power plants in the Philippines.

AT&T, Motorola, GTE, IBM and the Baby Bells are scrambling for market share in telecommunications. So are Alcatel Alsthom of France, Canada's Northern Telecom, Germany's Siemens, and Japan's NEC and Toshiba.

But it is not just the global that are gaining a foothold in Asia: many small companies are getting in on the action. Some prove quite successful because they are so much more flexible. Plus, many small firms secure a local partner who knows the terrain and understands the subtleties of Asian business cultures. Notes Robert Fernstrom, a vice president at Salomon Brothers in Hong Kong, "The ones that are really moving ahead are the ones with good local sponsorship."

Among the established and emerging regional players staking their future on the infrastructure boom are:

- South Korea's Anam Group, a $1 billion electronics concern, is developing truncated radio systems, successfully employed by Motorola in Japan, for transportation companies in South Korea and China.
- China Power & Light of Hong Kong will plan and design power projects in which it holds an equity stake in mainland China.
- Malaysia's IJM Corp. is known for completing projects on time and within budget. Major contracts are a $22 million industrial estate in Kedah state and two power-plant expansions for state-owned Tenaga Nasional Bhd. IJM is vying for a piece of the $30 million water-supply project for Ho Chi Minh City.
- IPCO International, Ltd. of Singapore proposed, helped finance, partly owns and runs a US $47 million water-supply system in Labuan, Malaysia. IPCO seeks projects in Indonesia, Malaysia, Thailand and China for the short term and Indochina and Burma over the longer term.
- Triveni Engineering Works Ltd., one of India's largest makers of steam turbines and sugar mill machinery, earns 40 percent of revenue from infrastructure development. Triveni recently completed the first stage of a sewage treatment plant for New Delhi and is building an effluent treatment facility for a steel plant in the state of Andhra Pradesh.

So there are deals to be made and many contenders. That the need is great is not in question. And many are willing to risk much for a great return. What many analysts and observers do question is whether Asia can *afford* to build all the infrastructure it needs. A more pointed question may be: can it afford not to? Enter the global investment community.

Funding the future

Asia's stock, bond and futures markets are undergoing phenomenal growth. In 1987, Asia's stock markets (excluding Japan) were capitalized at $195 billion. Today there are more than $1 trillion. Institutional investors, companies and individuals are plunging headlong into the world's fastest-growing financial markets.

The next 10 years will revolutionize Asia's capital markets, says *Asiamoney*. Portfolio managers and investment bankers in the West, it argues, will see Asia "as an integral part of the global market place for capital". The goal, of course, is to create the financial institutions and instruments to handle the investments Asia needs for its infrastructure.

In country after country Asia is modernizing stock markets, creating futures markets, and pushing banks into global competition. In the last three years, China, Thailand, India and Malaysia have established securities and exchange commissions to bring a semblance of order to their burgeoning stock markets.

Morgan Stanley became in 1994 the first US investment house to set up a joint venture bank in China. The American Insurance giant American International Group (AIG) launched a $1.2 billion fund that will take direct equity stakes in infrastructure projects, and then list those projects on local stock markets as an exit strategy.

Asia's stock markets come of age

Indonesia's stock market is fairly typical. Established in 1977, the Jakarta stock exchange listed only 24 companies one decade later, and despite the country's steady economic growth, capitalization was just $68 million. So the government took action. It simplified listing requirements, removed restrictions on daily price fluctuations, taxed bank interest payments, and permitted foreigners to buy up to 49 percent of listed companies and to

set up joint venture securities firms. By 1994 capitalization hit
$45 billion.

From 1987 to 1994 a balanced portfolio of the nine largest
Asian markets outside Japan returned about 22 percent a year,
calculated *The Economist*, compared with 15 percent from US
shares.

As might be expected, the path to relative stability is not a
smooth one for Asia's stock markets.

In China, a 40 percent plummet in a two-day period in
October 1994 prompted a flurry of companies to list on the
Hong Kong or New York markets rather than in their home
market.

India has a long history in stock markets — its first was in
the nineteenth century. The market currently lists more than
7,000 companies, but suffers from a lack of screen-based trading. Every transaction requires 35 different manual checks —
enough to send many traders elsewhere.

Going public

Pressure from all sides, including the need for funds to expand
regionally, to acquire new technology and to open new markets, business families intending to cash out, and pressure from
governments to redistribute wealth — Asian companies are
gearing up to go public. Some of the most tightly held private
companies in Asia are expected to list within the next few
years. For example, Philippines companies are looking to the
stock exchange for sources of funding. Market capitalization
grew from $5.9 billion in 1990 to $55 billion in November
1994.

Elsewhere in the region, merchant bankers are enjoying a
boom in their business of helping clients to list their stocks on
the exchange. The market is responding; besides the institutional investors, the increasingly affluent middle class are looking to the stock market to have a stake in the economy. Denway
Investment Limited from China, when listed in the Hong Kong

stock exchange in 1993, recorded 647 times oversubscription, attracting $31 billion to its offer of $52 million in a, to say the least, bullish market when China fever was over the top. Such spectacular oversubscription rates may not be repeated, but public offers are still being oversubscribed.

Intensifying regional competition

Asian governments are intent on developing and promoting the stock markets at home. Discontented that Hong Kong and Singapore dominated the financial and capital markets for the region, governments in Taiwan, Malaysia and Thailand are working on reforms and liberalization. For example, Malaysia recently announced a package of wide-ranging reforms in order to promote Kuala Lumpur as a regional fund management center. Officials in Kuala Lumpur believe that the quality of life in Kuala Lumpur and affordable cost should make the city more attractive against the rising costs of operation in Singapore and Hong Kong. Besides, Kuala Lumpur's market capitalization of $218 billion is more than double that of Singapore's — that makes Malaysia's bourse the largest in Southeast Asia and the fifth largest in Asia.

Stock markets are one vehicle of entry into global financial markets. Private capital, bond issues, securities, pension funds and insurance pools also are part of the mix.

Money finds its greatest return

Money is information and confidence in motion. Right now, and for the foreseeable future, the world is betting on Asia. Five years ago only a tiny proportion of America's $5 billion net equity flow went into Asia. By 1993 US equity investments in Asia hit $12.9 billion, one-third of the $40 billion total. Similar volumes of capital are flowing in from Japan, the UK and Europe.

But Asia's capital pool is swelling too: Taiwan's foreign exchange reserves are nearly $100 billion; Singapore's exceed $70 billion. "Economic growth has spawned mutual funds, pension funds and insurance funds that need solid but stable management," says *Asiamoney*. Hong Kong has $87 billion currently being managed, and Singapore will open up $28 billion for foreign fund managers in its effort to attract more fund management companies to relocate to Singapore. The fund management business in Asia is expected to double in the next five years, according to *Asiamoney*.

As Chapter 1 illustrates, Asia has extraordinary reserves of private wealth. The head of one international bank says the biggest foreign exchange positions — $250 million and above — are held by individuals, not by corporations. These individuals are increasingly taking positions in mainstream capital market deals.

Mobilizing savings

A sign of Asia's coming of age is when the corporate bond markets that cater to Asian companies issue long-term debt in local currencies to meet their local currency obligations. The recently initiated dragon bond market is a first step. "Dragon bonds are ordinary debt issues, denominated in a major international currency, aimed at raising capital from the growing pool of Asian wealth in the so-called dragon economies of South Korea, Hong Kong, Singapore and Taiwan," explains *Asian Business*.

Thus far, these have been restricted to solid corporations, governments and some issuers outside the region. But it demonstrates the level of sophistication toward which Asian financial markets are heading. Over $4 billion worth of dragon bonds have been sold; however, most of the issuers have been West European institutions, and most of the buyers Europeans as well.

Although Dragon bonds are listed in Asia, they are cleared

and settled through Europe's Euroclear and Cedel systems. In time, Asian corporates and institutions will be as comfortable issuing bonds in domestic currencies as they are in the international bond markets. The potential of Asia's bond market prompted Moody, the US-based credit-rating agency, to open an office in Hong Kong. Financial analysts around the globe acknowledge that the combination of pressing long-term financial need and an increasing deregulation in the financial industry will ensure a future for corporate bonds.

In the coming years, Asia will see a flurry of bank mergers, buyouts and takeovers similar to the anxiety-provoking US bank brawls of the late 1970s and 1980s. Banks owned by family conglomerates that operate on *guanxi* — personal connections — will continue to play a vital role, but so will foreign banks. Joint ventures between foreign and Asian banks will become commonplace. These efforts will be government sanctioned as the last barrier between maintaining a semblance of control over domestic capital markets and the uncontrolled international markets that move hundreds of millions of dollars through cyberspace in a matter of seconds.

This is clearly evidenced in Vietnam, where according to the *Far Eastern Economic Review*:

> "[the] rush to catch up with the rest of the region's economies has made the development of an efficient banking sector a priority. Reflecting this, Vietnam's banking sector has grown exponentially. Not only have over a dozen foreign banks been granted licenses to date, but domestic banks are now allowed to acquire the capital and skills they so badly need through foreign partnerships."

The Asian capital markets, the market solution, is the way forward in funding Asia's future.

What about the future of our children?

Asia must build an infrastructure to support its aspirations and empower itself to compete in the global information age, achieving in a matter of years what took the US and Europe decades.

Everywhere the pace of change is frantic. The impact on both people and the environment is not always positive. The distribution of wealth is often inequitable and the pace of development uneven within individual countries and the region at large. The first tentative efforts to redistribute wealth are under way, but lopsided growth will probably continue to trouble the region. Furthermore, corruption is alive and well. In many places political connections will guarantee profits in the emerging private sector.

Asian capitalism is not American capitalism, i.e. trusting market forces over state intervention (except of course for baseball strikes). Look at Japan's MITI (Ministry of International Trade and Industry), which, to the chagrin of some free marketeers, is one big reason behind Asia's success — and a great example of Asia following its own path. Borrowing liberally from various economic models, Asian leaders are fusing ideology and economic reality.

No one can turn back the clock, but many wish to slow down the rate of development long enough to examine the impact of growth on people and on the environment. In three years, China's economy expanded 40 percent. Steel production has helped China maintain that phenomenal growth rate. But sulfur dioxide emissions from the coal-fired blast furnaces have made Beijing one of the world's most polluted cities.

Pollution is evident in Hong Kong, Bangkok, Manila and in India's largest cities. In Indonesia, logging for paper and pulp has stripped the nation of its trees with no organized plan in place for reforestation. Major infrastructure projects like China's Three Gorges Dam will uproot tens of thousands of peasants. Many will drift to urban areas where there is little work for the unskilled and nowhere to live.

Drug use and commercial sex are on the rise throughout Asia, with a resulting increase in the incidence of AIDS. HIV is still rare in Japan where condoms are widely available and used, and intravenous drug use almost unheard of. But the problem is expected to become epidemic in India, Indonesia, Burma, Cambodia, Vietnam, and Malaysia. In Chaing Rai in northern Thailand, one in five young males is HIV-positive. In India's northeastern Manipur State, 55 percent of intravenous drug users have the virus.

Some fear economic development will take precedence over cultural preservation. Cultural sites such as temples and ancient cities hold enormous economic potential. Consequently, capital-hungry countries are turning them into tourist attractions, compromising the integrity of the fragile sites.

In many countries corruption is a way of life. Param Curaraswamy, a human rights activist in Kuala Lumpur, says: "Over the years, corruption has been allowed to continue, until now it has become a monster. Corruption in China has now reached epidemic proportions" and few escape the squeeze. In the countryside, local officials divert grain payments to real estate schemes. City folk must pay kickbacks for everything from telephone lines to treatment at public hospitals. As the economy booms, people can, and do, pay — which only encourages the corrupt officials. As one Western diplomat in Beijing puts it: "Where there's meat, you're bound to have flies."

The story is the same in India, where, of all the barriers to entry, the greatest is "debilitating corruption". The amounts of money that changed hands prior to selection of a cellular phone company in four cities were legendary. In the end, the Department of Telecommunications chose a different vendor for each city. Motorola, with the best service record in the world, wasn't selected. Those selected were four unknown companies with no history but lots of political clout.

Keeping the best in government

In Singapore, with a population of less than 3 million, the Prime Minister earns $797,000 a year. Top cabinet ministers earn $535,000. The country's per capita income rings in around $20,000 a year. In the US, with a population of more than 260 million, the President earns $200,000 and cabinet members make $148,000. Singapore government pays government officials on a pay scale based on private industry. And Prime Minister Goh Chok Tong says, the high salary is justified "against the cost to you for having an incompetent and corrupt government". In 1993, all Singaporean civil servants were given year-end bonuses equal to three-and-a-half months' salary.

Paying well keeps the best in government and eliminates the evils of corruption. Singapore hopes so. But increasingly talent is flowing to the private sector, where the rewards can even be greater.

The power of the market

Despite the imperfections of the market, the world has come to accept the free market system as the way to organize economic life. How the free market will evolve in each Asian country will depend on the ingenuity of its government and the vigor of its business leadership. The power of the free market is exciting. Consider the Philippines. When the telephone service was run by a state monopoly, 98 percent of Filipinos were waiting for a telephone, while 2 percent were waiting for a dial tone. Today, companies are competing for the loyalties of telephone users as they create a state-of-the-art telecommunications system for the Philippines.

A free market Asia is the key for the West

The Asian boom will provide the West, especially the US, with one-quarter or more of its total economic growth for the years just ahead, according to an analysis by *The Economist*. Asia and the US are the two places in the world that allow entrepreneurs free range to revitalize and build up their economies, and they are the two places that will truly prosper as we move toward the twenty-first century.

Nevertheless, many issues and problems persist — at least in the Western mindset — as barriers against the full potential of this economic bonanza. Let us look at a few.

Many in the West blame Asia for the accelerated loss of jobs at home. The response, they argue, should be more protectionist policies. But the main factors behind disappearing low-skilled jobs in Western societies are mobility of capital and technology, not Asia's new market competitiveness.

In reality Asia's infrastructure boom and the need for capital goods herald great opportunities for Western companies and their workers. Furthermore, low-skilled workers are at peril *anywhere* in the world. As this book frequently notes, Asia's mature economies lose labor-intensive, low-tech manufacturing to cheaper Asian locations. Hong Kong and Singapore are already putting programs in place to prepare themselves for the dominance of service and information in their economies.

Some Western companies have backed away from doing business in Asia because they think there is a lack of concern about the environment. My dialogue group in Singapore — one of Asia's richest countries, with a per capital GNP of more than $20,000 — was dominated by discussions of environmental deterioration. Strong voices on the subject are heard everywhere in Asia. If anything, I hear more people in Asia talking about environmental concerns than I do in the West.

As Asia grows richer, the environment will become a greater preoccupation. Asia will become more uncompromising about the trade-offs between the environment and economic development. Polls show that in South Korea, Taiwan, Malaysia and the Philippines, a significant number of people are prepared to have their earnings reduced in exchange for a less polluted environment. Many middle-class well-off urban people in Taiwan are moving out of the cities to build settlements in the quiet countryside. With the convenience and access provided by Asia's increasingly sophisticated telecommunications facilities, a small reverse flow from cities to the countryside has begun. The opportunity for the West is to help with its technological knowhow and experience in making existing Asian industries more environmentally friendly.

Western companies need an Asian strategy. The key is to demonstrate understanding, respect for and commitment to the region. Asian talents are increasingly motivated to work with Western companies who see their own future aligned with Asia's.

To begin with, a Western company should decide on a strategic city to anchor its operations. It does not need to be a capital city. Many Western companies, for example, operate out of Penang, Malaysia, rather than the capital city of Kuala Lumpur. In China, the capital city of Beijing is the place not to be. Most of the action is in Guangzhou, Shenzhen, Fuzhou and Shanghai. It depends on the industry and nature of the business. Also, discard the national border mindset. Select a location that allows maximum and easy access to the most efficient combination of land, talent, ideas, technology and markets, a judgement best made with the help of an Asian partner.

There is an acute shortage of management talent in Asia, and the situation will become more critical as the boom accelerates. But although professional managers are important, entrepreneurial talent will pay greater long-term dividends. Remember that Asia is a long-term project. Talent will be needed for a long time to start, build and sustain a business. With increasing demand for business talent, loyalty is waning, and job hopping is fast becoming a favorite pastime in some Asian capitals. Those companies that innovate and are more creative will keep the best talent. Commit resource to train and develop a talent pool.

The key is to be flexible and cultivate relationships to learn to operate in Asian cultures. As economies modernize, greater political openness will follow. But Westerners should not insist on Western legal arrangements. Quality partnerships and trust (as the ethnic Chinese have practiced for centuries) will prove far more successful. A Western legal system does not necessarily help. The Indian supreme court has more than 1 million backlogged cases, which at the present rate of disposition would take more than 300 years to clear.

Many Asian multinational companies are eager to bring in management experts, to develop management controls and more efficient structures. Opportunities for Western citizens with technical skills will grow dramatically — good news for those affected by all the downsizing in the West. Much in demand will be system and process engineers, architects and designers, financial analysts, telecommunications specialists, international fund managers, and environmental specialists.

On the other hand, Asian companies would be wise to avoid overcontrol and excessive professionalization, so as not to lose the communitarian touch, the soul of the enterprise.

The twentieth century began with a utopian view that communism could bring the best quality of life to everyone. It is ending with the realistic understanding that a market-driven society brings the greatest prosperity to the greatest number. By shifting to market-driven economies, Asia between 1970 and 1990 reduced the number of desperately poor Asians from 400 million to 180 million, even while the populations of its countries grew by two-thirds. Never before in the history of humanity has so large a number of people been raised from poverty in such a short time. A record 123 Asians made *Forbes* magazine's 1996 listing of the world's wealthiest people. Of the 123, 82 were non-Japanese, up from 27 in 1991.

Free market mechanisms and the technological revolution

have expanded the coverage of the market economies of the world from 1 billion to more than 4 billion people. Three-quarters of them are in Asia. The free market, a Western idea, and what it can do, is a triumph for everybody.

5

From Villages ⟶ *Supercities*

"At six minutes past midnight on December 5, 2006, the human being will become primarily an urban animal."

In ordinary times, people move from country to city, and city to country, and back again. Sometimes the shift is noteworthy, sometimes it is just a little hashmark on some census counter's tally. Old towns die and new ones are born as industry or agriculture shifts elsewhere. But in Asia these are not ordinary times. The rules don't apply.

People are migrating from villages to cities in such extraordinary numbers, planners and policy makers must come up with dramatic ways to cope. That is not easy. Jakarta came up with a plan: it declared itself a closed city (unsuccessfully, I might add). Beijing's city officials decided to charge new residents as much as $11,600 to move into the capital.

This chapter will describe some of the more successful innovations. One thing is certain. If current patterns persist — and there is little reason to doubt they will not — the ultimate shift from rural to urban will change the character and context of Asian society.

United Nations predictions paint a stunning portrait of urban life in Asia in 2010: 30 Asian cities will have populations greater than 5 million (compared with only two US cities and six in Europe). Shanghai and Bombay will each have 20 million

people. Beijing, Dhaka, Jakarta, Manila, Tianjin, Calcutta and
Delhi will have more than 15 million.

**Seven of the thirteen cities whose populations exceed 10
million are in Asia.** Some Asian cities double in population
every 10 to 15 years. By the year 2010, half of China's population will live in urban areas — up from 28 percent in 1994.

**In China, the urban migration of rural poor is so great
that ethnic ghettos — Chinatowns in China — are springing up.** Between 1984 and 1994, more than 400,000 moved
from Zhejiang province to Beijing. So many there is now an
area of Beijing known as Zhejiang village, which has its own
clinics and nurseries. Only the Zhejiang dialect is spoken.
Zhejiang migrants are known for their clothing production.

Country to country the statistics are mindboggling:

- Tokyo, with 30 million people, is larger than 162 countries.
- Vietnam's population has grown more than 60 percent since
  1975. Saigon's population surged from 2.5 to 4.5 million.
- Since 1960, Bangkok's population has tripled in size to 7.1
  million.
- Bombay's population has increased 400 percent since the
  1950s, and almost 300 rural Indian families move to Bombay
  each day in search of work or a better quality of life.
- Asia's urban population will increase by 600 million during the
  next 25 years.

The social and environmental costs are incalculable. Already
traffic, garbage and smog choke many Asian cities.
Unemployment and underemployment are epidemic and there
are chronic shortages of all kinds, including housing, water,
power and transportation. Yet for many, a modern, global community is an urban community. Despite the mind-numbing
problems, urban life offers opportunity and hope, both in short
supply in tiny rural villages.

"We have only two things in the countryside," says a rice

miller in the farming community of Yongchon, South Korea. "A growing number of graves, and a growing number of ageing people waiting to get there."

For that simple reason — and because urban migration furthers the economic goals of some governments — it will continue.

The Hong Kong model

Two places to find solutions are Hong Kong and Singapore, which successfully evolved out of poverty and decay to become models of urban planning and control.

In the 1950s, Hong Kong was a huge shantytown populated by Chinese seeking refuge from the communists. In 1953, fire consumed the homes of 50,000 people. Urban planners had to figure out how to house these people as well as the hundreds of thousands of Chinese who kept pouring into the country.

How did they do it? "We had to rehouse these people, and we realized we'd also have to keep building to house the other refugees as they poured in, or we'll always be just a huge squatters camp," explains Ted Pryor, Hong Kong's main urban planner. "The lesson we learned is that you begin rehousing as soon as you can, but you do it very conservatively and with very modern standards."

Forty years later, Hong Kong is a "magnet for urban planners who come to study how the colony works". Hong Kong residents have housing — more than half the population lives in modern public housing developments — and business has ample office space (albeit pricey). And, while the city has one of the highest population densities in the world, 50 percent of its land is reserved for parks, nature preserves, and farms. Hong Kong apparently learned its lesson well. In 1994 *Fortune* magazine named it the world's "best city for business".

The Singapore model

Arguably, Singapore is the world's most modern city if measured by its telecommunications infrastructure and definitely one of the most conservative, if measured by its paternalistic social policies. But it works for Singapore and urban planners flock to the tiny nation state to see what makes it tick.

So keen is the world's interest in Singapore, its Foreign Ministry created 80 positions to deal with inquiries and tours. In 1990, 48 foreign dignitaries came to study the Singapore model; by 1993, the figure was 231. What they found was a city built on a "malarial swamp" that had evolved into a model of efficiency with electronically controlled roads, fast-moving traffic and few signs of pollution.

While Bangkok builds more roads to cope with its traffic congestion, Singapore levies a hefty tax to make cars less attractive to residents. While many Asian cities struggle to apply, however loosely, basic democratic principles, Singapore's government officials rule with an iron glove. It wouldn't fly in most Western cities, and it is growing increasingly difficult to rule by municipal fiat in most Asian cities, but in Singapore the population seems willing to give up some basic civil rights in exchange for a clean, virtually crime-free, urban community.

On the opposite page are the elements that Singapore's officials see as the key elements of the "Singapore model", as summarized by *Asiaweek*.

Brigadier General George Yeo Yong Boon, a key cabinet minister in Singapore, comments:

> "We're somewhat embarrassed by the quite sudden interest in the Singapore experience in the last few years, not just by nations in the region, but also by big countries like China and India, and by distant ones like South Africa, Kazakhstan and the new Palestinian state. Singapore has become a ready-made model for them to study, not only for our successes, but also our mistakes."

1. Strong government
Decisive leadership is seen as providing all-important stability. The People's Action Party has dominated politics for nearly 40 years, aided by a weak opposition and supportive local media.

2. Long-term planning
Government guidance keeps the economy on track. Socialist in style, it supports the free market. Pragmatism rules.

3. Foreign investment
Instead of protecting its markets, Singapore puts out the welcome mat for overseas investors and multinationals.

4. Clean administration
Politicians and civil servants have a reputation for honesty; corruption is dealt with harshly. The government works to recruit the best and the brightest.

5. Education for all
Singapore's emphasis on educating everyone, including women, raised the level of skills and gave the country the ability to handle high technology.

6. No welfarism
Rejecting Western-style welfare policies, Singapore stresses working through the family and the individual, such as with the Central Provident Fund. It has also encouraged home ownership.

7. Family values
The family is the basic unit of society, the ultimate safety net. Fostering respect for authority has enabled the government to implement policies with little open dissent.

8. Law & order
To keep the crime rate low, leaders swear by harsh punishments such as caning and hanging. Internal security laws allow authorities to clear the streets of gangs and secret societies.

9. Communal harmony
Sensitivity to other cultures is stressed in a multiracial society. Everyone must know two of the four national languages.

10. Nationhood
Singapore promotes national identity over ethnic allegiances. Regular campaigns promote national "goals," from being more courteous to stopping smoking.

Building a mini-Singapore in China

Deng Xiao Ping was so impressed he encouraged China to tap into the Singapore experience. From this evolved the township of Suzhou, a "mini-Singapore", under construction in a coastal area 50 miles west of Shanghai. The planned community will encompass 28 square miles of residential, commercial, light industrial, and recreational areas. It is expected to be finished in 2009, when Singapore-Suzhou Township will be home to 600,000 residents and employ 360,000 people.

This extraordinary project is one-ninth the size of Singapore, and is located in China's fourth fastest-growing major coastal city. The township is being developed as a multi-company, multinational joint venture. Some 19 Singapore-based and Indonesia-based companies together own 65 percent of the project, 11 Chinese companies own the remaining 35 percent; $20 billion is being invested.

Modeled after Jurong Town, a self-contained suburb of Singapore, Suzhou is considered a showcase of what Singaporean leaders call a "transfer of software", or management and organizational skills, to China. Suzhou Mayor Zhang Xinsheng, a Harvard-educated former Minister of Tourism in China, is convinced that with Singapore's help the township will be able to merge Western civilization with Oriental style.

If successful, and there is no reason to believe that they won't be, Singapore officials plan to proffer the model elsewhere. "In five years, we'll see the beginning of Jurong Town Corporation taking shape in Suzhou, and in ten years we should be able to repeat the project anywhere else in China or Vietnam," explains Senior Minister Lee Kuan Yew. A similar development zone near the city of Wuxi, China, will have an estimated $6 billion in foreign investment by the end of 1996.

If you build them, will they come?

China is breaking ground — by creating new cities whole cloth.

Currently, an estimated 87 percent of the Chinese population lives in rural areas. The government would like to reduce that to 50 percent.

But the country's already overburdened urban centers cannot accommodate significant population increases. Hence, the "new city" concept. China created 50 new cities in 1994, increasing the number of urban centers to 620.

The government intends to move 440 million people — the equivalent of the combined populations of America and Russia — into new cities.

China will increase the number of townships, with 3,000 targeted for renewal by the year 2000. More than 500 townships have been chosen for a pilot urbanization project. In the Beijing–Tianjin–Tanggu area, towns will be built to serve the larger cities. In Heilongjiang, Jilin and Liaoning provinces, new towns will be built to serve as trading centers. And Nanyang in Henan and Xiangfan in Hubei will be transformed from grain producers to industrialized communities.

If planners are successful, by 2000, 45 percent of the population of Guangdong province will live in urban areas — up from 39 percent today. Since 1978, the number of Guangdong cities with populations exceeding 500,000 increased from one to eight. The province's small towns grew from 132 to 1,321.

In China, urbanization and modernization go hand in hand. Both are sweeping the nation. In just three years, the rural farming area of Pudong, across the river from Shanghai, was transformed into "a modern development zone", with conveniences like flush toilets and gas stoves. Residents of Pudong, which was created to ease Shanghai's congestion, can now commute to the urban center via a long suspension bridge.

Haikou, the capital of Hainan Island in China's largest economic zone, is in the midst of a $9 billion facelift that will replace farms and fishing villages with an international center of light and heavy industry, trade and tourism. It will be home to 1.5 million people.

Indonesia's Kampung Improvement Program (KIP), begun

in Jakarta and Surabaya in 1969, is a critical component of its city housing system. More than 500 *kampungs* (urban centers) have been rehabilitated. Integral to KIP's success is involvement with community residents during and after the process.

While policy makers focus on the immediate urban needs, others look to the future. In Japan, Taisei Corp.'s "Alice City" project would "move everything that need not be on the the surface, underground". The hub of its 100-hectare dream city is Alice Terminal, envisioned as a 120 meter wide complex going 180 meters down into the ground, covered with a clear dome. The surface of this subterranean complex would be landscaped with parks and gardens. It would be served by underground transportation which would link it with other similar complexes.

Although the Alice project is a long way from completion, Tokyu Construction's Geotropolis, an underground project, is already under way and should be finished by 2020. It will consist of three large commercial areas below Tokyo connected by underground transportation.

And in August 1995 Prime Minister Mahathir of Malaysia announced plans to build a new capital city by 2008, at an estimated cost of $8 billion. *The Economist* reports: "The new capital will be a 'garden city' and an 'information hub', linked to Kuala Lumpur by a 'multi-media supercorridor', featuring the latest in satellite and fibre-optic technology."

And the urban migration continues.

China's floating population

In China, as well as the government moving people, more than 100 million migrants — equal to 40 percent of the US population — have left rural communities in search of a better quality of life. Lured by the potential for wages that are three times higher than in rural communities, migrants flood into Beijing's main railway station at the rate of 1,000 people an hour. Officials estimate that 70 percent of the people riding Beijing's subways on any given morning are "rural job seekers".

The experience is the same in virtually every city in China.

Although the numbers are staggering and the strain on urban infrastructure enormous, China's government views the relentless urban migration not as a problem, but an opportunity. Called *mang liu* (blind flow), refugees from rural poverty are considered "the engine of China, an inexhaustible supply of cheap labor, a floating population helping to the build the country," reports the *New York Times*.

The *People's Daily* calls migration the "inevitable choice" for the peasant "looking for higher objectives". It is considered a stabilizing force, supplying much-needed labor in the cities while minimizing the economic strain on the countryside.

- Approximately 11 million migrants work in Guangdong — 1 million of whom sleep on city streets.

- More than 10 million migrants have flocked to the "golden triangle" of Shanghai, Nanjing and Hangzhou. Shanghai alone is home to 3.5 million.

- Six million people have migrated out of Sichuan, and another 4 million are "on the move" within the province.

- Between 1990 and 1995 more than 300,000 people left Duyun, a rural community back in the mountains of Guizhou province — ten times the number of people who worked in the province's industrial sector.

- In 1991, 200,000 farmers left Jiangxi province in search of higher wages. In 1993, that number jumped to 3 million.

"Migration has negative effects on transportation, infrastructure, birth control and social order," concedes the *People's Daily*, "but these problems can be solved, so we should not consider it something bad and stop it."

Fan Gang, an economist at the Chinese Academy of Social Sciences, thinks the tide of migrants is quite a positive development, so far. "It has helped transfer wealth from rich to poor areas of the country," Professor Fan argues. "If you don't have the problem in the city, you'll have it in the country."

A *New York Times* article says migrants are "one reason that 5,000 factories can be simultaneously under construction in China's coastal province".

Richard Blum, a political science professor at the University of California at Los Angeles, says migrants "cushion the transformation of the Chinese economy". They are a giant "shock absorber" flowing from one area of the economy to another.

Rather than discourage this massive rural outflow, China wants to control, organize, and apparently encourage it. In the next few years, it will set up 15,000 rural employment agencies and their urban counterparts. "Our goal is to coordinate employment between cities and the countryside," says Cai Haishan, a project manager with the Ministry of Labor. "Our system will make peasants part of city life."

Of course, this assumes economic growth will continue unchecked for the foreseeable future. If not, if there is an economic downturn or a recession, results could be disastrous.

As it is, by the year 2000, there are expected to be 268 million people unemployed in China — more than the entire population of the United States.

Richard Blum says:

> "It is a double-edged sword to be sure. They may be an efficient buffer helping to transform the economy, but they are also a large pool of marginal people subject to vagaries and insecurity of having no rice bowl they can count on. They are dying in grotesque industrial accidents, they are locked in the dormitories at night, and they create a pocket of potential human misery wherever they cluster."

Liu Binyan, a Chinese intellectual living in exile in the US, says migration to the cities "always" marks the end of a dynasty. "This is not to say the current government is about to fall," he says, "but if it reaches the point where this large floating population does not find work and does not have enough to eat, then there will be big problems."

Vietnam: cities booming, farms busting

In Vietnam, the story is much the same. *The Economist* comments:

> "Drive along Giang Vo street in Hanoi early in the morning and you will find lines of young men, squatting on their haunches on the pavements. They are casual laborers who have drifted into Hanoi from the countryside in search of work on the city's building sites."

No wonder. Hanoi and Ho Chi Minh City (Saigon) are sizzling along with 20 percent annual economic growth.

Economic reforms, including private enterprise farming, were planned for the rural areas, home to 80 percent of Vietnam's population. The government tries to locate industry in the countryside, in the words of *The Economist*, "to persuade reluctant oil companies to site a big new refinery deep in the country, rather than on the coast where they want to put it".

But apparently this is not enough, as 51 percent of the population is still below the poverty line. (By contrast, the percentage of the population in poverty in China is 9 percent; in Indonesia, 15 percent; and, in the Philippines, 21 percent.)

The World Bank concludes: "Vietnam needs to tackle rural poverty if it is to engage the bulk of its population in its development and secure sustainable economic growth for the longer term." It says that "broadly based economic growth — with policies that absorb and make productive use of the rural labour force — will expand employment and income-earning opportunities for the poor in Vietnam. Policies that fail to benefit farmers will bypass most of the poor."

Says *The Economist*: "The growing gap between the cities and the countryside also has uncomfortable social implications."

How ya gonna keep 'em down on the farm?

Other governments and business leaders are trying to stem the urban tide — and the problems that accompany it — by building a better life in the countryside

The South Korean government is investing $53 billion in rural improvement projects, including housing, education, and healthcare facilities.

In Thailand, one million people moved from rural homes to Bangkok and other cities during the dry season between November 1992 and May 1993. This alarming rate of migration prompted the development of the Thai Business Initiative in Rural Development — T-Bird.

"We wanted people in rural areas to have jobs in their home villages instead of coming to Bangkok, where they have problems," says Suchart Suksom, Production Manager with Canada-based Bata Shoe Company. "The quality of their production is very high." Bata is in good company. Others involved in the project include Mobil Oil, Bristol-Myers Squibb, American Express and 3M. It is a goal of the project developers to have 500 companies involved in T-Bird by 1996.

In Indonesia urban poverty is more common than rural poverty, because the government made rural development a top priority with policies like guaranteed rice prices, investment in irrigation, and subsidized fertilizer and pesticides. From 1960 to 1980, agricultural output increased 4 percent a year. The *Washington Times* reports:

> "A small scale farmer on the Indonesian island of Sulawesi, Mr. Asikin [Mohamad] has transformed his family's life from subsistence struggle to rural affluence. His 1.25 rice paddy in Lompengang Village, outside Barru, produces two to three times what it did for his father. The family's sturdy hut on stilts now has electricity, running water and a television. With money and motivation, his two children will most certainly finish secondary school, if not college."

Extending rural credit early on was a critical part of Indonesia's rural success story and proved a wise move politically and economically. In the early 1970s, Indonesia launched a "rural credit program for most of the country's 60,000 villages, and a commercial bank, Bank Rakyat Indonesia (BRI), that now reaches 2 million rural residents — one quarter of them women."

Indonesian rural policy radically cut numbers below the poverty line. In 1971, 68 million were counted as poor; in 1990, even with a 50 percent increase in population, the number of poor decreased to 18 million.

But Indonesia's recent surge in economic development may threaten those gains. The government seems to understand the need to keep productive, irrigated rice fields from conversion to commercial, residential or other use. But the temptation to use land and labor more profitably is always there.

In fact, in the not too distant future Indonesia could well become an importer of rice as its agricultural industry develops alternative crops for the hot and dry climate of its eastern islands, an area that so far has been bypassed by industrial development. These crops would be grown for export in an effort to give this rural area a share in the country's wealth.

"If so, Indonesia will be able to congratulate itself further," says Singapore's *Business Times*. "For if a policy of such importance as rice self-sufficiency were to outlive its usefulness in less than a generation in such a large country, that would be a startling achievement indeed."

Asia faces enormous challenges over the next decade or so as it shifts from a society that is rural and agrarian to an urban, industrial society. Country to country the shape and scope of challenge vary. But many find they must import the grains they once exported to the world.

Changing face of agriculture

"Considered one of the eight wonders of the world, the Ifugao rice terraces in northern Luzon is one of the Philippines' main tourist attractions," reports the *Bangkok Post*. The Ifugao tribes have sculpted a fantastic landscape out of Banaue's mountains. "But now Ifugao traditions are fading and the terraces that have ruled the people's lives for 2,000 years could go the same way."

Neither animal nor machine can work the "skyways" of these mountains, which are carved out of steep slopes that tower hundreds of meters above the valleys. Thousands of tourists come each year to see the splendor of the terraces. But that popularity, coupled with continued industrial development, is compromising the integrity of the slopes. Furthermore, young people are leaving the tedious way of life, which requires that the rice be tilled by hand and that the mud and stone retaining walls be maintained the same way. They prefer to make and sell handicrafts to the tourists or work the tourist trade in some other capacity.

Some believe the rice terraces will disappear in 15 years. For the people living in the Philippines' remote villages where "life retains the rhythms of the past, dictated by the seasons and instructions of tribal priests", the demise of the terraces is more than the loss of livelihood. It is the end of a way of life.

What is happening on the terraces of the Philippines is occurring elsewhere in Asia on a far greater scale. Industrial development is devouring agricultural land at a phenomenal rate.

In China, in 1994, more than 713,000 hectares of farmland was put to other uses. The country has diverted 400,000 to 466,000 hectares of farmland annually for non-agricultural uses. In Shandong province, the "breadbasket of China", peasants have learned how they, too, can prosper when they give up farming. On the fertile acres in the Yellow River's alluvial plain, grain crops have been replaced by a slaughterhouse, a drug-making plant, and a furniture factory. In Xishan, a farmer turned blue-collar worker boasts that, "Not even a single villager grows grain now. We're not country bumpkins here."

China is still one of the world's biggest grain producers. "But the rice capital of the world is facing an agricultural upheaval," says *The Asian Wall Street Journal*, which also concludes the trend spells opportunity for the "American Midwest, Argentina's campos and Australia's wheat belt: China is finding itself more and more dependent on the world to meet its food needs".

China's government claims to be working toward food self-sufficiency, but will not stop destruction of farmland for industrialization. If the pace of economic development is to continue, then so must the relentless plowing under of land. People's tastes have changed: Chinese eat greater quantities of meat. Much of the grain goes to feed livestock. Lastly, China's young people have embraced Deng's mantra "to be rich is glorious", and farming is not their avenue to riches.

"Other East Asian miracle economies went down this road," says *The Asian Wall Street Journal*. "In Japan, Taiwan and South Korea, once equally obsessed with food self-sufficiency, villages became towns, towns became cities, and industry crowded out agriculture." These countries are now among the top markets for farmers in the US, Australia and Argentina, which have a lot more farmland per person.

China is already a top wheat importer. But some estimates say that early on in the twenty-first century China will consume 30 to 50 million metric tonnes of imported grains annually. By 2030 China will import 90 million tonnes of wheat — about half the total of world grain exports today. As one might imagine, this is welcome news to countries — including the US — that have gaping trade deficits with China. China purchased $1.1 billion of US farm products in 1994.

"Would I tell Americans to put every fallow acre of land into production? Not yet," says a China-based grain expert who advises US industry. "Would I tell them to start gearing up? You bet."

There's no place like home

Perhaps the greatest challenge facing the countries of Asia is to renew a sense of belonging and purpose. As rural inhabitants stream into new urban centers and industrial development forces farmers from their land, the integrity and security of community are threatened. It is a natural — albeit, painful — part of the evolutionary cycle.

A story in the *Bangkok Post* described this need for community:

> "A mega-city of nearly 10 million people, Bangkok is the heart of the country's business sector, has the country's top educational facilities, and is the center of the country's service industries. It has attracted people from diverse cultural backgrounds and social classes from all over Thailand, and, indeed, the world. Yet when academics and Bangkok Metropolitan Administration officials got together recently to assess the capital's cultural strengths...they found themselves unable to come up with anything at all."

"People feel powerless and alienated because they cannot effect change in their environs," says Dr Ubonrat Siriyuvasak, a professor at Chulalongkorn University. "The sense of belonging will return if people have a chance to help right the wrongs that exist in their communities... A sense of community, which is lacking in Bangkok is crucial in bringing the Bangkokians together to solve their problems."

That sense of community is weakening everywhere. In Guandong, Shanghai, Beijing, wherever there is a plot of land with potential as a commercial development project, residents are relocated. Forced migrations from city centers to suburbs are occurring wherever escalating land prices tempt local authorities. *The Economist* reports:

> "One of the many certainties in China under communism has been a roof over the head, and it is likely to be one of the last to go. Governments do not want to see people thrown on to the streets where they could make trouble. But what the states gives, the state can reallocate, and much of the urban population is moving house, whether it wants to or not."

In Beijing center-city office space sold for $4,000 a square metre in 1944, and urban "villas" for $3,500 a square metre. Beijing's urban real estate is the fourth most expensive in Asia, after Hong Kong, Tokyo and Shanghai. What's more, developers are earning 50 percent to 85 percent on their investment. Small wonder local authorities think little of relocating thousands of people who pay as little as $1 a month to rent apartment space in the urban core.

In Shanghai's center, most of the old housing has been torn down. What was once the city's museum is now an office building. The local municipal building has been turned back into a foreign bank.

But what of the residents? Many have lived in Shanghai for generations. What happens to them?

In Thailand, during the past decade, the government attracted both Thai and foreign investors to its eastern coast. Once a beach and some rice fields, it is now "prime commercial real estate".

In 1969, the government invoked the Land Reclamation Act in Tambon Tungsukla in Chon Buri province, compelling villagers to give their land to the government. Says the *Bangkok Post*: "The much-touted slogan 'sacrifice for development,' means simple villages have no choice but to go when the government says so."

But the residents of Laem Chabang, a fishing village and one of the oldest communities in the area, are resisting government plans to make it the center of a new industrial zone. Nearby farmers have been forced off their land, denied compensation and relocated to areas where they can't grow rice. The fisherman fear the same fate, but also fear losing their homeland. As one mother said: "We were born here and have lived here all our life. We would rather die here than move out."

The love of land is a factor in the equation that government bureaucracy seldom allows for. Kastorius Sinaga, a lecturer in the Social Sciences Postgraduate Program at the University of Indonesia, Jakarta, writes about the struggle of poor farmers from the Parbuluhan village in Dairi Regency, North Sumatra, who refuse to give up their rights to over 1,300 hectares of communal land: "Viewed from a development perspective, the farmers' resistance seems to be counter productive. The existence of an agro-industrial plantation in this remote and under developed village will afford a long and glowing list of benefits."

What the government fails to take into consideration, argues Mr Sinaga, is the depth of attachment to the land. "For rural communities, resistance movements to land release plans are deeply rooted in existing local cultures and social beliefs about the meaning of land. With this in mind, one of the well-known reasons for resistance to development in rural areas is the love-of-land and love-of-birth-place phenomenon."

It is more than a love of land and it is not unique to rural communities. It is love of community, a need for the familiar, the reassurance that comes from a sense of belonging, of shared heritage, of standing on common ground. And as Asia continues its relentless drive towards modernization, this "clan identity" must be factored into the equation.

The Economist, not known for mushy liberal sentiment, describes a pitiful, moving scene:

"In the northern city of Tianjin, a man sits in a one-room flat that he took over from his grandfather. On the other side of the street there is a vast building site. It will gobble up his home within the next few months. He complains that although the authorities have promised him a flat in the high-rise block that is to be built on the site of his present home, the rent there will be very much higher. But is he not looking forward to having running water and an inside toilet? He looks at the walls of his flat, which have not seen a new coat of paint in decades, and at the metal bowl which serves as his bathroom, and says 'no.' His flat may not be much but, to him, it is home."

Symbol of success

Meanwhile, the tide of urban migration rolls on and development continues. Shanghai, Singapore, Kuala Lumpur, Taipei and Bangkok are Asia's emerging "supercities", each determined to supplant Hong Kong as the great commercial crossroads, or to in some way replicate Hong Kong's unparalleled success.

But Asia is now too large and too wealthy for just one more Hong Kong.

"There will be more than enough for competitive Asian capitals to grow and prosper," predicts Hong Kong Director-General of Industry Denise Yue.

Asian cities are also racing to put up symbols of success — by building the tallest building in the world.

Of the world's top ten tallest buildings scheduled to be completed in the 1990s, nine will be in Asia.

In the near future, Shanghai, Jakarta, Chongqing (China), Taiwan, Hong Kong and Kuala Lumpur will each have a tall building, symbolizing their economic arrival. Malaysia arrived first with its Petronas Twin Towers standing at 1,476 feet and 88 stories each, finished in 1996. The towers are the tallest in the world, topping the Sears building in Chicago by 22 feet — until they are overtaken.

In a sense this also symbolizes Asia's competitiveness with the West: the world's tallest building *will be* in Asia.

While tall buildings have in the West been symbolic of wealth and power, why must the East mimic such a gross lack of taste and efficiency? Asia has a great opportunity to demonstrate an Asian model of success. Eco-friendly work and a human-scale living environment would make a powerful statement. Asian city planners have a great opportunity to demonstrate to the world an Asian way of creating work and living space best for the inhabitants, the harmony of wind and water (*feng shui*). At a time when Asians are racing towards greater heights, one of the world's most successful companies is

putting things back into perspective. The tallest building in the
suburban corporate headquarters of Bill Gates' Microsoft near
Seattle is only three stories high, not as tall as the neighboring
Douglas firs.

The West can be key to the infrastructure

The considerations in the face of Asia's rapid urbanization are
wide ranging, from decisions to locate production, marketing
and operating bases to looking for opportunities for new products and services. Those new products, in turn, range from
childcare and eldercare (for nuclear families who now live away
from grandparents), to mobile phones, motorcycles, highways
and bridges.

The Thai Farmers' Bank reported that traffic jams in
Bangkok had caused demand for mobile phones and pagers to
soar. (Last year in Bangkok I got a call at 7.45 a.m. from the
sponsor of a speech I was giving that evening. He didn't really
have anything to say and after a few minute I realized he was
caught in a traffic jam and was making calls to entertain himself. Mobile phones as entertainment: the use of mobile phones
in Bangkok has grown in direct proportion to time spent in
traffic jams.) Net profits of telecommunications firms increased
by 140 percent in 1994 compared to 1993; net profits for the
mobile phone business jumped 150 percent in 1994.

The demographic landscape and cost structures (rent, labor
and amenities) in Asian cities are changing rapidly. Apart from
Tokyo, Hong Kong and Singapore, other Asian cities are fast
climbing up the cost ladder. For example, in Mumbai
(Bombay), one of the world's most densely populated cities,
rents for prime office space are the highest in the world —
slightly more than Tokyo and four times more than Manhattan.
Foreign companies rushing to gain a foothold in Asia must
examine very closely the fast-changing demographics and cost
structures so as not to incur very high learning costs. In

Mumbai, because of scarcity, tenants have to pay several years of rent in advance — sometimes as much as five years — before occupying the premises. Such costs can be avoided if you look at Asia, or India, as a whole and are not captive to a capital city or a particular country.

The greatest opportunities for Western companies are in introducing technology and design to build environmentally friendly dwellings for Asian cities and help build Asia's urban–suburban transportation systems.

From Labor-intensive
⟶ High Technology

Many Westerners still associate Asia with low-wage, labor-intensive industries. Workers in Japan are well paid, most recognize, but in Taiwan, Korea — and certainly China — people earn considerably less than their US or European counterparts, don't they? To a large extent, yes. That's one reason Asia is so competitive.

But as the global economy continues to shift from its industrial past to the full potential of the information-based future, the key to productivity will not be inexpensive labor but the best use of high technology.

Good news for the West, right? Good news for the leaders in high technology. For the US, Japan and Germany.

Not exactly.

In reality the countries of Asia have envisioned the future more clearly than most. Asian entrepreneurs and their governments, by and large, realize the fulfillment of high technology will weaken their primary strategic advantage — cheap labor. Furthermore, they saw the handwriting on the wall a decade ago. Larger global forces are converging to make all of us rethink what we are doing. While the US and Europe sank into the political quagmire of protectionism, Asia forged ahead.

Today Asia's sophisticated urban centers, its savvy, technology-seeking, incentive-supplying governments and global high-tech companies, as well as a new breed of US-educated and now repatriated business leaders, have consciously leapfrogged over the industrial age and are pioneering the information age.

There is, of course, the caveat this book's readers know well: the tale of two Asias. Hong Kong is said to have the world's most sophisticated phone system (Singapore might disagree). In Sri Lanka, however, it has been said to be "faster and easier to travel by car to any destination in the country than to try to make contact by telephone". If you can find a phone, that is.

In India there is less than one telephone per 100 people, one of the lowest penetrations in the world. But the state telephone company employs more than 500,000 people; the ratio of employees to telephones is one employee for every 17 telephones. As I exclaimed in Bombay recently, "That's not a telephone company — that's an employment program!"

That said, the point remains: the shift in Asia from labor-intensive to high technology is well underway. This chapter will forcefully illustrate that premise. It is happening even in Asia's developing countries.

The question is, what are the implications of Asia's headlong rush into high technology for the rest of the world? And in particular, for Asia's competitors in the US and Europe? That question cannot be addressed without a detailed look at the advanced, and very impressive, state of technology in Asia today.

The opportunities ahead

Virtually every country in Asia is creating policies and removing bureaucratic barriers that might impede progress toward a high-tech, fully wired future. Yet no matter how far each has traveled on the information highway, each Asian country must address the same three basic opportunities:

- Make current manufacturing operations more efficient through technologically advanced production techniques.
- Develop and support "home-grown", high-tech industries.
- Create a telecommunications infrastructure capable of supporting an information economy and integrating into the global information network.

Tigers and dragons and geese

What makes this drama so fascinating is Asia's unique approach to development, the so-called "flying geese formation" which jumpstarts regional growth. The "Four Tigers" are already prosperous. But success brings rising costs. Where is a new millionaire to invest? In Asia, the answer is often right next door. Malaysia, the Philippines, Indonesia and Thailand, where costs are still low, attract their neighbors' wealth.

The result is the creation of interregional growth hubs, each component of which offers a critical element in support of industry. One such hub ties Singapore to Southern Malaysia and the Indonesian archipelago in support of a burgeoning electronics industry. Singapore brings the technological knowhow, and the telecommunications and transportation infrastructure, while Malaysia and Indonesia offer labor, water, and electric power. It's a dynamic triad, win–win–win situation. A similar effort links Malaysia and Indonesia to Thailand.

The powerful economic links between China's southern Guangdong Province and Hong Kong are legendary — even though there are no official trade links due to unresolved political issues. Throughout Asia politics is giving way to pragmatism.

Taiwan: a microcosm of the region

If you want to understand what is happening in Asia, look at Taiwan, which has been transformed from an agricultural backwater to an economic colossus — in just 40 years. GNP growth averaged more than 9 percent in the 1960s, 10.2 percent in the 1970s, and 8.2 percent in the 1980s. GNP is expected to increase between 6 and 9 percent in the late 1990s.

Much of Taiwan's prosperity was built on exports, which continue to soar. In 1995, total exports amounted to $111.7 billion, while imports totaled $103.6 billion. Taiwan held the world's second largest foreign-exchange reserves in 1995.

In decades past Taiwan exported labor-intensive manufactured products such as textiles and footwear. No more. Now the island nation is a leader in high technology.

Success drives up costs

Economic prosperity improved Taiwan's standard of living, but also drove up the costs of labor and land, and put a strain on the country's infrastructure. The very attributes that attracted manufacturers there in the first place were being compromised. Taiwan's government and people faced the choice of giving up on manufacturing or creating a strategic plan to make existing industries more competitive, while at the same time increasing the country's attractiveness to high-tech companies. Taiwan chose the latter. Then, in 1991, Taiwan embarked on a whopping $300 billion six-year national infrastructure development plan (since scaled down).

Taiwan realized its comparative advantage in traditional labor-intensive manufacturing had begun to decline, says Fred C. H. Feng, Deputy Director, International Cooperation Dept., Ministry of Economic Affairs for Taiwan. "We now have to increase our productivity and upgrade our industries away from labor-intensive products to more high-tech products with greater value added," says Feng.

That is a smart, sophisticated vision. But how was a country like Taiwan supposed to implement it?

Basically through strategic alliances with leading global companies. Taiwan needed their state-of-the-art technology and determined to create an environment so hospitable, the world's information leaders could not resist.

Taiwan's goal — to become a regional center for international corporations — was realistic considering its position in the middle of northern and southern Asia, its nearness to China, skilled laborforce, immense capital and a long tradition of supporting the manufacturing needs of multinationals. Taiwan's incentives to companies with expertise in its newly selected "strategic industries" include the loosening of banking and financial regulations (foreign banks can now open branch offices in Taiwan) and relaxation of rules forbidding foreign institutional investors from buying and selling securities.

As a sign of Taiwan's new political pragmatism, The Mainland Affairs Council considers all matters dealing with cross-Straits relations, and aims to work toward a smooth reunification. Meanwhile, although China and Taiwan technically remain in a state of war, economic bonds between the two countries grow stronger.

Taiwan becoming principal source of foreign investment capital

As a holder of large foreign-exchange reserves, Taiwan rapidly became a main source of investment capital. Taiwan's Ministry of Economic Affairs says that the country is the world's seventh largest overseas investor.

The vast majority of this investment is in Asia, mostly mainland China. Taiwan has invested more than $20 billion in China alone. Much of its investments have been in labor-intensive manufacturing, partly because land and labor costs have increased so much at home.

Taiwanese have also invested in Vietnam (where it is the largest foreign investor), Malaysia and Thailand (where it is the third largest foreign investor) and Indonesia.

Taiwan's investment is happily received by its Asian neighbors, but some say it drains money away from the country's own industries. Taiwan's domestic economy is undergoing restructuring, moving up the value chain.

If Taiwan is to navigate the straits of global information society, not to mention convince top information companies to invest millions, it must invest significant resources at home. Thus the six-year infrastructure development plan. A critical first step is its commitment to a fully digitalized telecommunications network by 1996, on the heels of Singapore's digitalized network completed in 1995. The race is on in Asia to go fully digital.

Industries of the future: Taiwan's top ten

Although observers who espouse the "let the market decide" model might wince (this author is with the wincers), Taiwan's choice is clear. It will follow the Japanese approach and "pick favorites".

Taiwan offers significant financial incentives to companies in these ten "strategic" industries: telecommunications, information, consumer electronics, semiconductors, precision machinery and automation, aerospace, advanced materials, fine chemicals and pharmaceuticals, healthcare and pollution control.

Companies in these catagories stand to reap an impressive set of benefits including administrative and financial assistance. The Industrial Development Board "may subsidize up to 50 percent of the financial management, quality control, production management, material management, marketing, in-service training and design costs of a company that meets the strategic-industry criteria," reports the *International Herald Tribune*. Such companies also enjoy "a five-year tax holiday and may be exempt from import tax on equipment imported for R&D work".

Taiwan serves as an economic development model for the region as the government explores all avenues to prosperity in the twenty-first century. Taiwan also targets expatriates who left the country for academic reasons and stayed away for political reasons. Now they are encouraged to return home to build the country's future.

Strategic asset: reversing Asia's brain drain

Hsinchu Science-Based Industrial Park, south of Taipei, is a sort of haven for repatriated engineers. **Of the park's 155 companies, more than half were founded by Taiwanese engineers who returned to Taiwan from the US.** H. Steve Hsieh, the park's director general, who has a PhD from the University of Wisconsin, says:

> "The original thought was that since there were so many Taiwanese scientists and engineers in Silicon Valley, that if we could get some of them to come back and start businesses, they could help us start a high-tech industry here. Many people went to the United States...because Taiwan was under martial law. Some of these people got into a middle-age crisis. So we've tried to recruit them to come here and start high-tech companies."

Middle-age crisis, as well as long stints with certain US firms, can certainly create an entrepreneur.

Nobel Laureate **Dr Lee Yuan Tseh** returned in 1994 to Taiwan to head the Academia Sinica, Taiwan's most prestigious research institution, at the invitation of President Lee Teng Hui. "In the 1960s, most young people didn't feel that there were good opportunities in Taiwan. The best and brightest went to America," he says. Dr Lee sacrificed a comfortable life and gave up his US citizenship to return. In his new position, he is now crusading for the return of the diaspora of Taiwanese intelligentzia worldwide, including such prominent figures as Harvard paleontologist Chang Kwang-chih, physicist Frank Fang and botanist Yang Shang-fa. He set up the Foundation for the Development of Outstanding Fellows, which raised almost $30 million from business circles to help scholars and scientists relocate to Taiwan, to teach and conduct research.

"I'd been at IBM long enough," says **Wu Tao-yuan**, a

Stanford University PhD in electrical engineering, and head of R&D for IBM in Silicon Valley. "I saw that my future was limited there because of the nature of the beast. Taiwan presented a much greater opportunity for me."

"I was at Stanford in applied physics," says **Yau You-wen**, who returned to Taiwan from the US in 1993. "[I] went on to Honeywell, and later IBM. What brought me back were the opportunities." Yau is now the Director of Quality at the Taiwan Semiconductor Manufacturing Company, the country's largest fabricator of integrated circuits.

The 155 companies in the park are privately owned but have received money from the government's National Science Council for land, buildings, and research. Total 1995 sales were expected to total $9 billion. By 2003, Hsieh expects sales to hit $50 billion. US-educated Taiwanese engineers are largely responsible for the park's success. Around 1,500 returned expatriates now work in the park. Several of its tenants are among the country's largest high-tech firms. Microtech, for example, founded in 1980, captured 15 percent of the world market for desktop scanners.

In the past five years, an estimated 6,000 experienced managers and engineers have returned to Taiwan, many with doctorates. Says Hsieh, "I want to see a whole series of little Singapores created here in Taiwan." A second park will be built near the southern city of Kaohsiung (the world's third largest container port after Hong Kong and Singapore). Hsieh envisions a third in central Taiwan and two more by the year 2020. Hsinchu is also expanding.

In the wake of generous government incentives, Taiwan, Hong Kong, Singapore, South Korea and others may offer this new generation even greater opportunities for professional growth than US high-tech firms.

As this chapter illustrates, Asia does a lot of things right when it comes to technology. But this new move to reverse the brain drain, more than any other single action, should give US information giants pause.

Shifting the balance of power in technology development

The commitment to bring thousands of US-educated Asians home introduces the very real possibility of a dramatic shift in the balance of technology power. *Business Week* says nearly half of the 1993 engineering PhD recipients at US universities were foreign nationals, many of whom stay in the US to work in Silicon Valley or top research and development centers such as AT&T Bell Laboratories. These talented foreigners are vital to the success of US technology-based companies. *Business Week* says:

> "As more of these high-tech journeymen head homeward with their skills and network of contacts, they are closing the technology gap. Take the case of South Korea. Thanks partly to U.S.-trained researchers who have returned over the past decade, Samsung Inc. is in a dead heat with Japanese chipmakers to dominate next generation memory chips."

Business Week points to the more than 100 AT&T Bell Laboratories "alumni" who returned to Taiwan, making the island "an export power in semiconductors and multimedia gear". It calls Hong Kong "a hotbed of telecom and audio gadgets, with hundreds of entrepreneurs", and cites Allan C.Y. Wong, a US-educated former NCR Corp. electrical engineer who built VTech Holdings Ltd., a $500 million plus maker of educational toys and cellular phones, into a global company.

The new repatriated technology masters **"tilt the balance of technological power toward the emerging markets in the next century,"** concludes *Business Week*.

At the very least they will accelerate the pace at which Asia plays catch-up with the West. In the past three to five years, the technology playing field has been leveled. In many areas US, Europe, and Asia are on an equal footing. Asia's far-sighted governments are doing everything in their power to pave the way for the transfer, from creating special high-tech parks and economic zones to investing in research and development initiatives to secure a future for home-grown innovations.

R&D pays off

Few have been as successful as Singapore in setting goals for technology development and achieving them. Its sophisticated telecommunications infrastructure grew out of the 1986 National Information Technology Plan which aimed to create the first fully networked society — where all homes, schools, businesses and government agencies are connected through an electronic grid. That will probably happen by 1999.

Singapore has a superb track record in shifting from imported to indigenous technologies. "Just 10 years ago, the island's economy was still heavily geared to basic manufacturing. But since then, the city-state has turned itself into a hotbed of R&D activity, with local labs busy working in areas such as computers, medical technology and basic engineering," reported *Asian Business*.

The Institute of Molecular and Cell Biology (IMCB), which receives funding from the government and the private sector, has a multinational group of 200 scientists, including more than 100 with PhDs and a support staff of 60 technicians. The Singapore government is making a long-term investment in R&D, and the island's Ministry of Education has a special $35.7 million budget for basic research at the island's two universities. The R&D focus covers biotechnology and pharmaceuticals, microelectronics, computer software and computer imaging. South Korean companies increased their R&D spending by 25 percent in 1995, to $3.9 billion.

According to *Asian Business*:

"South Korea's R&D efforts to move into hi-tech have secured a prominent position for its semiconductor industry. Now the country is the third largest exporter of memory chips, after the US and Japan. South Korean producers

hold about 30 percent of the market for the 4-megabyte
dynamic random access memory (DRAM) chips that have
become standard equipment for the latest generation of
personal computers."

Asia's answer to Silicon Valley: India, Inc.

India first offered incentives to high-tech companies in 1986.
Today Bangalore, with seven software development parks and 5
million people, is one of the world's largest exporters of computer software. Bangalore's population has doubled in recent
years, attracting many returning emigrés.

Pradeep Singh spent 10 years in the US at Texas
Instruments and Microsoft. Returning to Bangalore, he
launched NetQuest (India) Private, which sells electronic services and software products.

G. Jagannath Raju earned a PhD from the Massachusetts
Institute of Technology, and started Systematics Inc., a
Lexington, Massachusetts-based robotics company. Government incentives lured him back home after 20 years. He
plans to build robots for India's nuclear power plants, mining
industry and aircraft manufacturers.

India's software development firms are connected to US and
European customers through a telecommunications network
that was the brainchild of some Indian software writers. Infosys
now has sales of $28 million.

"Passengers traveling by many international airlines, including American Airlines, Swissair or Singapore Airlines...have
software companies in India to thank for the fact that these aircraft run anything like on time," writes Dewang Mehta,
Executive Director of the National Association of Software and
Service Companies (NASSCOM). The London Underground
runs on an Indian program, too, he says. So do bank accounts
at Citibank, American Express, Deutsche Bank and Hong Kong
& Shanghai Bank.

Mr N. Vittal, Secretary to India's Department of

Electronics, comments:

> "There was a time when the world used to speak about Japan Inc. What is now emerging is India, Inc., particularly in the area of software. The government of India has provided all the requisite inputs — training for manpower, high-speed data communications, red-tape-free systems — in fact, a veritable red carpet for the industry."

Government strategy is paying handsome dividends. Since 1989, India's software exports have averaged a stunning 40 percent increase a year, hitting $1.2 billion in 1995.

What's more, India's software industry is no longer selling programming skills, but what Ed Yourdon, author of *Fall and Decline of the American Programmer,* calls "expertise in managing entire projects". The engineers' identity is almost irrelevant, he says. Customers care about cost, quality, and on-time delivery. "Indian software firms offer considerable project management expertise, high quality testing and quality assurance capabilities, and an overall 'infrastructure' to assure that the project will run smoothly."

China's urban centers will also compete in the high-tech bonanza. In 1985 China established special economic zones for technology. By 1994, there were 27 state-level zones along the coast, 16 inland, and 9 in remote districts. Another 25 regional zones have been upgraded to state-level zones. "Electronics Street" in Zhongguan, a district of Beijing, is the site of numerous universities and research institutes.

In 1993 Shanghai's computer industry rang up $80 million in annual sales. It aims for $2 billion by the year 2000. A high-tech software development park will be home to 30,000 engineers. They can only hope to be as successful as Bangalore.

Aiding and abetting the transfer of technology power are the global companies that came to Asia in search of cheap labor and discovered a wealth of talent, energy and an extraordinary work ethic.

The global workforce — Asia benefits

Singapore's R&D effort aimed to attract global information giants. Result: a who's who in electronics — Motorola, AT&T, Digital Equipment, Hewlett-Packard, IBM and Matsushita — arrived to take advantage of government incentives.

- US-based Motorola Electronics opened an R&D facility in Singapore to develop consumer electronic products aimd at Asian markets. It was Motorola's fourth R&D unit, and only its second outside the US.

- National Semiconductor chose Singapore for its high-tech R&D center, which will be the only facility outside the US making semiconductors to US military standards.

- The $35 million Motorola Innovation Center develops pagers in Singapore. It was here the Scriptor pager was developed almost entirely by Singaporean industrial designers using software developed in Singapore. The plant employs 75 local engineers.

- Hewlett-Packard opened a plant in Singapore in 1970 to put together computer keyboards. It is now worldwide R&D and production center for HP's portable ink-jet printers.

Major US information firms are making a home in India, which, after the US, claims the second largest pool of English-speaking scientific talent. India boasts more than 100,000 software engineers and technicians. Hundreds of companies, many locally owned, supply software to Western customers, says *Business Week*, which predicts the number of engineers could double by the year 2000. An Indian engineer with five years' experience earns $800 a month and a slot in the upper middle class.

The training edge and skills crisis

Penang, Malaysia, is home to Hewlett-Packard's worldwide base for microwave components and is taking over from a Palo Alto site responsibility for hard-disk drives.

Global shifts in production responsibility, R&D and assembly would not be possible but for the intensive emphasis on training in the cutting-edge companies cited.

Penang's Skills Development Center, a 360-student polytechnic institute for high school and university graduates, was funded by 57 foreign firms and the Malaysian government. Intel contributed a $140,000 microprocessor lab. Seagate Technology, Inc., operator of a hard-disk plant, donated a 20,000 sq ft "team building park" for leadership training. Motorola gave $320,000 for PC software training and a bachelor of science program.

"Originally, they set up plants in Asia chiefly for cheap labor," writes *Business Week*. "But many of these assembly shops have gathered so much knowhow that they now do critical design-and-engineering tasks."

Multinationals still get what they came for — inexpensive labor. A circuit board designer in California earns between $60,000 and $100,000 a year. Comparable talent in Taiwan makes about $25,000. In India or China you can employ the cream of the crop for less than $10,000. And today Asia's labor is as well trained as the West's. Plus, many employers find the work ethic and attitude superior.

There are even greater savings on the "back end", the painstaking work that produces software, reports *Business Week*. Nursing a concept from blueprint to computer code to prototype or test model takes hours and hours of work. In China, where a keypunch operator earns $75 a month, a graphics designer $400 a month, a company like Bilingual Education Computer Inc., which designs interactive CD-ROM programs, can produce a product for one-quarter to one-tenth the cost of US production.

Advances in telecommunications mean knowledge-based

operations can be located anywhere. Software shops in Taipei, Singapore or Penang can serve end-users in New York or Frankfurt. "Conventional notions of comparative advantage are getting blurred in the process," writes *Business Week*.

Similarly, "Citibank taps local skills in India, Hong Kong, Australia, and Singapore to...develop products for its global financial services... And everyone from law firms to US non-profit groups cut costs in managing and analyzing documents by hiring 'outsourcers' such as International Data Solutions Inc. in Herndon, Virginia which employs thousands of workers in the Philippines."

According to the research firm Dataquest Inc. there are an estimated 350,000 information-technology engineers in Chinese research institutes and state companies, with average salaries of about $105 a month. Since China's list of priority industries includes electronics and telecommunications, its academic institutions will undoubtedly begin cranking out engineers at a rapid clip.

Improving product quality

"As recently as five years ago, a China-products fair could still bring a wry smile to the faces of browsing foreign traders," says a story in *Nikkei Weekly*. "The clunky toaster; the cheesy looking welder; a tank-sized refrigerator looking as if it belonged at the head of a May Day parade. At best functional, always 20 years out of date, Chinese products were destined almost exclusively for Third World markets."

But now international market analysts believe that within three to five years, China will export consumer and industrial products equal in quality or better than Japanese products.

How is such a turnaround possible? The answer, of course, is technology transfer. Since the late 1970s, the heart of China's industrial policy has been acquiring foreign technology. To date, Chinese companies have signed over 5,600 technology-transfer agreements with developed nations worth more than $40 billion.

No other developing country has purchased as much foreign technology as China.

No wonder China's domestic steel industry is rapidly overtaking Japanese imports, helped by joint ventures with the Japanese themselves, mostly in Dalian. The high yen is part of it, but the main reason is the vast improvement in the quality of Chinese steel. China is also moving into the high-tech steel market, once Japan's domain.

Still, consumer electronics remains the greatest concern to Japan's manufacturers. Already, China's acquired expertise in color-television production technology allows it to crank out TVs on a par with anything Japan exports.

Japanese consumer electronics exporters worry about Taiwan's new reputation for high-quality, affordably priced goods. "Leading the 'Made-in-Taiwan' charge," says a Taiwan ad in *Business Week*, "are two corporate visionaries — Frankie Hong, Chairman of Proton, whose TV and other electronics products are penetrating global markets, and Stan Shih, chairman of Acer, a hot computer maker. Acer, in fact, is by far the largest brand-name exporter in Taiwan."

One high-end, top-quality product to emerge from Taiwan's newly revamped manufacturing sector is Philips Taiwan Brilliance 1720 monitor, a favorite of software programmers and graphic designers the world over. It followed exhaustive research to learn what end-users really needed.

Proton's state-of-the-art TV, the wide-screen, fully digital DT-3660, is setting the standard for interactive capabilities. It is programmed to handle every known signal from a laser disc to a camcorder or TV game. It is an all-purpose, interactive entertainment center equipped to replace PC monitors, telephones, fax machines and videocassette recorders.

South Korea's Lucky-Goldstar, Hyundai, and Samsung are making their mark on global high-tech markets. Samsung is No. 1 worldwide in the production of D-RAMS, memory chips that store computer data. The company just broke the record with its 256 megabyte D-RAM, the world's most powerful chip.

Goldstar is creating alliances with GE Appliances, Zenith Electronics, Texas Instruments, Hitachi, Siemens and others to secure a global position similar to its leading position at home in consumer electronics. It is a leading player in the memory-chip market, and is out to capture the market for thin-film transistor liquid-crystal displays presently held by Sony and other Japanese producers. *Business Week* reports:

> "No longer the so-called Hermit Kingdom that treasured its privacy after countless invasions over the centuries, South Korea today is opening its windows to technology and trade as it has never done before. And nowhere is this happening more visibly than in the offices of the country's highly diversified conglomerates, now facing free-market competition at home and in foreign markets and, as a result pouring $35 billion into new plants and products to improve their competitive advantage."

These are exhilarating times for Asia. As the region takes its place among the global community, it is emerging as an economic powerhouse, a sophisticated producer of high-tech products. Only two factors could slow down the region's headlong rush towards prosperity: education and telecommunications capabilities. If either were insufficient to meet the challenges of the information age, growth could come to a screeching halt.

Where will the engineers come from?

"In our view, the biggest challenge of all facing Asia is education," reports Hong Kong-based Political & Economic Risk Consultancy Ltd. "China can pump all the billions of dollars it wants into its phone and rail systems. It will be money wasted, however, unless those responsible for operating these systems are educated in efficient management techniques."

Well said. And they are not the only ones who think so. The World Bank estimates "one quarter of all investment in rail systems, power plants and other infrastructure is wasted through technical inefficiencies largely due to poorly trained operators".

Asians have made extraordinary gains both in academic and hands-on training. This chapter has cited the thousands of repatriated engineers and hundreds of thousands of home-grown technical graduates. Is it enough to keep pace with the region's development?

Not even close.

"The shortage of skilled workers is so serious [in Asia] that in some places it threatens to derail growth," claims an article in the *Far Eastern Economic Review*.

Malaysia, Thailand and others in the region face serious labor shortages:

- In Thailand, some 6,000 engineering students graduated in 1993; the demand was for thousands more.

- Malaysian universities graduate fewer than 6,000 engineers each year; annual demand is for 10,000.

- In 1994, Hong Kong allowed 1,000 Chinese professionals to emigrate, hoping to meet the need for more computer experts.

- South Korea expects to increase the number of engineering students from 280,000 to 340,000 by 1999. Already, South Korea engineers with graduate degrees number more than 60,000 annually, but it is not enough.

- Demand for India's 20,000 computer science students is so high that industry wages are increasing 20 percent a year.

"It's a very serious problem," says Somsak Tambunlertchai, an economist at the Asian and Pacific Development Center in Kuala Lumpur. "These countries need to move up the comparative-advantage ladder. And the lack of skilled manpower is a serious constraint."

Comments Don Carkeek, managing director of Digital Equipment Corporation (Thailand) Ltd., who supervises 300 sales and service people in Thailand: "The demand for skilled, talented, well-educated people far exceeds the supply. Look at the daily newspapers — the classified ads go on and on and on about requests for people with a skills background."

Business fills the gaps

As a matter of survival, business attempts to fill the educational gaps. In South Korea, Samsung, Hyundai, Kia Motors and Pohang Iron & Steel built their own high schools, guaranteeing that the skills of graduates match the needs of the business. Daewoo supports a university, and Pohang's Institute of Science and Technology took top honors as South Korea's best institute of higher learning — winning out over the prestigious Seoul University.

Elsewhere in the region, Toyota's Shenyang plant trains employees on site. Microsoft gave 25 personal computers to a training facility in Shanghai. Honeywell provided the CAD/CAM systems, and Matsushita Electric Works Ltd. gave the machinery to develop robots. Labs and high-tech sites will be opened.

At Motorola's training center in Beijing, workers learn to brainstorm, define goals, and understand the concept of corporate vision. Difficult as it is to find skilled workers, people with management expertise are even harder to find. That is one reason repatriated Asians are in such high demand. Motorola sent employees from its Singapore office to Copper Mountain in Colorado for an "Outward Bound" type of team-building experience, to strengthen collaboration and employee bonds.

What's more important, one might ask: education or infrastructure? For Asia to prosper, the infrastructure must be developed even as educational needs are identified and filled. It isn't either/or. It's both.

The information age is here

AT&T sold China a high-speed digital transmission system between Hong Kong and Guangdong province that can carry "more than 30,000 voice and data calls over a single optical fiber line". It is said to be as good as, if not better than, the lines linking New York and Washington, DC. "This technology is as advanced as anything we have commercially available," says Christopher Padilla, AT&T's Director of Government Affairs. "In effect, we're helping China lay down its first information superhighway."

Since the end of Cold War era export controls, high-tech manufacturers in the West have sold enormous amounts of technology to China. During the last six months of 1994, AT&T sold China more than $70 million in previously restricted equipment. "Only a few years ago," writes *The Asian Wall Street Journal*, "such a voluntary transfer of Western brainpower to a Communist country would have been unthinkable."

- France's Alcatel SA received $1.2 billion in orders for telecom equipment in China in 1994 — more than double the 1993 orders.

- Motorola will invest another $1.2 billion in its China operations. Of that, $360 million will be used to add on to a plant in Tianjin which makes cellular phones, pagers and semiconductors. Motorola is intent on creating a wireless system for China.

- IBM is helping China build an information infrastructure, and Digital Equipment also sees a bright future in China.

- During 1996 China will spend $11 billion on fiber-optic lines, switches and phone connectors, plus an additional $49 billion by 2000.

Asia gets wired

Forget fax machines, fiber optics, satellites and cable. In much of Asia, the issues are telephones and transmission lines. Asia without Japan has more than half the world's population, but just one-tenth of its telephones. In the next decade, China will install 98 million telephone lines. But that will only be one for every 10 people. The number of telephone lines in China is expected to increase from 48 million in 1994 to 110 million by 2000.

To accomplish its goal, 10 million to 11 million new lines will have to be installed every year until 2000 — the equivalent of installing Britain's telephone network every three years — at a cost of more than $100 billion.

Asia's developing countries must spend $90 to $120 billion by the year 2000 just to meet basic phone service, reports the World Bank.

Singapore has one of the highest phone densities in the world, one of the most sophisticated telecommunications infrastructures and among the most ambitious plans for growth. What officials in Singapore realized early on is that it isn't land-based phone lines, or cellular, or fiber optics, or microwaves, or satellites — it's the mix of all of those technologies.

- Bangladesh wants 150,000 phone lines installed as soon as possible.

- India has 9 million phone lines — one line per 100 people — and would like to increase that to 20 million phone lines by 2000. The price tag: $13 billion. There are four million people on the waiting list for telephones in India, and some have been waiting for five years.

- Indonesia will spend $10 billion on telecommunications by the year 2000, much of it on phone lines. There are now 1.65 lines per 100 people, most of those in Java.

- Malaysia will spend $20 billion to bring its telecommunications system closer to world standards.

Converging technologies

"In places like China and India, the information superhighway will have to be wireless, because it is cheaper and faster to install," notes Paul Kan, Chairman of Champion Technology of Hong Kong, a company that plans to have around 50 ventures in China in 1997.

Wireless is one route, but it is not the only way to go. China already has 36,000 km of fiber-optic lines and plans to install 17 fiber-optic trunk lines by the year 2000. Fiber-optic submarine systems connect Hong Kong with Japan, Malaysia, Singapore, Taiwan, Thailand and Vietnam. Hong Kong, Singapore and Japan all plan to connect every home via fiber optics.

South Korea will spend $60 billion on its information super-highway through 2015. One of the first projects will connect 80 major cities by fiber-optic cables by 1997.

Meanwhile, mobile phones are a hot item throughout Asia, most notably in Hong Kong where more than 737,000 people carried a cellular phone in January of 1996; 167 times the esti-mated number of users in 1985. Between 1990 and 1994 the number of mobile phones in Beijing increased from 20,000 to 1.57 million. By 1997, there will be more mobile phones in Thailand than land-based ones. In 1996 the number of people in China with pagers will surpass the number of people in the US with pagers.

Between 1984 and 1994 the number of outgoing calls in China and Vietnam increased close to 30 times. Eight of the ten countries with the fastest increase in outgoing overseas calls are in Asia.

Keeping all these people talking could require at least 20 to 30 new telecommunications satellites for the Chinese market alone (including Hong Kong) in the next decade, reports *The Economist*. Inmarsat, a London-based consortium of telephone companies in 75 countries, plans to have 12 high-orbit satel-lites, from which people can call anywhere in the world from a hand-held phone.

The latest trend is in "low earth orbiting" satellites which offer greater clarity through smaller and lighter-weight phones. By early 1995, there were 11 low earth orbiting satellite services planned. Among them are Motorola's Iridium project, which will connect 66 satellites, and TRW's Odyssey, connecting 12 satellites.

Virtually every country in Asia has an aggressive plan to link up to the global economic village. Already aficionados of the Internet, it is only a matter of time before all of Asia can reach out and touch someone anywhere in the world anytime via computer, telephone, fax, cellular phone or satellite.

It is increasingly clear that the West can no longer count on maintaining leadership in technology development.

The Chinese network's talent pool

One of the more surprising and interesting sights in Hong Kong is at the tiny park in front of the huge Hong Kong & Shanghai Bank, where on weekend afternoons as many as 2,000 Filipinos, mostly maids, gather to pass the time during their time off. They are only the most visible of the foreign workers needed in Asia, now a land of labor shortages. Finding, training and retaining employees are some of the few restraints on growth in the region.

Only a trickle now, in time we are likely to see a major migration of workers from West to East. This shift is now being led from the high-end, highly educated professionals, many of them part of the returning brain drain.

Up to 50 percent of 220,000 Taiwanese who went abroad for master's degrees and doctorates since 1970 have returned to Taiwan. According to the Hong Kong government, about 12 percent of the 462,000 people who emigrated during the last 10 years have returned. The Hong Kong Institute of Human Resource Management estimates that for every 100 professionals who emigrated two years ago, 20 others returned from overseas. Among the returnees:

Woo Chia Wei, the founding President of Hong Kong University of Science and Technology, a physicist, became the first Chinese-American to head a major US university when he was appointed President of San Francisco State in 1983. Since heading the University of Science and Technology, Woo has recruited more than 450 mainly US-trained scientists, engineers and management specialists. About 75 percent of his faculty are ethnic Chinese educated in the West.

Dr Chris Tan, a noted biotechnologist in Canada and the US, returned to Singapore to head the National University of Singapore's Institute of Molecular and Cell Biology. Since his return in 1987, Dr Tan has helped the Institute recruit more than 300 research fellows, most of them Asian returnees who have earned doctorates and lived and worked in North America.

Millions of Asia's best and brightest went to the West during the past 30 years, primarily to the US, Canada and Australia. *Asia Inc*. estimates that there were about 8 million who did so. The current reverse brain flow could develop into a tidal wave of returnees as Asia seeks to lure them back to help drive the growth into the twenty-first century. Ronald Skeldon of the University of Hong Kong described the attraction to the reverse flow: "In Hong Kong and Singapore, you have high-salary, low-tax economies; in North America, you have low-salary, high-tax economies."

There is also an increase in the number of Western expatriates flocking to Asia. In Hong Kong, for example, the number of Americans, Australians and Canadian expatriates — including ethnic Asians who hold foreign passports — more than doubled from 45,300 in 1985 to 97,000 in 1994.

For productivity to increase, the quality of human resources matters more than quantity. Asia has been smart in pouring its resources into primary and secondary education rather than higher education. Now, as the Western world passes into the information age, and some parts of Asia leapfrog into the new age, Asia is in urgent need of development and reform in higher education. Education services in science and technology, and research and development, could become a major Western export to the East.

Asia is in a relatively stronger position to enter the information age than most people think. The region has several advantages:

● Asia has a young population that makes it more technology comfortable. Asia youth are so fascinated with technology that they are willing to try anything. An expatriate executive at Microsoft in Singapore was amazed at how much interest the teenage kids have in computers compared with their peers in the US. He said, when he goes home to the US, the common talk among teenage girls is about becoming beautiful, going out for a big date, and other stuff about having fun. In Asia the girls are talking about Pentium, how many megabytes you need to run a certain software, and about *Windows 95*. They are ready for cyberspace.

● As a latecomer to development, Asia has a golden opportunity to install the latest state-of-the-art infrastructure. A new airport in Asia can install the latest air traffic controllers' computer system. Almost all the airports in the US have computer systems from the 1970s. Moreover, the young population need not be retrained; they don't have to unlearn the systems of the industrial period.

● Although there is a shortage of engineering talent, concerned governments are making efforts to remedy the situation. There is endless talk about education reforms and some are already going forward. Increasingly, Western engineers are being hired and efforts are made to recruit from Western companies. Many of the high-tech and telecommunications projects around the region are managed by expatriate engineers and experts. Many more will be needed.

A promising direction for the West lies in collaboration with Asians. Technology-hungry Asian companies and governments are eager to make joint ventures and form strategic alliances with Western companies that possess the technology, knowhow and personnel. The synergy of capital, market and talent in East–West collaborations will do wonders for the world in the spread of scientific and technological innovation.

With the reversing of the Asian brain drain will come the emergence of strong global enterprises with large capacities to buy talent from the West. If Asia can find a way to achieve economic growth and better integrate quality-of-life values into its societies, it will become an attractive alternative workplace for many people, especially young people in the West.

The famous Asian work ethic may require some getting used to for people from the West, but if the quality of personal and professional fulfillment is significant, it may be a price that many will find worth paying.

Technological leadership, the West's domain for many years, will probably continue in some areas — no guarantees. But technological applications, proving the power of technology to millions of new participants in the global economy, will depend on many highly educated and skilled people with an understanding of ways to use science and technology for improving people's quality of life. From this standpoint, India and China will dominate the twenty-first century in the sheer number of skilled technicians who will be able to deliver new products and services to the world. The future of professional services may, in the process, shift from West to East and the prosperity associated with these services will follow.

7

From Male Dominance
➤ *Emergence of Women*

A tiny Buddhist nun living on the eastern shore of Taiwan has created a massive medical enterprise and transformed a mining town of 350,000 into a cradle of compassion. Starting with nothing, she built, and now runs, an 800-bed hospital employing 140 full-time doctors, 500 nurses and 900 staff members, as well as a nursing college and a medical school. Her followers, 4 million strong, some 90 percent of whom are women, raise more than $100 million a year to support the work of this remarkable entrepreneurial women.

It is a measure of the high regard in which she is held by her disciples that one of them told me that Master Cheng Yen is 6′ 2″ tall. In fact, she is 5′ 4″ and weighs no more than 90 pounds. This 59-year-old dynamo with deep-set eyes and a powerful gaze is testimony to the change ahead as the women of Asia extend their extraordinary energies into economic, political and community life.

It is in fact a revolution that has already begun. A quiet, yet powerful revolution.

Although most still live by centuries-old traditions, millions of affluent, professional Asian women will enter the twenty-first century as a force the entire world — not to mention Asian men — must reckon with. Educated and business minded, they are pioneering new roles in politics, demanding a full partnership with men and playing a leading role in the entrepreneurial explosion of the Pacific Rim. A new generation of women, including daughters of well-to-do Chinese overseas, are taking the reins in the family business or launching family-financed businesses.

Granted, Asia's women leaders are an elite in a continent where wealthy states sit alongside countries still racked with poverty. And there is great disparity in achievement and opportunity between urban and rural women. Still, the patterns that will change the lives of hundreds of millions of Asian women are already in place. First, women are well educated. In Taiwan, for example, women aged 20–24 match the college graduation rates of their male counterparts diploma for diploma. As any Asian will tell you, education is the first step.

Second, Asian women have made substantial, mostly unrecognized, inroads in the workplace. Country by country, all across Asia, the labor force participation rates for women compare favorably with those of Europe. Against this backdrop of widespread structural change, this first generation of Asian women professionals, politicians, company presidents and corporate managers have achieved financial independence comparable with other women worldwide and with their male colleagues. A sample of statistics from across Asia tells the story:

- In Japan, nearly all currency traders are women.
- The number of female managers in Singapore has nearly tripled in the last decade.
- One in five management jobs in Hong Kong is held by a woman.

And yet Asia's quiet, women-led revolution is not simply the story of women managers. It is the story of women farmers and

laborers, too. In retrospect, Asia's economic miracle would not
have been possible without their participation.

● Korea's industrial base was built by a legion of women working
  at the repetitive, dead-end and poorly paid jobs in the electronics, textile and toy factories.

● Thousands of rural women, predominantly indigenous Malays,
  migrated to the cities, to work in the electronics factories of
  Malaysia. They have over the last decade successfully helped
  the nation make the transition from a largely agriculture-based
  economy to one that is rapidly industrializing.

● Singapore's early industrial expansion in the manufacturing of
  electronics was made possible by the thousands of pairs of
  nimble hands of women in the assembly plants.

Education and financial independence will deliver what Asian
women may value most — **options**. In a part of the world
where women's lives have been role bound for centuries, new
options are emerging, as Chapter 3 indicates. But, as ever, new
opportunity does not come without challenge. Assuming new
roles can be a confusing, exciting, and painful process. Yet, as
the stories, quotes and statistics in this chapter will illustrate, for
millions of Asian women there is no turning back.

Sally Solo writes about Japanese women in *Fortune* magazine:

> "This is a revolution without marches or manifestos. There
> is little confrontation, because of the nature of the change
> and the nature of those who are changing. For one thing, it
> is a revolution based on economic necessity, not ideology."

Confluence of circumstances accelerates evolutionary process

A confluence of trends has accelerated women's entry into Asia's
economic life and heightened the enthusiasm with which they

embrace these new opportunities. The three critical factors are:

● **Opportunity**. Asia's exploding economy and the small populations of some Asian economic powerhouses (Singapore has only 3 million people, Hong Kong 5.5 million, Malaysia 20 million) mean labor shortages and full employment. Business must tap all human resources. Furthermore, many international companies with facilities in Asia are accustomed to hiring women.
● **Education/demographics**. Women in Asia possess the educational preparation to exploit these new opportunities. They are more educated than their mothers (in some cases than their male colleagues), are marrying later (if at all) and having fewer children. Many Chinese couples choose to remain childless. In Shanghai, 85 percent of couples prefer a one-child family. In large cities, more than 10 percent of couples are childless, and in 70 percent of these families, women are making the decision.
● **Technology**. Instant access to global events via international broadcast systems gives Asian women a window on a world that earlier generations could not even fathom. And, in the workplace, the new technology is gender blind.

Singapore's *Business Times* reports:

> "Women in Asia have made far greater inroads into business, partly because the shortage of educated talent has overcome prejudice more rapidly, partly because business families have recognized the value of commercial talent. Thus, in only one generation some Asian countries have created a corps of career women who are upwardly mobile, globally minded, affluent and ambitious. That is no mean feat."

Indeed, one could argue the time frame is more like one decade. Furthermore it has happened with no coordinated effort, no affirmative action in business or government, no well-organized women's movement. In some countries, women are creating organizations to help other women, but that effort is quite recent and not widespread. In Asia, the feminist movement to all intents and purposes is non-existent.

Still the trend from male domination to a partnership society where women take their place beside men in business, academia, and politics is evident throughout Asia — and gaining momentum.

Voices of Asian women

The combined influence of education, technology and rapid economic growth has set the stage for Asian women to become more assertive about their rights, more aggressive in pursuing their ambitions. Women seek to establish a new order, a fairer, more open, equal social system.

But in Asia, women who speak out risk being accused of "aping the West blindly", as one local newspaper put it. Comments Miss Kanwaljit Soin, a nominated MP in Singapore:

> "When women's groups call for steps to be taken to change attitudes which are lagging behind social and economic realities, policy makers tend to respond by suggesting that these are the shrill cries of a minority of women who are selfishly demanding doctrinaire equality and symmetry for their own ends."

Soin is asking the government of Goh Chok Tong to create a taskforce to consider policies that might help balance the dual demands of family and work. She laments the strains on Singapore families, who, she argues, must confront "ever higher standards" at school, the office and on the shopfloor. "[The issue is not a tussle] between so called liberated women and men and families," she says, "but it is essential that society reexamine how best adjustments can be made on attitudes and in work conditions that will allow for a better balance between the demands of family life and economic activity."

From property ownership to inheritance rights, from employment to abuse and domestic violence, women are demanding prompt social change. In Malaysia, for example, Minister Datuk Napsiah Omar, a woman, got the country's parliament to pass a domestic violence bill at the eleventh hour, and the Sisters of Islam, a study group of Muslim professionals, called for the creation of a comprehensive gender policy within Muslim culture that takes into account contemporary realities.

Women in Thailand, Taiwan and Hong Kong are beginning to speak out on gender issues. Charatsri Teepirach, Governor of the Thai province of Nakhon Nayok and Thailand's first and only woman provincial governor, says:

> "I always say if females are kept down, you lose half of the country. I don't fight for women's liberation, but if we utilize this portion of human resources, we can do things... As a lady, I feel I have to work harder, because I am being watched. If I fail, there will be a good excuse for them [the ministry] not to appoint anymore women as governors. So, I have to work hard."

Others argue that women must first look within to find the road to success.

"If we want to see advances in the careers of women or their success in business, the woman has to remove those limitations, her self-imposed limitations," says Gloria Tan Climaco, Chairman and Managing Director of SGV & Co., Asia's largest management and accounting firm, and an affiliate of US accounting firm Arthur Andersen. Such limitations, she argues, may exist because of the tradition — "years of subtle messages that this is what you should do as a good woman, as a good mother, as a good wife," she continues. "It takes someone to sit down and think through what she wants to do with her life, to figure out whether she wants to remove the limitations."

Women workforce participation rising rapidly

If the percentage of women in the workforce is any indication, many Asian women have followed Climaco's advice. Women are represented in the Asian workforce in percentages that look remarkably like Europe:

● Vietnam	47%		● Taiwan	38%
● Thailand	46%		● Hong Kong	37%
● Indonesia	45%		● Philippines	36%
● China	44%		● Malaysia	35%
● Japan	41%		● Sri Lanka	27%
● Korea	40%		● India	24%
● Singapore	50%			

Labor shortages spell opportunity

According to a World Bank study, Indonesia alone will need an estimated 26,000 people each year to fill mid-management positions. A University of Indonesia Management Institute study concluded that the number of new management jobs created each year in that country was closer to 100,000.

Elsewhere in Asia, the same "problem" — full employment, due to expansive economic growth — is creating monumental opportunities for women. Companies that might have discriminated against women are in such dire need of talent, they promote without regard for gender — unless, of course, a position is deemed unsuitable for women.

Changing economic structure

Asia's rapidly expanding service sector will create greater employment opportunities for women. Taiwan, Singapore and Hong Kong's service sectors already comprise 61, 68 and 77 percent respectively of those countries' GNP.

In some countries, women are already dominating in the service sectors. For example, in Korea, women hold 60.6 percent of service sector jobs, Japanese women hold 54.9 percent.

. As one male executive commented to a reporter who was conducting a survey for the magazine *Asian Business*: "You can't afford to ignore 50 percent of your talent."

In Thailand between 1974 and 1990, the number of female managers grew almost fivefold, compared to a twofold growth in the number of male managers.

In Singapore the majority of women managers, 51 percent, are in commerce. The percentage of women managers in finance, insurance and real estate is around 18 percent; in manufacturing, 14 percent; and in community, social and personal services, 9 percent.

Indeed, the growth of women managers in Singapore tells a dramatic story. Over the past 10 years, their numbers have increased from 8,644 to 22,580. Some 62 percent of female managers are between 20 and 39 years of age; the percentage of male managers in that age group is 47 percent.

In Malaysia, women have been successful in human resources and personnel management, public relations, job training and education. Few hold positions in engineering and law. Similarly, in Taiwan, women hold managerial positions predominantly in personnel, advertising, mass media, or research and development.

While professional women in Singapore, Taiwan and Hong Kong participate in Asia's financial and trading sectors, thousands of well-educated Filipino women took over the management of their households and care for their young and old. Hundreds of thousands of Filipino women work as maids in the affluent urban centers of Asia.

High achievers/high finance

Against all cultural norms, Asian men are slowly accepting the presence of women at work. At least women are honest, they rationalize. But it also appears that women's traditional role as family money managers has opened doors to women in the global world of high finance. In any event, that is an area where Asian women achieve marked success.

Elizabeth Sam, Senior Executive Vice President with Overseas-Chinese Banking Corporation Ltd. (OCBC), directs the bank's Investment Banking & Treasury Division and manages the investments of the bank, its subsidiaries and customers, as well as directing investment banking, the stock market, and the provision of nominee and trustee services and treasury operations.

A former Chief Manager of the Monetary Authority of Singapore and a Main Board Director of Mercantile House Holdings plc, a UK listed company, Ms Sam joined OCBC in 1988. She is Chairman of the Singapore International Monetary Exchange Limited.

Rosario N. Lopez held the position of Chairman of the Philippines Securities and Exchange Commission, for which she had previously served as Chief Legal Counsel.

Chin Ean Wah, a Chinese Malaysian educated in Singapore, runs the Morgan Stanley Institutional Fund, Inc. Asian Equity Portfolio, which realized a stunning 106 percent return in 1993. Chin is successful, she says, because she and her four associates visit 300–400 companies a year. "In Asia, far more than elsewhere, the company is synonymous with the man behind it, usually an entrepreneurial founder. We need to know his motives, connections, and how he treats shareholders."

Two other Asian women at the pinnacle of success in high finance are **Naoko Takemura**, Associate Director of Asset Management at Nomura Trust, who is responsible for Nomura's Japan Fund, Asia Fund and Asian Emerging Market Funds; and **Chok Kwee Bee**, the Senior General Manager at Arab Malaysian Merchant Bank. Chok oversees the bank's activities regarding the listing of Malaysian companies and mergers and acquisitions.

Throughout Asia, women dominate the world of fund management and currency trading. In fact, as already noted, in Japan almost all currency traders are women. One explanation for this phenomenon is that women are better at foreign languages then men — a key skill when dealing with international monetary markets. Or maybe women are just better at managing money.

An article published in the *Far Eastern Economic Review* entitled "Where to Put Your Money" featured a "How the Experts See It" column. Three of the five experts quoted were women. They were: Diahann Brown, Senior Fund Manager at Thornton Management (Asia); Winnie Lee, director at Aetna Investment Management; and Elizabeth Tran, chief investment officer for Asia at IDS Fund Management.

Asia's dual income and high savings rate

In Asia's rapidly growing young families, women's income is needed to supplement the household income in order to cope with the rising cost of living, both in the acquisition of consumer and luxury goods, and the high cost of education and retirement.

Although discrimination between sexes in payment of wages is banned in most Asian countries, in Japan the average wages of women account for only about 60 percent of those of men — even among full-time employees.

So the wage gap is not just a women's issue but a family issue, and demands for pay equality can be expected to rise.

Furthermore, Asia's high savings rates were in part due to women having control of the family's pursestrings. Most Japanese men turned over a big proportion, if not all, of their salaries to their wives. This is also widely practiced among Chinese and Muslim families.

Up against the glass ceiling?

Dr Irene H. S. Chow, a senior lecturer in the Department of Organization and Management at the Chinese University of Hong Kong, reports that in Hong Kong, one in five managerial positions are held by woman. Yet her research also showed that while men and women say they respect the skills of their female managers, they would still prefer to be managed by a male. Presenting a research paper at the Conference of Women in Management held at the University, Dr Chow concluded that women in Japan and South Korea lag far behind women in Hong Kong, Singapore and the West, but that all women face barriers when attempting to reach the boardroom.

2.5 million Japanese women run their own businesses.

In 1994, China honored seven women who had overcome enormous obstacles, not the least of which was prejudice, to achieve positions as chief executive officers. Yet, when the session of the local Shenyang People's Congress nominated Zhang Furong as a candidate for the 37-seat standing committee, the protests were loud and vigorous.

"Some people questioned my qualification, asking why the congress should need a female entrepreneur as the member of the standing committee when there are so many male CEOs in industry and business," says Zhang. She didn't flinch. She stood her ground and won the seat, noting in an interview that, "There are still very few women who have reached the top of the business, industrial as well as political echelon. I have only one or two women colleagues whenever there is a gathering of business and industrial CEOs in the city."

For many women, the struggle for respect and responsibility isn't worth the energy. They would rather stake their own claim in the business world. Entrepreneurship is flourishing among women in Asia.

The long march to equality

To appreciate how far Asian women have moved toward equality (and how far they have to go), one must understand the Confucian-like ethos present throughout Asia, even in non-Confucian societies. Developed from ancient religious practices, the Confucian rule of life relied on rites, family, social attitudes and hierarchy to impose and maintain order. Controlling one's feelings, for example, is considered necessary and desirable to achieve moral serenity.

Within Confucian social order, men and women have defined places and roles for the purpose of achieving harmony — *yin* and *yáng*. Males are strong and aggressive (*yáng*); women passive and nurturing (*yin*).

From the Asian perspective, being subservient is not necessarily undesirable. In the Confucian system, women are to be revered. Children are taught to be filial to their mothers. Daughters-in-law are told to respect their mothers-in-law (who in many cases are the most powerful person in the household), and in traditional polygamous Confucian families, the first wife enjoys prestige and enormous power over subsequent wives. In exchange for total submission, women are promised lifelong care. First they are looked after by their fathers, later their husbands or brothers.

These norms, stitched into the very fabric of Asian society, will not easily change. Asian society believes that, while there should be mutual respect between husband and wife, nonetheless the husband sings, and the wife accompanies.

Although revered, they remain subordinate to men and are expected to live according to the three obedience and four virtues (*san cong sì dé*) for women's right living. While at home, daughters submit to their father (*zài jia cóng fù*), once married she submits to her husband (*chu jià cóng fù*) and in old age to her sons (*láo lái cóng zǐ*). The virtues include the codes on good morals (*fù dé*), right speech (*fù yèn*), appropriate work (*fù gong*) and proper looks and attire (*fù róng*). Confucius also opined that "a women without talent is a virtuous women".

In their excellent book *China Wakes*, Nicholas D. Kristof and Sheryl WuDunn note that for thousands of years, girls had to bind their feet, remain illiterate and try to survive with no identity or dignity of their own. When Mao Tse-Tung declared that "Women would hold up half the sky" the Communist Party decreed a number of changes to improve the status of women. "The party outlawed prostitution, child marriages, the use of concubines and the sale of brides." Women's organizations were formed, and consciousness of the respect and equal treatment of women was instituted for the first time. "The party encouraged women to join its ranks, to become officials, to run factories and to do things they have never done before." China witnessed a dramatic increase in the number of women participating in the industrial force, from 600,000 in 1949 to more than 50 million today.

After Deng Xiao Ping's economic reforms, women faced greater economic opportunity, but not without discrimination and abuse. Millions of women now work, churning out electronics, shoes, apparel, toys and all kinds of labor-intensive consumer products in congested, dirty factories.

As women grow more independent, more active in society, more influential in their communities, a new ethos will take the place of ancient traditions. Meanwhile uncertainty reigns. Still, women are in the workforce. They are increasingly visible and vocal in local and national politics. And there is no turning back.

A women-led entrepreneurial explosion

"The greatest concentration of entrepreneurial talent the world has ever seen is dispersing throughout the Pacific Basin, and establishing the most extraordinary commercial network in history," said Paul Meo, Chief of the World Bank's international trade division.

Meo made that comment at the beginning of the decade.

Today the world is feeling that entrepreneurial explosion in Asia, and discovering that women are a critical part of its driving force.

Five out of six new businesses in Japan are created by women. Women own some 2.5 million businesses, most of them with fewer than five employees. While women managers are still rare in big companies, women are starting and managing small and midsize firms in increasing numbers.

- In Singapore, 38 percent of women managers own their own firms; and about 20 percent of business owners are women.
- In China, women make up one-third of the self-employed. A new program has now been designed to integrate women business owners into the modernization process.
- In Indonesia, women, in particular those in the powerful Javanese ethnic group, have traditionally been active in the labor force and decision makers in the family. In Jakarta, a growing number of women are opting for entrepreneurism.
- In the Malaysian state of Kelantan, women are generally the breadwinners. They own most small and midsized businesses in the community.
- In Thailand, women-owned businesses are concentrated in agriculture, services, retail and manufacturing.
- In Singapore, most women-owned businesses are in fashion, food, travel or employment, but not all. Throughout the region, women own highly successful businesses in many economic sectors.

The trend setters

Thailand-based Dusit Thani Group, the country's leading hotel chain, ranked in the top 100 best-managed businesses by *Asiamoney* magazine, was founded and is managed by Chanut Piyaqui, who serves as Chairperson. Ms Chanut launched the business in 1970, with no family resources to draw on. She mortgaged her home and sold her jewelry. Today, her international corporation has 63 hotels in 17 countries. She was honored with the title Khunying, awarded to women of outstanding achievement by the King of Thailand. Ms Chanut simply says of her success, "I wanted a hotel like the ones I stayed at in America."

Another successful entrepreneur in a non-traditional business is **Mrs Mutiara Djokosoetono**. After graduating from law school, she pursued a successful career in academics for 12 years. Left with three children after the death of her husband, she turned two rented cars into a taxi company at a time when such vehicles were scarce in Jakarta. Today, she is President Director of the Blue Bird Group — the largest taxi company in Indonesia with a fleet of over 3,000 vehicles operating in Java, Bali, and Sumatra.

Western China is home to **Rabiya Kadir**, an ethnic Uighur Muslim, living in Urumqi, the capital of Xinjiang Province. When Deng Xiao Ping began his economic reforms in 1978, Kadir was a housewife with an unquenchable entrepreneurial spirit. Beginning with the equivalent of $10, she bought and sold textiles, clothes and food to local residents. In 1982, she invested her profits in a small shop, which, in the next decade, she transformed into Arkida Industry & Trade, a huge complex of trading and manufacturing interests. Its profits quadrupled between 1992 and 1993. Mrs Kadir's personal net worth is an estimated $15 million. Says Kadir modestly, "I am just an entrepreneur. I concentrate on making money and how I can contribute to the economy of Xinjiang Province."

Independence through entrepreneurism

Throughout Asia, thousands of women like those described above, full of ambition and energy, are starting new businesses in record numbers. Explains Singapore's Claire Chiang, Human Resource Director of the Wah Chang Group, and former President of the Association of Women for Action and Research: "There is nothing like being on your own. I think women will increasingly feel the need to control their life situations, finances and their time. We want it all, work and family. We can have it especially through entrepreneurship."

Ms Chiang sees the entrepreneurial explosion among women as a reaction to on-the-job discrimination and the glass ceiling. Chiang is an entrepreneur herself and one of the first two women to be elected to the Council of the Singapore Chinese Chamber of Commerce.

Kuala Lumpur's Khatijah Ahmad realized she had hit the glass ceiling at age 30 while managing a department of 2,500 at a semi-governmental enterprise. "I could see I would always be No. 2." So, she negotiated a 60–40 venture with international money broker Atley & Pearce. Khatijah offered better deposit and loan rates than local banks, and turned a profit after just three months. Now her KAF Group, a multi-services finance house which is listed on the Kuala Lumpur Stock Exchange, turns in $2.3 billion a year and has 500 employees. Market capitalization is $243 million.

Of her extraordinary success Khatijah says, "You agonize for a short period of time, then you take the plunge. After that first decision, I just took one step at a time." Her timing also was flawless, as the Malaysian government was deregulating the financial market creating unprecedented opportunity.

Women in fashion

Joyce Ma is credited with single-handedly creating an international fashion market for Hong Kong. Born in China, Ma moved with her family to Hong Kong in the early 1950s. In 1969, recognizing a dearth of designer outlets for the increasingly fashion-conscious Asian women, Ma launched Joyce Boutique Holdings. Today the company has 27 Hong Kong outlets, several stores in Taiwan, two in Manila and plans to expand throughout Southeast Asia. Ma recently spent $7 million to refurbish and expand the Joyce Boutique in the Kowloon Regent Hotel. There are more than 27,000 Joyce credit cardholders, and company revenues doubled in the last two years.

Says Ma of her success: "What I've tried to do is create a space in which human beings, not shoppers are free to dream."

Hanoe Mori is described as "the first Japanese designer to break into the international fashion scene...the doyenne of the industry". Opening her first shop in central Tokyo in 1951, in 1965 she had her first show in New York. By 1977, she had become the first Asian given membership in the Chambre Syndicale de la Couture Parisienne. Members of this exclusive association include Yves St Laurent and Christian Dior. She also was awarded the Order of Merit, considered "Japan's highest cultural honor". And, she enjoyed the honor of designing the bridal dress for crown princess Masako Owada.

Mori now presides over an empire worth more than $450 million, with more than 70 stores worldwide. She is considered one of Japan's most successful businesswomen.

Martha Tilaar has spent 20 years developing a line of cosmetics that blends traditional Indonesian mixtures and treatments with products discovered in her travels around the world. She comments, "I had always thought that everything from the West was the best, so it was a great shock to me...[when people] told me to go back to my own country, study my own culture and develop my own beauty products. It changed my behavior and my way of thinking. It told me that I had to be myself, that I had to be an Indonesian." Tilaar's cosmetic business is now a multimillion-dollar operation.

Media

"The power of women can especially be seen in the media," says **Diane Ying**, who along with two colleagues started the economic monthly *Commonwealth* in the early 1980s. Today, the Chinese-language periodical is Taiwan's number one financial and economic magazine, and is regarded as the "beacon" for the business community. The magazine attracts more advertising dollars than any other monthly magazine in the country. Ying is the only women to sit on the National Unification Commission, which advises the President on policies towards the Chinese mainland.

Taiwan's two largest newspaper groups, the United Daily News Group and China Times Group, also are managed by women.

Hong Kong's **Sally Aw Sian** runs a flourishing newspaper empire. Her group controls Hong Kong's third most popular Chinese paper, *Tin Tin Daily News*, and the English language *Hong Kong Standard*, along with the flagship Chinese language dailies: the morning *Sing Tao Jih Pao* and the evening *Sing Tao Wan Pao*. She is also a world leader in newspaper publishing for Chinese communities in North America and Europe.

Women excel in science and technology

It is not just in "women friendly" enterprises that Asian women excel. **Dr Choo Yuen May**, for example, is the Senior Research Officer for the Palm Oil Research Institute of Malaysia and is a recipient of the World Intellectual Properties Gold Medal for Best Women Inventor. Dr May graduated from Waikoato University, New Zealand, with a Bachelor of Science and a Master's degree in Science, and received her PhD from the Malaysia Institute of Chemistry. She has won numerous awards, has 143 publications to her name and holds 12 patents.

Pearleen Chan is the Managing Director of Singapore Network Service Pte Ltd., which she founded in 1988 to implement the first nationwide trading network — Tradenet — which she introduced to Singapore Electronic Data Interchange Technology. Throughout Chan's 20-year career in information technology she has been an integral player in development of the country's state-of-the art telecommunications infrastructure, widely reported to be the most sophisticated network anywhere in the world.

She played an active role directing the computerization of the Civil Service at the ministry of Finance and National Computer Board (NCB). She is Chairperson of both the Asia EDIFACT Board and the national IT Standards Committee, and is a board member of the Information Technology Institute/Institute of Systems Science Common Management Board.

Spearheading the development of high-tech industries in China is **Dr Yu Ching Yu**, President of Asia Simulation & Control System Engineering Ltd. Sent to the US by China to learn simulation and control technology, Yu now heads a team of 200 engineers and scientists in a design and simulation engineering company based in the southern city of Zhuhai, China. Her factory is a "showcase" for the progress China has made in technology development and is a frequent tour destination for visiting dignitaries, including Deng Xiao Ping, Li Peng and Senior Minister Lee Kuan Yew.

Women transforming politics

In Asia's future, many of those visiting dignitaries may be women.

- In China, women make up 21 percent of the parliament.
- In Taiwan the government reserves about 10 percent of its locally elected seats for women.
- In Bangladesh, Hong Kong, India, and the Philippines women make up 10 percent or more of the legislatures.

"If we want to bring about major change, we have no choice but to get into politics," says D. Rounnag Jahn, a Bangladeshi political scientist at Columbia University. "And while it is in our interest to join politics, it is also true that women are better equipped to transform politics."

Some would disagree that women are better at transforming politics, but no one can deny they are moving into the political arena.

Three Legislative Councillors in Hong Kong, **Anna Wu**, **Christine Loh** and **Emily Lau** — called ACE by the media (for their first initials) — represent a new phenomenon: women as "professional politicians". They are "leading challenges to the sacred cows of Chinese and colonial tradition...giving gender issues a broader airing and helping dispel the still-strong notion that politics is an art best left to males," says the *Far Eastern Economic Review*.

Hong Kong is a bellwether for political change in Asia, and these three women are leading the charge. Christine Loh pressed for changes in rural inheritance laws, and in 1994 the government repealed the law barring women from inheriting rural property. Anna Wu came to office in 1991. Early on her agenda was pressing Hong Kong to sign the United Nations Convention to Eliminate All Forms of Discrimination Against Women. Now she is challenging the government to set up a commission on **human rights**.

All of Asia is being "politicized". Throughout the region, women are making inroads. Even in staid, conservative Japan, women are taking their place beside men in the political arena. **Takako Doi**, former chairperson of the Social Democratic Party of Japan, is the first woman Speaker of the lower house of Japan's Diet. "There was the general perception that female candidates could be used like equipment to gather votes," says Doi about women appointed previously into office. **But now, the number of women elected to the lower house is increasing steadily.**

"The most politically active and passionate among Asian women are perhaps to be found in the Philippines," says *Asiaweek*. A woman became President in 1986. Although she reluctantly came to power after the assassination of her hus-

band, President **Corazon Aquino** gave women more prominence in her administration than in previous ones.

In the May election of 1995, women had a strong showing.
Gloria Macapagal Arroyo topped the elections to the powerful Senate, the first woman to do so. She is considered a serious
contender for president of vice-president in the next election.
Three other women were elected to the Senate in the 1995
elections, as were 19 to the 215-seat House of Representatives.

Miriam Defenso Santiago came close to winning the
Presidency of the Philippines in 1992. A former judge and head
of immigration with a reputation as a corruption-buster, she is
tooling up to compete again in the next presidential contest.

There is a growing awareness of the value of having women
in positions of political power. Some key leaders are actively
encouraging women to get involved. In Thailand, for example,
Khuying Supatra Masdit, who at the age of 29 was the
youngest person ever elected to the parliament, after four terms
decided not to run again, but to turn her attention instead to
encouraging and helping women win political office.

To achieve her goals, she founded the nonprofit Center for
Asia-Pacific Women in Politics. Based in Manila, its purpose is to
"give information and training to women on how to get elected,
how to govern, how to make policies, build constituencies and
maintain a political base. We also support women who are already
in office." Masdit was the convenor of the Women's Forum at the
UN's Conference on Women held in Beijing in September 1995.

Focus on "soft issues"

"My government and I will continue our quest for peace," says
Chandrika Bandaranaike Kumaratunga, Sri Lanka's first
female president. She has vowed to end the civil war with the
Tamil separatist rebels. Chandrika follows in the footsteps of
her mother, Sirima Bandaranaike, who became the world's first
female Prime Minister after the assassination of her husband,
Soloman Dias Bandaranaike.

Bangladesh's former Prime Minister, **Khaleda Zia**, widow of President Ziaur Rahman who was assassinated in 1981, worked to increase education and vocational training, particularly for girls. She also set up no-collateral loans to enable women to pursue business opportunities. Sheikh Hasina Wajed won the 1996 election.

Women in government and civil service

In China, women faced tremendous difficulties in getting to the center of power. Women *are* in the top leadership, although in very small numbers. According to a government white paper published in 1994, there are 16 female deputy and full ministers in government. Eighteen women are serving as provincial governors and deputy governors. In China's 517 cities, there are 317 female mayors and vice mayors, and 21 percent of the representatives in the People's Congress are women. Women now hold jobs in more than half of China's township administrations, achieving the goal set by participants at a 1990 conference on the empowerment of women. Beijing now has 86 women in the executive and People's Congress — up 56.4 percent since the previous session. Women hold positions of influence in 88 percent of Beijing's towns.

Clearly, women in China are more actively involved in government than at any time in history. A few, like Wu Yi, Minister of Foreign Trade and Economic Development, often called the "part Dragon Lady", have risen to national prominence. Wu is the only women cabinet minister in the male-dominated PRC.

Wu played a key role sorting out tariffs, trade barriers, copyright laws, the complex process China must complete to rejoin the world's international trade organizations. Her stately manner and dignified air attract notice wherever she goes. She is frequently mobbed by fans requesting her autograph. A legend in her own time, she is said to have spurned the advances of Yang Shankum, then China's President, by stating that she was "far too humble to accept such an exalted position".

She made a sensational debut in her first confrontation with US trade delegates. When a peeved American counterpart supposedly exclaimed: "We are negotiating with thieves!" she calmly replied. "And we are negotiating with robbers. Look at your museums. Do you have any idea how many of the items were looted from China?" In charge of $200 billion in Chinese foreign trade, she has wooed and won negotiators from around the globe.

Women are becoming more visible elsewhere in the region.

- Charatsri Teepirach, a Provincial Governor in Thailand, is an architect by trade. She comes from a position as Director-General of the Interior Ministry's Town and Country Planning Department.

- Anson Chan, who serves as the Chief Secretary of the Hong Kong government, is the highest-ranking civil servant. She is considered to be in the running to head Hong Kong after the 1997 takeover.

- Malaysia's Minister for International Trade and Industry, Rafidah Aziz, has been enormously successful in promoting foreign investment.

- In Singapore, Dr Chan Heng Chee, a former Ambassador to the United Nations, is now the head of Singapore's Institute of Southeast Studies, a thinktank that specializes in research on political and economic affairs.

Opportunities for advancement will increase as legions of women assume responsibility for government programs at every level. In Pakistan, for example, Prime Minister Benazir Bhutto, now in her second administration, is implementing "women-friendly" policies. She appointed Khalida Rashid Peshawar as High Court Judge. Sindh's Majida Rizvi, also appointed by Bhutto, was the first woman provincial judge. That should change soon — henceforth 10 percent of government jobs are supposed to be held by women.

Karma, gender imbalance and techno time bombs

Asia's historic preference for male offspring and the horrific practice of female infanticide, still practiced in rural Asia, especially China and India, is extracting a sort of karmic retribution in the form of gender imbalance — which will potentially create endless social problems. With the arrival of ultra-sound scanners and the strict enforcement of the one-child policy, many couples abort a female fetus so that they can later try for a son. Because of this widespread practice, it is estimated that by the end of the century, China will have some 70 million bachelors destined not to marry.

South Korea's demographic profile is even more unsettling. Kim Min Kyong, head of the National Statistical Office's population statistics section, says that "By 2010, for every 100 girls, 130 boys will reach the marrying age". Some 30 percent more unmarried men than women.

In India there are already just 929 women for every 1,000 men. Realizing the seriousness of this gender imbalance, governments are banning "technical means" of determining a child's sex and advising people to let nature takes its course. The gender imbalance is sure to shake up age-old assumptions about women, marriage and family. Already India's social activists have been pushing the government to work towards uplifting the status of women. In rural India, where three-quarters of India's 940 million people live, government studies have documented parents' neglect of their daughters.

Elsewhere in the region, as the communities become more modernized, the cultural and economic imperative to bear sons seems to have subsided with increased prosperity. "That may soon happen in China, India and Korea. But if it doesn't, those societies will learn the hard way that it doesn't pay to fool with mother nature," opines *Asiaweek*.

An ounce of prevention

Thailand's Charatsri Teepirach, governor of Nakhon Nayok province, hopes education will help wipe out child prostitution in the province. "If they have higher education there will not be many prostitutes out here," she argues. She visits known haunts of child prostitutes to encourage them to go to school and sends doctors to educate girls about the dangers of AIDS and other sexually transmitted diseases.

In Asia, where the sex trade is big business, young girls are often kidnapped, even sold into prostitution by their families. But education is a way out. "Girls who go on to secondary school have a 99 percent chance of staying away from prostitution," says Mechai Viravaidya, Chairman of the Population and Community Development Association.

Some 90 percent of Asian prostitutes joined the sex industry with a sixth-grade education or less; more than half never completed fifth grade, reports Chakrapand Wongburanavart, Dean of Social Sciences at Chiang Mai University and Director of Thai Women of Tomorrow. If girls stay in school beyond sixth grade, he argues, "they will likely continue their education and...reject the idea of becoming prostitutes. Then they can be trained for other jobs."

Thai Women of Tomorrow has already given 1,000 scholarships of $120 each to high-risk sixth-grade girls in Pha Yao and Chiang Rai provinces. Half the money comes from US foreign aid, half from private donations. The girls study to be secretaries, dressmakers and healthcare assistants.

According to Amihan Abueva, head of the Manila-based Salinlahi Foundation, a child-welfare organization, "In Thailand, the Philippines, Sri Lanka and Taiwan there are around 200,000 [child prostitutes]." And that's considered a conservative number. "If you include India, Bangladesh, [and] Pakistan, the number can easily reach more than 1 million in Asia. Recently, child prostitution has spread to Cambodia, Vietnam and Korea." The foundation is part of the 19-country network End Child Prostitution in Asian Tourism organization (ECPAT). It is ECPAT's goal to make people aware of child prostitution and to force governments to take action against it, including making available educational opportunities.

Harnessing the energy

Increasingly, entrepreneurship is seen as one way to lift women and children out of poverty. A new breed of financial institution is harnessing and directing that entrepreneurial energy to address the pressing issues created by poverty.

A main goal of the Friends of Women's World Banking Association of Thailand is to encourage and support women in business. It offers information on starting and managing small businesses and guarantees the loans women take out to finance their self-employment activities.

Similarly, the Dhaka-based Grameen Bank in Bangladesh lends money to individuals to help them help themselves. Started in 1976, the bank has loaned around $1 billion to 2 million families. The repayment rate is an incredible 98 percent. Most borrowers are women. The bank now has 1,042 branches and 11,000 employees serving half of Bangladesh's 68,000 villages.

State-owned companies in Indonesia donate 1 to 5 percent of profits to a fund which the Young Indonesian Pribumi Business Association helps manage. The fund provides money and training to small business owners. Additionally, Indonesian banks are required to set aside a fifth of their funds for small businesses.

Lastly, India's Self-Employed Women's Association (SEWA) offers credit to poor, self-employed women working as weavers, garment workers, embroiderers and domestics. The SEWA bank has about $1 million in working capital, which comes from its 46,000 members. Repayment rates for women borrowers are 96 percent. Other banks wish they could claim such stellar repayment rates.

Throughout Asia, women have demonstrated that given the

opportunity, they can accomplish whatever they set out to accomplish.

Education as equalizer

If knowledge is power, then education is the great equalizer. In Asia, where literacy rates are high, women increasingly pursue higher levels of academic achievement.

"The real hope for women lies in education," says Chua Jui Meng, Minister of Health in Malaysia. When women and men both continue their education, she argues, "we have achieved parity."

In Asia, women's education levels have improved dramatically in the past decade. In some countries, women achieve higher levels of education than men. As a result, women are increasingly well prepared to assume positions of authority in politics, business and society.

Singapore government statistics demonstrate that women's participation in the labor force increases with education and is substantially higher for women with secondary education. In 1991, more than 80 percent of women with university education were active in the labor force. What's more, these women are usually "better educated than their male counterparts". About 60 percent of working women have at least a secondary education; the comparable statistic for men is 48 percent.

In Thailand, as in most countries, education is the single most important route for women's advancement into managerial positions. As early as 1990, the number of female students at college level exceeded that of men.

In Hong Kong, more and more women are studying management. Women, for example, made up half the graduates in the full-time undergraduate business program at the City Polytechnic of Hong Kong in 1991 — and 75 percent of the graduates in international business. Furthermore, in 1990 women made up 38 percent of students earning business degrees from the Hong Kong Baptist College. The number of women studying business administration at the Chinese University of Hong Kong jumped from 5 percent in 1979 to 11 percent in 1989.

In Taiwan, 10.4 percent of women and 10.5 percent of men between the ages of 20 and 24 were either "in or had completed four-year universities and colleges" in 1992. Taiwanese parents place tremendous importance on education. In some ways, women college graduates have an edge over their male peers. Men must serve two years of military duty after school, whereas women can go right into a job. By the time their cohorts return to the labor force, women already are more advanced in their careers.

Women breaking new ground in Asia

In Malaysia, the percentage of women in technical studies jumped from 4 percent to 36 percent between 1970 and 1990. Female undergraduates make up 50 percent of physical science students at the Universiti Malaya (UM), Universiti Sains Malaysia (USM) and the Universiti Pertanian Malaysia (UPM). On the postgraduate level women make up 60 percent of the students at UM and UPM.

A training program in the Philippines teaches women non-traditional skills like carpentry, welding and masonry.

In Tujia autonomous county of Shizhu in Southwest China, in the area of the Three Gorges Dam, Li Shuqing is raising rabbits using modern farming techniques. In 1994, she earned 20,000 yuan ($2,366) selling rabbit fur: a handsome sum anywhere in China, but particularly in rural areas. Some 100,000 women in the country have already learned similar techniques. Many women now contribute to family finances, and win leadership positions in their community.

In Indonesia, a largely female Environmental Bamboo Foundation (EBF), led by designer Linda Garland, is pioneering a global movement to create an industry using bamboo as a wood substitute for products ranging from spectacular bamboo "hardwood" floors to water filters, construction materials, musical instruments, pharmaceuticals and food. Bamboo's use as an environmental tool, for eco-tourism and sustainable business, is now being integrated into the policies of several Indonesian ministries, an example of a bottom-up, grassroots movement eventually taking hold at the highest levels of government.

Education is the "alternative to being bound, ignorant, and kept in a 'golden cage' through early arranged marriages," said the Javanese noblewoman Raden Adjeng Kartini, who spent her life expanding women's chances for education. She is remembered throughout Indonesia every year on "Kartini Day", which "celebrates the progress women have made over the past century".

A tale of two worlds

In the wake of rapid social change, the emergence of women is a trend many Asians (both men and some women) may view as undesirable. Asians value family, and by having women stay at home in the past, the twin tasks of bringing up children and caring for the old were taken care of. With women's emergence, child rearing is viewed as shared responsibility. Motherhood gives way to parenthood. This is new. It is making many men uncomfortable, undermining traditions, and changing roles of the sexes. But whatever people think, women will continue to question cultural traditions as they search for new roles that work for them.

In Asia's first regional conference for women managers and entrepreneurs held in December 1994 in Kuala Lumpur, a women in her late twenties, dressed in the traditional Muslim veil and long-sleeved, ankle-length clothing to the floor, congratulated the speakers for their success and said that she was encouraged and inspired by them.

She also shared her predicament with the group: "Her husband," she insisted, "would be uncomfortable" if she were to raise her profile. She asked if women have to be high profile in order to succeed. And she commented to the audience: "I find that it's better for me to work behind the scenes to avoid scenes at home."

Such simple words speak volumes about the varying degrees of progress women have made, and the pressing, but difficult challenge of changing social norms and cultural traditions that date back centuries. Although Asian women have made greater progress in less time than women in any other area, it has occurred more out of economic necessity than out of any will of the masses to make it so.

One manager, a Malaysian woman, dismissed the need for affirmative action. "Look at the Malaysian women. They are in that enviable position where they work hand-in-hand with men in the development of Malaysia. Why? Because there are not that many Malaysians. There are only 18 million Malaysians. So, every person counts."

Demographics help, no doubt about that, but as one journalist put it in *Asiaweek*:

"Abuses and discrimination against women [still] exist in Muslim communities. These have their own unique laws and regulations to protect females and nurture their lives...[but] safeguards don't always work... Many women don't know they have a right to divorce their husbands and think Islam permits their spouses to beat them. And a great number regard a role beyond wife and mother as unthinkable."

Similarly, in rural China and India, where more than 2 billion people live:

"the rhythm of birth, life and death has changed little from when Confucius and Buddha walked the earth. Farmers with no income other than what they harvest rely on strong sons to help work the land — and support them after they have hung up their hoes. If a son is born, a daughter is a burden. She is less productive in the fields during her youth — and after her marriage guarantees only her in-laws' comfort. In India's predominantly Hindu society, a daughter is 'outside wealth' that is handed over to a husband, usually with a hefty dowry payment. For some, too many daughters can literally lead to bankruptcy."

This is the tale of two worlds for women in Asia. There is still the very real world of arranged marriages at an early age, of women as chattel, or "outside" wealth, and of bride burnings and child prostitution. In the other world live women who are college educated and as prepared as their male counterparts to take advantage of exploding economic opportunities. These are the women who are marrying later, if at all, and having fewer children, if any.

Women in transition: changing the mindset

There is a dramatic shift in mindset, especially among young Asian women. Their assertiveness is expressed in leading a totally new and revolutionary lifestyle, which Asia's rapidly changing society is learning to adjust and respond to. Among the changing aspects are:

- Marriage — from when? to why?
- Choice of partner — from the man chosen by the family to my own choice.
- Children — from how many? to why have children?
- Relationships — from husband and family first and always to what about me?
- Options — from no to marriage to yes to motherhood.

The evidence of these changing lifestyles is to be seen everywhere.

In **Japan**, women are abandoning the old aspirations of getting married as soon as possible and are embracing a new indifference. The social stigma attached to being single, especially for those in their 20s, is much weaker now. At the beginning of this decade, more than half of the women in Tokyo between 25 and 29 were unmarried. Japan now contests with Sweden for having the oldest median age for first-time marriages, 27 for women and 30 for men.

Women are having children later, and some not at all. Increasingly child bearing is perceived as a burden. Rates in Korea and Japan have dropped to among the lowest in the world: fewer than 1.54 children for women of child-bearing age in Japan and 1.7 in Korea.

Women are intitiating divorces everywhere in Asia. Between 1979 and 1990, divorce rates doubled in China, and they jumped another 300 percent between 1991 and 1994, mostly among intellectual women. In Japan, Taiwan, Singapore, and even conservative Kuala Lumpur, many women are ending marriages and exploring new options.

In **Singapore**, so concerned were the authorities about the high ratio of unmarried professional women that a new department called Social Development was created to play Cupid, developing ways to persuade women to marry, and creating opportunities to meet potential partners (including loveboat cruises and weekend barbecues).

Some women are deciding on motherhood without fathers, risking social displeasure. **Unmarried mothers are on the rise in Asia.**

Becoming your own role model

The rapid pace of social change, coupled with society's own coming to grips with the new realities, a new social order will finally emerge. Taiwanese author Liou Fey Ying perhaps put it best:

"Women only managed to shake off centuries-old bondage in recent decades. There are now role models for the women of the future. Everyone can become a pioneer. There is a wide spectrum of possibilities: becoming an entrepreneur, a professional manager, a wife and social activist. The time has come for a thousand flowers to bloom."

Women-driven economics

The average male reader — Western or Oriental — might greet the emergence of Asian women with a skeptical response: a trend, perhaps, but a megatrend? Surely not.

I believe such a reaction rates as somewhere between ignorance and pure folly. No businessman can afford to ignore the economic implications of the emergence of Asia's hundreds of millions of women consumers, entrepreneurs, community leaders and voters. Let us explore just one.

Time is money, or so the saying goes, and in years past Asia achieved astronomical savings rates because non-working housewives "made" money by transforming their time into bankable savings. Non-consumers to the core, they spent their days comparison shopping, avoiding expensive clothing and luxury items, and they banked their husbands' salaries.

Their daughters are a different breed. The Japanese secretaries with $1,000 Chanel bags and Hermès scarves are now legendary.

But of greater structural importance is the simple fact that working women must shell out for transportation, lunch, childcare — and a decent working wardrobe.

The banker's nightmare is a marketer's dream. Such is the "progress" of civilization, the "lifestyle" of a maturing economy.

In a couple of years, those male economists who were blind to the emergence of the women megatrend will scratch their graying heads, pondering the steady drop in Asia's savings rates.

You will know better.

A few numbers. There are 9.9 million women in Taiwan, 4.35 million of whom have a full-time career. There are 5 million households in Taiwan: the woman in each of these households commands a disposable income or spending power of $25,000, a total of $125 billion. Women have control of the family purse; they wield the real economic power. This pattern is the same elsewhere in urban Asia. Marketers the world over will put themselves at risk if they do not start taking a real interest in Asian women. Asian governments know full well that women voters can tilt the balance of power at the ballot box and completely alter the course of their political fortunes, and women are increasingly becoming the targets of their campaigns. They will alter the balance of power and change the course of fortune in the marketplace as well.

Many Western businesswomen have been hesitant to bring their talents to a male-dominated Asia (not to mention short-sighted companies who ban women from jobs in the region). But Asia in the twenty-first century will find leadership in its own women and they, in turn, will find partnership with women in the West, moving toward global critical mass. Fast-changing societies cannot afford to leave half their talent behind.

The rise of women will not have to be at the expense of men. Labor shortages will abound in Asia for the foreseeable future — especially educated labor. As women gain greater access to educational opportunities, their talents will contribute to the development of new legal systems, new economic systems, and new social infrastructure.

Asian women will find their own way, blending religious commitments and cultural traditions with new work styles and economic and political leadership. They will redefine feminism the "Asian way", providing an additional dimension to the richness of ways of improving our common humanity.

8

From West ⟶ *East*

Through its dominance in market, technology and capital since the Second World War, the West had an overpowering influence on the world, especially on Asia. The world used to mean the Western world. But a confluence of circumstances is converging to alter the global balance of power forever. Today, as this book has made clear, global forces are forcing us to confront a new reality: the rise of the East. It is becoming apparent to the East and to some in the West that we are moving towards the Easternization of the world.

In the global context, the West is still important, but no longer dominant. The global axis of influence has shifted from West to East.

Global political, economic and cultural forces are reshaping the world. It is no longer just what America and Europe can do. It is what America, Europe and Asia can together do to reshape the world. When Latin America and Africa are integrated at a later stage, there will be total and complete integration of a world system, the single market global economy.

Only 35 years ago, East Asian economies including Japan contributed 4 percent of the world's output. Now they contribute 24 percent, the same amount as the US, Canada and Mexico. By the century's end, if current trends are played out, they will be responsible for one-third of world output. The

World Bank estimates Asia will account for half the expansion in global trade. The rise of the East began with economic power. Political clout and cultural influence will follow.

The Western world in transition

The twin forces of global change — first, the decline of Western dominance and the rise of the East, and second, the shift from industrial to information societies — are producing painful adjustments. The shock waves are enormous in speed and magnitude. Sitting governments who cannot make a timely paradigm shift will become helpless, economies that cannot restructure will create many unemployed, unhappy voters. Yet this time of change also holds unlimited opportunities for the West — if, that is, the West is willing to join in a new world where collaboration replaces domination, where diversity and convergence are far more attractive alternatives to homogeneity.

The time has come to fully recognize and accept the East. This acceptance is as profound as was accepting that the world is round. And the East is not just Japan and China. The countries of the ASEAN group — Thailand, Malaysia, Singapore, Indonesia, Philippines, Brunei and Vietnam — have a population of 450 million, and the Indian subcontinent's 940 million people are powerful forces and players in the reshaping of the world economy.

Beginning of a world reshaping itself in Hong Kong

The year 1997 is symbolic for the Chinese, as well as the West. In Hong Kong, colonial rule officially ends on 30 June 1997. When Macau returns to China in December 1999, the final chapter of Western domination in Asia will be closed.

For the first time in 400 years, every inch of Asian soil will be controlled and managed by Asians.

When in 1995 the high-profile Royal Hong Kong Jockey Club jettisoned the appellation "Royal" and became the Hong

Kong Jockey Club, reality started to sink in. The West must now look at Hong Kong through a new pair of lenses, seeing Hong Kong as China, not as some Western outpost taken back by China. Those same new lenses must examine all of Asia, beginning now.

For Hong Kong, China is the new master. People feel it already. Hong Kong, like a son who has been given away, must now return home. Hong Kong's new official symbol, the five-petaled bauhinia which has already replaced the likeness of Queen Elizabeth II on coins, is a symbol of its new identity. The international community is well aware of the integration of the mainland and Hong Kong. Any mishandling of Hong Kong will not be in China's interest.

Enter the dragon

Distrust and suspicion of the mainland Chinese leadership will remain for some time. Martin Lee, the leader of the Democratic Party in Hong Kong's legislature and a leading barrister, is dismayed and skeptical. "China wants Hong Kong to be the most prosperous Chinese city. They will tolerate Hong Kong as a Chinese city. They will have control of the executive, the legislature and the judiciary. They will control the universities and the press."

But isn't Hong Kong a Chinese city?

Tsang Yok Sing, an official Hong Kong adviser to Beijing, finds Martin's fears ludicrous. "We believe China understands very well that to keep the social and economic system in Hong Kong, a democratic system has to be developed [here in Hong Kong]. Most people in Hong Kong know they are Chinese. If you ask me, I say it is my country. You can't get away from it." Hong Kong's Chief Secretary Anson Chan reiterated the sentiment, "I am Chinese through and through. I never regarded myself as British. I want to see China succeed."

Fortune magazine ran a cover story in June 1995 proclaiming "The Death of Hong Kong". Not death, but birth. I say a new Hong Kong is being born. **A Chinese Hong Kong —** which may not fit Western standards, which the West may not be comfortable with. In fact, China itself may not be entirely comfortable with the return of Hong Kong.

"Ultimately what is required of China is a different mind set," wrote Karen Elliott House in *The Asian Wall Street Journal*. "A society that counts its 1.2 billion people as interchangeable commodities is being asked to understand the value of six million people as unique individual assets." House suggested that the US offer visas to Hong Kong citizens who wish to emigrate.

Years ago, that would have been an attractive proposition, but with the explosive growth in Asia in general, and China in particular, how many in Hong Kong want US passports? Some would, but ever pragmatic, they would eventually return to Hong Kong to make money. When movie producer and actor Raymond Hui was asked about his Canadian passport, he said that it is just a travel document. The Canadian High Commissioner in Hong Kong offered to help him get rid of it.

China has made it clear: those who stay in Hong Kong or return to Hong Kong before 1997 will retain permanent resident status. Those returning after 1997 must stay for seven years to requalify as permanent residents. The moment of truth has dawned: West or East, the people of Hong Kong must choose.

Hong Kong 1997 is symbolic of a world reshaping itself.

The East is taking over, superseding the West's influence. K. C. Chen, former editor of the Chinese-language Hong Kong-based *Huanan Economic Journal*, said, "for years, people complained that it is difficult to adjust and to fathom the Japanese, theirs is a very different world. It is even more difficult to understand and try to work with the Chinese. But Japan is only 126 million people, China has 1.2 billion." The question is obvious: who can afford to ignore China?

Hong Kong's governance is a domestic issue of international concern. How its governance is decided will represent a new chapter in the history of a China reclaiming her former glory.

China: the new superpresence

The question of China becoming the new world superpresence is not "if" but "when". China's economic resurgence, followed by the rise of political clout and potentially huge military presence, are certainties the world must deal with in the twenty-first century. The China challenge will preoccupy the sphere of international relations, especially between China and its immediate neighbors in Asia. Eventually, the world will accept China's return to dominance as a political, economic and military power. China will be a global power, if not the global power. The question is, how can the world influence what kind of a global power China will become? Among other things, it will be inseparable from the ethnic Chinese network.

China's economic fortune depends on the open markets of the US, and investment and technology from the Asian newly industrialized economies. The world is driven by the allure of the Chinese market. The rise of China will be on a scale the world has never seen before, and a policy of containment in dealing with a supernation returning to its former glory just won't work. The short-term concerns of conflicts and flashpoints are testing grounds for the development of a longer-term engagement strategy with China. An Asian- and China-driven solution is needed.

Unlike Japan in the 1930s, China's interest is not conquests. The complexities of domestic conditions, the need for capital to fund growth, the widening of the rural/urban gap and impending social instability, the weakening of Beijing's control and authority on the provinces, and a whole range of political and economic concerns will all undermine China's potential hegemonistic intentions or ambitions. However, the same reasons could force China to reach out to secure valuable resources, such as control over oil and gas reserves in the South China Seas, to address domestic needs at home.

The fears and concerns on the negative aspects of the return to glory of the world's former giant are understandable. It will forever change the balance of power between West and East.

What the world must now think about is the predictable Asian way of dealing with China: that is, to accept and let China reestablish its leadership role in a hierarchical pattern of international relations. By identifying economic and political interests with China, and acknowledging China's supremacy, countries in Asia could accommodate the rise of China and Chinese hegemony. This could be the alternative to conflict and instability in the region.

Towards equal partnership

In the context of this changing balance, Australia has accepted reality, and come to terms with becoming Asian. Paul Keating, Prime Minister of Australia, wrote in Asiaweek:

> "Engagement with Asia has been a major part of Australian public policy for over a decade now… For as never before Australia's economic, strategic and political interests now coalesce in the region around us…and importantly, finding a place for ourselves in Asia is also about finding our own identity. Asia is no longer the 'Far East.' It is the 'near north.'"

Australia is experiencing Easternization on a major scale. Half of Australia's immigrants now come from Asia. One-third of Australia's exports went to Asia in the early 1980s. By 1994 it had increased to 60 percent or $38.3 billion. Japan and Korea are the largest export markets, followed by ASEAN countries (counted together). In 1994, more than 60,000 students from Asia studied in Australia. The West is learning to adjust to Easternization, beginning with Australia.

A relocation from East to West: Asian companies move manufacturing to Europe

Once US and European megamanufacturers outsourced labor-intensive operations to low-wage, low-skill Asian nations — today, as Chapter 6 outlined, that tide is turning. For some time now, companies in Hong Kong, Singapore, Taiwan and South Korea have moved manufacturing operations to less developed Asian nations. Now wages and incomes are rising in those countries as well, and it is now more cost-effective to manufacture and distribute in the countries to which goods are destined to be delivered.

There are ten big South Korean manufacturers in the US and nine from Taiwan, half of which opened their doors in the last several years. South Korea has 36 companies operating in Britain, Taiwan has 67. Hong Kong has 16 manufacturers in Britain, mostly in textiles and electronics. As the former British colony prepares to become part of China in 1997, some Hong Kong companies are moving elsewhere.

The birth of an Asian network

Will Asia dominate politically? Will Asian nations unite like the European Union? The answer is no. Alliances to date have been motivated almost solely by economic self-interest. While Asian countries such as those in ASEAN and the growth triangles sort out the political priorities, they will create economic groups, benefiting from each other's market, labor, resources, capital and technology. Because the marriages are based on economics, they work. And collectively, the countries of Asia are very powerful. Asian governments provide the leadership, create the necessary conditions; private business carries out the integration. Western multinationals have played their role, but it is the Asian companies that are raring to go regionally and globally. For now, Asians are eager to engage the West in reshaping the world.

If the US takes a myopic view of Asia, the results could be

devastating. *Wall Street Journal* columnist Albert Hunt argues:

> "in the final analysis, the simple fact is that Asia is so big and bustling that the U.S. ability to affect change is limited. But at the margin it's critical that U.S.'s influence be constructive rather than destructive. Otherwise, America will be a mere observer in the Pacific century."

A massive shift in the balance of power is in motion: from West to East.

The world's future is in Asia

The East will not take away jobs from the West. The predator is technology and not cheap labor in Asia. Asia itself loses jobs with new technologies. But with the great reduction in the labor content in manufacturing, it does not make much sense for companies to relocate, except for those in textiles and clothing where labor costs can make the difference, and they are already there. According to a study by Charles Oman of the OECD, the share of low-skilled labor in production costs has been rapidly falling — from around 25 percent in 1970 to 5–10 percent today.

The markets are in the East, both for consumer and capital goods. The US Department of Commerce has designated 10 priority markets as vital for the growth of all American exports; all these markets are developing countries.

The US already exports far more to Asia than to the mature markets of Europe, while Europe ships twice as much to the developing world as to the US.

The Asian way restated

The typical Western view of modernization which encompasses ideals on civil liberty, freedom of speech and democracy is strongly challenged in Asia. As Chapter 3 stressed, Asians place a high priority on family first and seek to devise a more communal and equitable form of development. Centuries of political chaos have so scared the Asian psyche that they will do anything to preserve social and political stability. "Harmony is the goal in our pursuit of modernization," said Korean Scholar Professor Dr Sang-Woo Rhee of Sogang University, Seoul.

The West prefers diverse lifestyles. Asia emphasizes discipline and conformity. The West delights in open debate, while Asians abhor confrontation, preferring to persuade. But East Asia's success may set a new model for the world.

Building a new Asian model raises many questions for those in the region. What in the West is good that we want to make it our own? What does the West have or do that we want to avoid at all costs? Do we need to reinvent cities? Do we need to create big corporations? In Asia's diverse environment, small and flexible operating units with a common belief system have been the standard. Asia was built on that. Will success and ambition blur our vision? Will we fall into the trap of equating size with success? How do we build on past successes? In family and social welfare considerations, how much do we want governments to intervene? Is Asia at a competitive advantage because it does not have a social welfare system that bogs it down?

The welfare debate

Many Asian governments and citizens are debating welfare and safety nets. Not just in the developed economies. China's media is discussing social security, because of the risk of social instability resulting from massive unemployment when loss-making State-owned enterprises are scrapped.

Massive employment programs in the form of state enterprises in China and India face the greatest challenge. Welfare demands do not follow affluence in democracies. In socialist societies, they are the state's *raison d'être*. Asia's affluent newly industrialized economies (NIEs) will increasingly have to deal with the welfare debate. The challenge is to design systems that do not kill personal responsibility and self-reliance, the cornerstones of individual and country competitiveness.

Comprehensive Western-style welfare systems are not on Asia's list of development priorities. Most Asians favor preserving self-reliance and enterprise, as evidenced by the proliferation of small and midsize businesses in the region, especially in the Chinese-based economies.

- Over the past five years, South Korea has put in place a national pension scheme and is going forward with a comprehensive health insurance program.
- Malaysia and Singapore have State-regulated savings schemes that encourage home ownership.
- Thailand has recently announced plans to care for the elderly, the disabled and those below the poverty line.

It's the system, stupid

Welfare state disincentives and safety nets can erode personal responsibility. A recent US census study found that more than 30 percent of Southeast Asian households in the US depend on welfare. Among Laotians and Cambodians in California, 77 percent of households survive on welfare. Southeast Asians represent the highest incidence of welfare dependence for any US ethnic or racial group.

An effective and workable welfare system provides opportunity, encourages enterprise, promotes personal responsibility and preserves self-reliance.

Hong Kong's Jimmy Lai, publisher of *Apple Daily*, is a great champion of the free market and individual enterprise. His is a spectacular rags-to-riches story. "In the marketplace," he says, "you vote with your dollars, you vote with your own self interest, your children's interest."

Ow Yang Hsuan, Chairman of the Board of Governors,

Singapore's Institute of Policy Studies, maintains that it is avoidance of Western-style welfare and emphasis on family self-reliance that have helped Asia on its road to prosperity. The World Bank noted that "from 1965 to 1990 the 23 economies of East Asia grew faster than all other regions of the world". The growth was due to hard work. There is no miracle. The Chinese diaspora (see Chapter 1) shows how self-reliance works as a strategy for upward mobility.

The Asian-American experience

The pivotal players in this new global configuration will be Asians living in America, and Asians born in America. It is in America where East and West truly meet. Many Asian-Americans are as comfortable in the Western world as they are in the Eastern world. As growing numbers of American-born and/or US-educated Asians return to their native country to take advantage of the region's explosive growth and dynamism, this Asian-American population will become an important bridge between the two hemispheres.

Bilingual Asians in growing demand

"Once upon a time code phrases like 'language barrier' and 'cultural differences' were used to keep Asians out of the choicest jobs in American businesses and professions," says *Transpacific* magazine. "But today, being Asian, especially a bilingual Asian, may be the best qualification for a high-paying career. The former 'language barrier' will soon be called 'language advantage' and 'cultural differences' will soon be considered one of the most necessary attributes for top ranked executives", where the future will be dominated by Asians.

This is not to suggest discrimination is not an issue for Asians in America; it certainly is. The number of Asians in the top ranks of America's corporations is still quite small. But the tide is changing. According to Kiuchi "Kris" Aoyama, a partner with Heidrick & Struggles, the world's oldest executive search firm, "there's a tremendous demand for executive managers with a bicultural background." With the right qualification, in fact, Aoyama feels an Asian executive in any corporation "can write their own ticket".

Heidrick & Struggles surveyed 4,000 CEOs in 1993, asking what they looked for in an executive or manager, or what they needed to succeed. "Almost all of them independently, Asian, Caucasian, Black or Latino, gave the same elements," reports *Transpacific* on the survey:

- a background in the Asian Pacific
- more than two languages
- at least one advanced degree, preferably an MBA from a top US school
- degrees from two countries

Clearly, more Asians in America and American-born Asians fit that profile than do representatives of any other population group. While they gain greater acceptance in the corporate world, many Asian-Americans will be eager to follow in the entrepreneurial footsteps of Bill Mow of Bugle Boy, David Chu of Nautica, and David Lee of Qume Corp.

Action of the big deal

Transpacific magazine recently profiled six Asian men in America who "live for the action of the big deal". Three of those profiled were investment banker Warren Woo, venture capitalist and self-made millionaire Yosh Uchida, and high-tech dealmaker Dennis Paul Kim who brokers investment deals between technology-hungry Korean companies and small high-tech companies in the US.

The world of independent film making is full of young, ambitious Asians, including Ang Lee, Tommy Chang and Greg

Araki. Until recently Asians were noticeably absent from the executive teams of major entertainment conglomerates. No more. Stephen Chao ran Fox Studios, and went on to head QVC's new spin-off channel. Teddy Zee held executive positions in several studios, and is now at Columbia Studios. Chris Lee is Executive Vice President at Tristar. Alex Kitman Ho has won Oscars for producing *JFK* and *Born on the Fourth of July*. Janet Yang is Head of Development for Oliver Stone's Ixtlan Productions.

Fastest-growing minority group in US

According to the 1990 US Census, Asian-Americans are the country's fastest-growing minority. More than seven million people (in 1990), a little less than 3 percent of the population, trace their ancestry to Asian nations, up from 1.5 percent in 1980. Most are from China, the Philippines, Japan, India, Korea and Vietnam. Already there are 1 million Asians in Los Angeles. There will be 20 million Asian-Americans by the year 2020.

There are an extraordinary number of successful entrepreneurs among Asian-Americans. Asians excel academically, have entered the professions in large numbers, and have the highest household income of all racial groups. They are beginning to exercise their political clout, to realize they have the power of the purse.

Asian-Americans are finally being acknowledged for the invaluable contribution they have made to modern American society, but it is an acknowledgement that comes after decades of discrimination.

A growing Asian-American middle class

Says *American Demographics*, "Forget Chinatown: most Asian Americans live in middle-class suburbs." In general, they are educated and have more disposable income than big-city

Asians. Although assimilated Americans, they tend to preserve their customs. Asian suburbs include Filipino Daly City (south of San Francisco) to Chinese Monterey Park (near Los Angeles). Some 25 metropolitan areas in the US had at least 25,000 Asian-American suburbanites in 1990, or 76 percent of suburban Asian-Americans, says American Demographics. Four of the top ten high-growth areas for suburban Asians are in the Western part of the US. In Atlanta, Riverside–San Bernardino and Dallas, the number of Asian-American suburbanites more than quadrupled during the 1980s. In Middlesex–Somerset (New Jersey) and Houston, the number more than tripled.

Explains Eleanor Yu, President and Chief Executive Officer of Adland and Adland Worldwide, a San Francisco agency specializing in the Asian market:

> "Historically, inner-city Chinatowns in Los Angeles, San Francisco, and New York were created because of discrimination and because the Chinese were not ready to assimilate. Today, many Asians — even recent immigrants — are ready to assimilate. They speak English, they've been exposed to culture, and they're buying estates in San Marino, Westchester, and Monterey Park."

Wealthy Asians have global business interests, professional careers, and travel frequently.

"Asians in the suburbs assimilate like anyone else," Yu said, but "they do maintain a certain level of Asianness". They watch Chinese TV, among other channels, and you are sure to find stacks of Asian-language newspapers in their homes.

Jeff Yang is counting on that certain level of Asianness. This 27-year-old Harvard graduate recently launched *A.*, a magazine created for the Asian-American community. He and his thirty-something partner, Phoebe Eng, are modeling the publication after similar lifestyle magazines such as *Ebony* and *Hispanic*. Yang and Eng are not the first to try to tap into the Asian-American population. Ten-year-old *Transpacific*, believed to be

the longest-running Asian-American publication, is different
from *A*. as it covers lifestyle and business trends in Asia. *A*. will
focus only on Asians in America.

Entrepreneurs create their own opportunities

Eng and Yang are among a growing group of Asian-American
entrepreneurs who are striking out on their own. This trend is
dramatically evident in California's Silicon Valley, where Asians
have long worked as engineers in America's fast-growing computer companies, yet never made it to the executive suite.

These entrepreneurs are both ambitious and frustrated.
Many Asians who came to the US to study and stayed to work
are now ready for more responsibility and greater success. Some
say it is not easy for Asians to advance in US firms.

"Many Asian engineers are not being looked at as having
management talent," says David K. Lam, one of the first
Chinese entrepreneurs in Silicon Valley. "They are looked upon
as good work horses and not race horses."

Dr Lam, who grew up in China, Vietnam and Hong Kong,
holds a PhD from the Massachusetts Institute of Technology
and spent many years at Hewlett-Packard. When passed over in
favor of a white American hired right out of college, Dr Lam
quit and founded Lam Research, now a publicly traded company that makes equipment used in chip making. In 1985 he
started Expert Edge, a software firm. Like many Asian entrepreneurs in America, Dr Lam started Expert Edge with financial backing from investors in Asia.

Among the companies Asian-Americans started in Silicon
Valley are Everex Systems, which manufactures personal computers; Komag, which produces data storage disks; Wyse
Technology, a terminal and computer maker; Qume, a printer
company; and Solectron, which assembles products for other
companies and was awarded the United States' Baldrige Award
for Quality.

Long aware of the value of networking and the informal

information chain, Asian-American entrepreneurs formed their own groups to replace what they lost in stepping outside the establishment. The Asian American Manufacturers Association, the Chinese Institute of Engineers and the Chinese Software Professionals Association keep executives in Asian-owned companies in the know. The Mount Jade Association, comprised of high-level executives from both the US and Taiwan, encourages business relationships between East and West.

Asian-Americans: the "model minority" assimilates in the Asian way

At the Vien Dong International Supermarket in the Linda Vista area of San Diego, incense burns and Vietnamese music is piped in over a sound system. Lettuce, tomatoes and onions rest in bins next to Chinese cabbage and ginger root. Customers can select a 2 lb bag of Uncle Ben's converted rice or a 50 lb bag of rice imported from Thailand; New England perch or milk fish flown in from Taiwan.

Vien Dong is one of 40 supermarkets in San Diego owned by either Chinese, Korean, Japanese, or Vietnamese immigrants that give equal shelf space to foods native to their country of origin and to American brands.

Opening in 1989, Vien Dong began as a specialty store selling Chinese gifts and firecrackers. Since then, it has grown into a four-store chain. One of its locations is an old Safeway store. What makes it remarkable is that the community it serves is less than 20 percent Asian. Vien Dong's success is not an isolated phenomenon.

Yaohan Plaza, in the prosperous Chicago suburb of Arlington Heights, draws Asian consumers from as far away as Michigan, Ohio, and Kentucky. Yaohan Plaza, according to *American Demographics*, "caters not only to the Japanese Americans who account for half of its customers, but also to a Chinese and Koreans (30 percent) and non Asians (20 percent)". Through a direct mail list of 12,000 regular customers, the mini-mall announces sales and promotions that keep its parking lots full.

American Demographics reports:

> "Del Monte canned peas are stocked next to Azuki beans; Starkist tuna sits adjacent to broiled eel. Quantities sometimes seem larger than life, with 25-pound bags of rice stacked on pallets and one-gallon cans of soy sauce. On the other hand, the Asian taste for junk food seems sated by unimpressively small bags of potato chips.
>
> "Chinese come for jasmine rice, very sweet cookies, and special varieties of green tea. Koreans buy extra-thin shaved beef and ribs for barbecuing, as well as dried cuttlefish. The store sells more than a dozen types of tofu, and eight varieties of fresh mushrooms, even in the dead of a Midwest winter."

Despite excellent revenue growth and an obviously loyal customer base, including many non-Asians, store manager Shuji Kono hopes to expand his non-Asian customer base. "The Japanese people, they're happy," he says. "But that is not enough. We need American people." His strategy: "We're going to introduce Japanese culture with food."

Beaverton, Oregon, is home to several Asian markets including the India Emporium, Hyundai Oriental Food and Gifts, Han Kuk Market and Manila Import and Export.

The Asian way

Introducing Japanese culture with food. How simple, how profound, and how very Asian. Although each country is unique, there are a certain cadence and rhythm common to Asians, an attitude and way of thinking that are distinctly Asian. It is part Confucianism, part Taoism, part Buddhism, and part Hindi. It is what has made it possible for immigrants and refugees, artists and intellectuals from Asian countries to make a home for themselves in the US, yet maintain their own style and identity.

To be sure, each immigrant group has been discriminated against and oppressed by the groups that came before, but eventually they were absorbed into the vast multiethnic population of Americans. This has not been the experience of Asians in America in the past because they cannot appear as "all American" as an Irish or German American could. It is true, partly because of continued discrimination, but also, in part, because Asians choose to do things the "Asian way".

A convergence of cultures

"The East is always interested in the West and the West in the East. We always find that which is different from ourselves to be intriguing and desirable," says Japanese designer Issey Miyake.

It seems that in the world of fashion design, Asia is in and Asian designers are hot. Established Western designers such as Ralph Lauren, Jean-Paul Gaultier, and Betsey Johnson have all introduced a bit of Asia into their lines. For Lauren it is "Vietnamese pajama pants and long patterned Balinese silk skirts," reported *The Asian Wall Street Journal*. Gaultier called his fall line "The Long Journey: Mongolia, Tibet, China and Eskimos", while Johnson used Asian models to show off her spandex catsuits in 1994.

Meanwhile, Asia-born designers are striving for acceptance as international designers with a more eclectic influence. **Rei Kawaubo**, founder of the revolutionary Comme des Garçons line more than 20 years ago, says one of her greatest milestones was to have her work finally accepted as her own and not as a Japanese phenomenon — a feat that took almost 10 years.

Indonesian designers **Ghea Sukaya**, **Bijan** and **Prayudi** were recently featured at a gala benefit for the Environment Bamboo Foundation in Bali. CNN's "style" host Elsa Klensel filmed the event for international broadcast.

When Hangzhou-born **Han Feng** describes her fashions, the word Asian is not on her lips. "I'm trying to get away from being called a Chinese designer making Chinese things. My designs are international," says Ms Feng.

After a quarter of a century of spreading Western fashion style in Asia, **Joyce Ma**, called the "First Lady of Hong Kong" is doing the reverse — bringing the East to the West through her $100 million fashion empire.

Canton-born designer **Vivienne Tam** takes a universal view of fashion. Based in New York, she sells her designs at Barney's and Saks Fifth Avenue as well as in her three boutiques in Hong Kong. "I wondered how well the traditional pieces would sell in Asia. But whatever style is selling the best in New York sells the best in Hong Kong. This somehow exemplifies the way the world is merging together," says Ms Tam.

This convergence of East and West is also in evidence in the art world.

In the January 1995 issue of *Art in America*, critic Janet Koplos reviews "Scream Against the Sky", a travelling exhibition of Japanese avant garde art since the Second World War. Her critique is entitled "How Japanese Is It?" In it, she describes what influenced the work of Japanese artists of this period, many of whom have not lived in Japan for decades. In her critique, Koplos makes a profound observation — one that is particularly appropriate to a discourse on Asia's influence over the West. She writes:

> "A complicated question that the show evades is just who or what is a 'Japanese artist.' By the end of the '60s, a number of contemporary artists had left Japan. For Munroe [curator of the show], they remain eternally Japanese, regardless of residence or preference or even citizenship, and regardless of where their influences derives from."

That, of course, is the question. Because of their uniquely Eastern heritage, do Asians who immigrate to, or seek refuge in, the West remain forever Asian? Are they destined to be strangers in a strange land, or do they, like immigrants before them, assimilate and become Westernized? Or does something quite different happen, do they take the best of what is Asian and the best of what is Western and carve out a wholly new identity? And vice versa, can the West ever understand the subtleties of Eastern thought, which has so great an influence over social conduct?

The drama of acculturation is now being played out on the world stage. As the global community becomes irrevocably linked by a seamless information highway, and one's business partner is as likely to be halfway around the globe as on the next block, the experience and influence of Asians in America could well become a model for emergent multicultural communities everywhere.

The modernization of Asia is not to be thought of as the Westernization of Asia, but the modernization of Asia in the "Asian way". Similarly, the integration of Asian immigrants into American society is not to be thought of as the Americanization of Asians. Asian-Americans have the same aspirations and expectations as all other Americans. They expect to be accepted into American society, to work where they choose to work and that their work be valued as highly as the work of their peers. At the same time they have not abandoned, nor will they abandon, their cultural heritage. They will be Americans in the Asian way, and both the American and the global community will be enriched as a result.

A bridge between East and West

In the global village, Asian-Americans, as well as Asians who are educated and have worked in America, will be a bridge between East and West. Having lived in both worlds, they will act as mediators and interpreters to a business and political community that is so interrelated that national borders and regional boundaries are irrelevant. And the Asia Pacific–American community will be mimicked. The best of what is Asia, the best of what is America, and the best of what is Europe will converge, and there will emerge an entirely new community model.

This convergence of cultures was described by Kishore Mahbubani, Permanent Secretary of Singapore's Ministry of Foreign Affairs, and Dean of the Civil Service College. In an article entitled "The Pacific Way", published in the journal *Foreign Affairs*, Mahbubani writes:

> "The Pacific community will be a completely new creation. It will not be an Asian community, nor will it be an American community. If the Pacific has emerged as the most dynamic region of the world, it is because it has drawn on the best practices and values from many rich civilizations, Asian and Western. If this fusion continues to work, there could be explosive creativity on a scale never before seen...
>
> "The real success of the Pacific community will come when the learning process in the Pacific becomes a two-way street rather than a one-way street. It took a long time for China and other East Asian societies to accept the common-sensical advice of Yukichi Fukuzawa, the Meiji-era reformer: to progress, learn from the West. Many American intellectuals still believe that all the deep wells of learning are in Europe. Those who travel across the Pacific come to learn about, but not from, East Asia. There is a profound difference between these two approaches. In the past few years, many Americans have been disconcerted by lectures from East Asians, as have many East Asians by American preaching on democracy and human rights. It will take time for both sides to learn to listen to each other."

It may take less time than he thinks. Americans are a pragmatic lot, and Europeans, although still clinging to a belief in their inherent superiority as a rich and venerated bastion of culture and intellectual thought, will ultimately learn to celebrate differences in culture and to accept that diversity is a path to universal prosperity.

Furthermore, there is emerging in the global community a new cadre of leaders who are both idealists and pragmatists.

They are risk takers who also believe strongly in consensus building. They are open, aware, change oriented and seek a balance between material success and spirituality.

Leadership for the future

A new breed of leaders is emerging in Asia. The young Asian leadership in politics, government, business, intellectual and academic areas is reshaping the direction of Asia and the world. Forty-something and ready for their ascendancy to positions of power, representatives of this group can be found in every corner of the globe. Pakistan's Benazir Bhutto, 43, Sri Lanka's Chandrika Kumaratunga, 50, and US President Bill Clinton, 50, are already in power. Malaysia's Anwar Ibrahim, 48, Singapore's Lee Hsien Loong, 43, and the Philippines' Richard Gordon, 50, plan to be there soon. "Behind them are a legion of well connected, highly educated technocrats, entrepreneurs, artists and community activists who together will lead Asia into the 21st Century," says *Asiaweek*.

In my travels around Asia, what impresses me most is the knowledge Asian leaders have of the West. There is a far greater number of people in positions of power and influence in Asia who know about the West than there are in the West who know about the East. This knowledge will put them in a more advantageous position in dealing with the West.

After the flap with China over his attendance at his class reunion, we all know that President Lee Teng Hui of Taiwan received his doctorate from Cornell University in the US. More than 70 percent of his cabinet ministers were trained in the West and 60 percent hold doctorates from Western universities. President Fidel Ramos of the Philippines is a graduate of the US Military Academy at West Point, and Pakistan's Prime Minister Benazir Bhutto is a Harvard alumna. Many of Indonesia's top economic planners hold doctorates from the University of California at Berkeley. Throughout Asia there are government leaders, corporate executives and second-generation business leaders of Asian family companies who were trained and educated in the West.

These new Asian leaders are unique among emerging global power brokers. Although politically active, many are not politicians, but rather successful businesspeople with a keen interest in maintaining economic stability. Many embrace spiritual ideals, but not religious zealotry. While politicians in the West wave the flag of family values when railing against moral decay, Asian leaders are products of Eastern religious thought which values family over all else. For the most part, members of this group support democracy in principle, but not necessarily the Western application of democracy. *Asiaweek* says:

> "Under the tutelage of their elders, they have been the backbone of East Asia's awesome economic advances. Now they are about to take charge just as the region is becoming a world-class economic power... They are creatures of their time. In many parts of East Asia they will be the last to know what it is like to grow up in poverty — and to have deprivation as a motivating force in their psychological and ethical makeup."

For the most part, Asia's new leaders embrace the guiding principles articulated by Malaysia's Deputy Prime Minister, Anwar Ibrahim, in an address to the 49th gathering of the UN General Assembly:

> "Development is the only secure foundation for global peace and security, for the origins of conflicts are often buried deep in socio-economic deprivation and disparities.
>
> "As for civil society, its growth into maturity requires the establishment of institutions for a stable and responsive social order, a democratic participatory arrangement as a means to channel political energy, and a conducive environment for culture to flourish.

"In all these, it is the people that matter, their freedom, security and development. All great traditions of mankind, East and West concur in the sanctity of the human person, the family as a fundamental unit of society and the primacy of moral ethical values as the foundation of civilization."

Muslims' ascendency to leadership in corporate Asia

Tajudin Ramli, Chairman and Chief Executive Officer of Malaysian Airlines, took command of the national carrier after engineering the largest corporate buyout in the country's history. His satellite and telecommunications companies are also well positioned to capitalize on the opportunities presented by rapid economic growth in such a huge region. Tajudin Ramli and a rising crop of corporate leaders who hold to the Islamic faith constitute a new phenomenon in Asia.

For a long time, an entrenched perception has had it that Islam is incompatible with profit, and Muslim participation in Asia's corporate sector has been minimal. A question often asked is whether Muslims can participate in the stock market or in banking. Interest is un-Islamic, although fees for services can be charged. There is no straightforward answer regarding their participation. It all depends on whether in the course of a transaction, one violates any of the Islam principles of business. However, a fact unknown to many is that Islam is generally not incompatible with trade and commerce. The Prophet Muhammad has been reported to have said, "A truthful and trustworthy merchant will be gathered [in the day of Resurrection] together with the prophets, martyrs and truthfuls."

In Asia's corporate world, more Muslims are taking the reins, led by many prominent Malaysian businesspeople of Islamic faith, together with their counterparts in Indonesia, and an increasing number in Pakistan and India. These leaders, many of them very young, thirty- and forty-something, are ambitious, articulate in English — many of them were educated in the West — and are completely at ease with science and technology. Leaders with Islamic faith are fast becoming important players in Asia's economic modernization.

The rise of Muslim leadership in Asia's corporate world will become increasingly visible. In response to this new Muslim visibility, many restaurants in the region are now including halal menus, sensitive to the special way the non-pork-eating Muslims prepare their food.

Many people in the world, especially Americans, associate Islam with the Iranian hostage crisis, fighting in the Middle East, and terrorism. These incidents created stereotyped images of Islam, which are a gross distortion of the mainstream religion. Today the American Muslim community is the US's fastest growing religious minority. The US has 4 million Muslims and 12 percent are Arabs.   The groundbreaking endeavors and success of Muslims in Asia will help change the world's perception of this major religious group.

Dealing with the East

Raymond Wong, a business consultant from Kuala Lumpur, complained about the lack of understanding of Asian cultures by Western businesspeople. "If the West want to do business with us, they must make it a point to get to know us." He recounted at length how warmly he and his colleagues received their Western counterparts while they were in Asia, and how this warm reception was not reciprocated when they visited the US at a later date. The cultural divide, especially in styles and expression, is a common source of friction and frustration. Asians are indirect, non-confrontational. It takes patience and perseverance to navigate cultural sensitivities.

Challenge of Asian languages

Learning the culture begins with mastering the language.

Many Asians have implied, "When we deal with you, we

speak English. Our children speak English, too. It would be best if you can understand and speak our language." (Being Asian, they will not say this directly to your face, and you will never know how they feel.)

Given the diversity of the region, a whole range of local dialects and native languages are spoken. Just to acquire a working knowledge calls for total devotion.

Fortunately, however, the greatest benefit of the Western legacy to Asia is the English language. Because of Asia's colonial past and the US presence in postwar trade and investment, English became the language of commerce and education for some Asian countries. English has been dominant in the business communities and, with the region's rush to join the world economy, there has been an upsurge in learning English, especially in Korea, China, Thailand, Indonesia and Vietnam. Even long-time nationalistic Malaysia is reversing its language policy and beginning to reemphasize the importance of English as a medium to embrace science and technology, so essential for the country's transition from labor-intensive to high-tech manufacturing.

English will remain the language of commerce and international communication in Asia, and its importance will grow as the region continues to liberalize and open up. But in time, a second language will become dominant. Mandarin will move center stage as the language of Asia.

Mandarin moves center stage

Cantonese is a dialect of the people of Southern China, and because the Chinese overseas in Southeast Asia and in the West were mainly from the southern region, there is a distorted perception that Cantonese is the language of the Chinese people. Mandarin is the language of China; Cantonese is only a dialect. Both China and India have many dialects, but all of China has a common written language. Everyone can understand the same written word. In India the dialects have different written languages.

It is now commonplace to overhear conversations in Mandarin in airline cabins and hotel lounges. Mandarin will become the dominant language of commerce in Asia. Communication in Mandarin, especially the written language, has been a challenge, even for Chinese and other Asians. China, Singapore and Malaysia use simplified Chinese characters or Kanji, while Taiwan staunchly retains the complex traditional version. There are so many characters, a typewriter needs different keyboard trays that have to be switched around. But computers have changed all that. Intelligent software can interpret both simplified and traditional characters, avoiding the need to master the tedious process of remembering the phonetic guide to 3,000 essential characters. Technology has enabled the language to be widely used in business tasks, but the challenge lies in its full adoption in contractual and legal realms.

Mandarin's grammatical simplicity has made for less than exacting contractual language (which Hong Kong lawyers and consultants experienced in their dealings with Chinese officials). Additionally, a lack of standardization of terms used in translating foreign words complicates the situation. Despite these challenges, the economic value of the language will accelerate its elevation to international use. Already efforts are being made in that direction. One example is the standardization effort launched by a Hong Kong-based 24-hour Mandarin television channel, the Chinese Television Network (styled to be the CNN for the Chinese communities in the world and launched in 1994).

Looked on for a long time as the language of high culture, Mandarin is spreading in Asia, and more will realize its economic value in the coming century. Paradoxically, it is also fast becoming the language of pop culture. Pop singers around the region, especially those from Hong Kong, are fast churning out Mandarin versions of their original Cantonese pop songs, called "canto-pops" by the local English media. It sure makes a lot of sense if the music and lyrics can be understood and appreciated by 1.2 billion people.

- In opening a dialogue between Confucianism and Islam, Malaysia's Deputy Prime Minister, Anwar Ibrahim, an ethnic Malay, quoted important verses from Chinese scholars in Mandarin. Southeast Asia's "China-driven" orientation has heightened interest in Mandarin.
- Since 1979 Singapore's authorities have actively promoted Mandarin as the "mother tongue" of its ethnic Chinese citizens. "School children are already learning Mandarin from a very young age," says Ho Kah Leong, senior parliamentary secretary at the Ministry of Information & the Arts. "Those who want to enter university — and who doesn't in Singapore — have to pass stringent tests of proficiency in Mandarin," reports *Asiaweek*.
- Mandarin is now widely spoken in Hong Kong, which for a long time spoke only Cantonese, and news broadcasts in Mandarin are on most channels in the region's television and radio stations.

When Japan was at its peak, many speculated that the world would have to speak Japanese. That never happened. One reason was that the Japanese never encouraged it. Mandarin is a different story. Because of the large ethnic Chinese population in Southeast Asian countries, the language has been commonplace for a long time. With increased confidence stemming from affluence, Mandarin will be embraced much more enthusiastically than Japanese. East Asians partially understand the written Kanji used in Japan, Korea and Taiwan. Standardization is urgently called for to accelerate wider application of the language.

A winning strategy in Asia

The East–West divide centers on the fundamental differences in the two systems. The rule of law, or the lack of it, and human rights issues remain the most explosive minefields in relations between East and West. The West believes that only the rule of law keeps governments from riding roughshod over people in business and in the protection of personal and civil liberties. Without a well-defined legal system and respect for individual rights, the view is that businesses cannot be assured of security.

Asia, especially China, has a long history of rule by man (*rénchi*). Asian cultures are "relationship driven" rather than "rules" or "system driven". Asians dislike formal conflict resolution, preferring to work out difference through negotiation. The Chinese people deal with emotions (*qíng*), logic (*lǐ*) and law (*fǎ*), in that order, in the organization of interpersonal relations. "The Chinese dislike technical and legalistic solutions, because the sophisticated background to implementing them isn't there," says Andy Sun, Executive Director of the Asia Pacific Legal Institute and Adjunct Professor of Law at George Washington National Law Center in Washington, DC. Many Asians believe that harmony in long-term relationships is preferred to reliance on the legal system, as once in court "face" is destroyed. In Chinese minds, everything, including differences, is negotiable as long as "face" is preserved. You now know why *guanxi* — personal connections — is so important in dealing with Asians.

But acceptance of the rule of law will evolve as Asia modernizes. The enlightened middle class with their new-found wealth will push for change bottom up. In Asia, navigate gently, don't push to gain ground. If you need a buffer, get an ethnic Chinese partner.

East–West harmony

As the East grows more materialistic, and high tech, spirit-starved Westerners grow more Eastern.

The West is importing Eastern spiritual traditions with an almost unquenchable enthusiasm. Yoga and meditation are mainstream fare. Chinese acupuncture and Japanese acupressure are available in many major European cities, and even skeptics swear by their healing powers. Reincarnation, Kundalini energy and Right Livelihood pepper everyday conversations of many Americans and Europeans. Korean ginseng is sold out at the local healthfood store, and Chinese herbs are coming on strong.

Millions of women who are interested in Goddess psychology might have a little Kwan Yin statue next to a Virgin Mary icon. The person doing Tai Chi in the park is either an 80-year-old Oriental or a 30-year-old Occidental.

Far from this being a passing fad, the real aficionado has moved on to the next layer of Eastern wisdom and embraces it with great gusto: getting Jin Shin Jyutsu treatments, investigating a psychic surgeon in the Philippines, studying Korean Shamanic tradition, Vispassana and Metta meditation, and Taoist meditation, not to mention Qigong, the 4,000-year-old science of internal energy cultivation.

How rich will the world be when West and East converge? What a great time to come to Asia. Young people, go East.

The Asian model?

John Hung, an expatriate Westerner who has lived for a long time in Hong Kong, and I were talking about the difference between Eastern and Western societies. He said, "A bus driver looking from his window at a passing Rolls Royce said to himself, full of hope, 'I may not sit in that car, but my son will.'" In contrast, Hung added, Westerners have a strong entitlement mentality, on a wide range of things. They insist on their rights, "whereas Asians aspire".

During the last 150 years of progress and prosperity enjoyed in the West, much of Asia was in poverty. Now, Asians are on their way to a renaissance, an opportunity for them to reassert the grandeur and glory of their past civilizations. Combined with science and technology, Asians could present the world with a new model, one that takes modernization and combines it with the virtues of Eastern and Western values, one that reconciles freedom and order, individualism with communitarian concerns. The most profound consequence of the rise of the East is the birth of a new model for modernization. In giving new meaning to modernization, Asians will give birth to a model for the new civilization.

References

Chapter 1: From Nation-states → Networks

14   Bustanil Ariffin's statement from *Business Times* (Singapore), 24 October 1994.

15   Hong Kong banker quote from "The New Power in Asia", *Fortune*, 31 October 1994.

17   Yoji Hamawaki information from an interview by the author.

19–20 Billionaires profiles from "The Bamboo Network", *Forbes*, 18 July 1994 and "Asia" in the 15 July 1996 issue. Nina Wang quote translated from "Profile of the World's Richest Chinese", *Forbes Zibenjia*, June 1994.

24–5 Robert Kuok quote from *Business Week International*.

25   Wang Gungwu quotes from "The Chinese entrepreneur and his cultural strategies", a paper given at the Second World Chinese Entrepreneurs Convention, Hong Kong, 22 November 1993.

29   Li quote from an interview by the author.

30–31 Shih quotes translated from the Taiwan-based *Excellence* magazine and Hong Kong-based *Yauzhou Zhoukan* magazine.

31   Lee quote from the Second World Chinese Entrepreneur Conference in Hong Kong in 1993.

34   Yukiko Oharo statement from "Japanese Banks' Bad Loans Constitute Bigger Burden Than U.S. S&L Debacle", *The Wall Street Journal*, 7 June 1995.

34–5 Terry quotes from *World Business*, January 1995.

40   Takeshi Nagano, Morita and Aoshima quotes from "Bring on the Clowns", *Far Eastern Economic Review*, 20 April 1995.

41   Ishihara quotes from *Boston Globe*, 15 April 1995.

43   Retired government official quotes from "Focus: Japan", *Far Eastern Economic Review*, 15 June 1995.
     Mihio Watanabe quote from "Should Japan be Sorry for its Conquests? A New Furor Erupts", *International Herald Tribune*, 6 June 1995.

Chapter 2: From Export-led → Consumer-driven

48   Gallup Poll data and Burkholder quote from "First Poll of China Finds Materialism Alive", *The Washington Post*, 16 February 1995.

50   Gray quote from "Middle Class Top Dollar", *Asian Business*, March 1994.

51–2 Description of purchasing power parity from *Global Paradox*, by John Naisbitt, Nicholas Brealey Publishing, 1994, pp 180–81.

54   Ferrier quote from "The Hard Sell, Advertisers Target Asia's Affluent Consumers", *Far Eastern Economic Review*, 24 November 1994.

      Kanoui statement reported in "Economic Liberalization", *The Asian Wall Street Journal Weekly*, 10 October 1994. Car data from "A New Taste for Quality", *Far Eastern Economic Review*, 7 December 1995.

55   Credit card data from various sources, including "Will They End Asian Frugality?", *Asiaweek*, 10 March 1995; "Citibank Blitzes Asia", *Forbes*, 6 May 1996; and "The Card that Could Rule Our Lives", *Asiaweek*, 3 November 1995.

56   Malls in Bangkok reported in "The Mall, the Merrier", *The Economist*, 27 August 1994; and "Retailing in the Philippines" in the 18 May 1996 issue.

57   Brooker quote and auto industry decline information from "Asia: Last Hope for Car Makers", *Asian Business*, May 1994.

58   Quote regarding the people's car from "China to Churn out Personal Cars", *International Herald Tribune*, 23 September 1994. Quote on incentives from "Chinese Will be Encouraged to Buy Cars", *Financial Times*, 28 September 1994.

58–9 Information on industry response to China's request for family car design from "China's Quest for Inexpensive Family Car", *The Asian Wall Street Journal Weekly*, 21 November 1994. Meyerand quote from "Boom-at-a-glance", *New York Times Magazine*, 18 February 1996.

59   Smil quote from "China to Churn out Personal Cars", *International Herald Tribune*, 23 September 1994.

60   Information on automotive industry in Asia from "World's Car Makers Prefer the Thai Tiger", *Financial Times*, 9 November 1994.

Proton information from "Malaysian Car Group Seeks Fresh Inroads", *Financial Times*, 31 January 1995.

Ford data from "Ford to Pay $50m for 7% Stake in Indian Car Maker", *Financial Times*, 17 October 1994.

61   Lee Yuen Tseh quote from an interview by the author.

Quote on California fantasy from "Raising Wealth Gives Asians Urge to Buy Package Tours", *The Asian Wall Street Journal Weekly*, 27 October 1994.

61–2   Sutch and Eddington quotes from "Congee at 35,000 Feet", *Far Eastern Economic Review*, 24 November 1994.

62–3   IATA data, airport quotes and data from an article by Jay Khosla in *Business Times* (Singapore), 19 November 1994.

64   Ebbs quote from "Middle Class Top Dollar", *Asian Business*, March 1994.

China's "star" rating information from "Five Stars Over China", *China Daily*, 8 April 1995.

65   Quote on Asian attitudes towards boats and cruise information from "Slow Boat to China", *Far Eastern Economic Review*, 24 November 1994.

Pélisson quote from "Accor sees Asian-Pacific Region as Hospitable for Expansion", *The Asian Wall Street Journal*, 20 December 1994.

66   *Far Eastern Economic Review* survey information from "LifeStyles, Special Report," 27 August 1992 issue.

66–7   Quote on food chains in Asia from "US Restaurant Chains Tackle Challenges of Asian Expansion," *Nation's Restaurant News*, 14 February 1994.

67–8   Information on companies selling goods in China from "How Not to Sell 1.2 Billion Tubes of Toothpaste", *The Economist*, 3 December 1994.

68   Procter & Gamble quote reported in "Unilever Turning Up Heat in Shampoo War in China", *The Asian Wall Street Journal*, 3 October 1994.

Pepsi and Coke wars described in "Cola Wars Heat up in Asian Market", *AdWeek*, 21 March 1994.

68–9   List of advertising agencies and quote from "Foreign Advertising Firms Grapple with China Chaos", *The Asian Wall Street Journal Weekly*, 25 February 1995.

Asian advertising expenditures from "The Hard Sell", *Far Eastern Economic Review*, 24 November 1994; "Winding Up for the Big Pitch", *Business Week*, 23 October 1995; and *Ad Age International*, April 1996 and June 1996.

69   Statistics on numbers of televisions in Asia from "An Asian Sky", *Asiaweek*, 19 October 1994.

70   Information on cable in Shanghai from "Asian TV Growth Sets Dizzying Pace", *International Herald Tribune*, 7 December 1994.

Prazwol Pradham information from "Ready for Prime Time", *Far Eastern Economic Review*, 26 January 1995.

Damrongchaitam quote from "Control Freaks", *Forbes*, 4 April 1995.

Faridah Stephens quote from "Pushing the Limits", *Far Eastern Economic Review*, 4 August 1994.

71   Shanghai talk radio fans and Yuan Hu quote from "Shanghai", *National Geographic*, March 1994.

Information on Taiwan talk radio and Chen Cheng-teh quotes from "Radical Radio", *Far Eastern Economic Review*, 15 December 1994.

73   T. Ananda Krishnan profile and quotes from "Multimedia Mogul in the Making", *Business Times* (Singapore), 3–4 December 1994.

74   Childcare quote from "Who's My Mommy", *Asiaweek*, 27 March 1992.

Toddler stress in India reported in "Flunked at 3, 1 Symbol of Middle-class India's Angst", *Washington Post,* 31 October 1994.

75   Zhu Xiaoying quote from "China's New Rich Pay Big Money for Child Education", *Korea Times*, 28 March 1995.

Teen market quote from, "Young and Free Spending", *Business Times* (Singapore), 8–9 October 1994.

76–7 Jagdeep Kapoor quote from "Changing Demographics", *Advertising Age International*, 17 October 1994.

77   Padamsee quote from *Far Eastern Economic Review*, 13 July 1995.

Information on urban Chinese money from "China, Stuggle for Control", *Fortune*, 1 November 1993.

Chinese earnings reported in "Find the Hidden Middle Class", *Business Week*, 6 June 1994.

Kabel and insurance quotes from *Asia Inc.*, March 1995.

78   Information on auctions in Singapore from *Yauzhou Zhoukan*, a

Chinese-language weekly magazine published in Hong Kong.

79 Masanor Fukoaka quote from "Indian Art Market", *Asian Art News*, May/June 1995.

80 Christie's auction in Hong Kong reported in "Jaded", *Far Eastern Economic Review*, 18 May 1995.

81 Statistics on art buyers from *Asia Inc.*, April 1994.
George Fisher quote from "Kodak's New Focus", *Business Week*, 30 January 1995.

82 Vitachi quote from *Far Eastern Economic Review*, 13 July 1995.

84 McDonald quote from "Sitting Pretty", *Far Eastern Economic Review*, 21 December 1995.
Ng quote and information about car sales from *Financial Times*, 19 August 1995.

Chapter 3: From Western Influence → the Asian Way

87 Lai quote from "The Information Rebellion", *Far Eastern Economic Review*, 14 April 1994.

88 Quote by Chen Li from an interview by Foong Wai Fong in Beijing.
All Lee quotes in this chapter, unless noted, are from "Culture is Destiny", Foreign Affairs, *March/April* 1994.

89 *Asian Values and the United States: How Much Conflict*, by David I. Hitchcock, Center for Strategic and International Studies, Washington, DC, 1994.

92 Anwar Ibrahim quotes from his speech at the Islam and Confucianism Civilization Dialogue on 13 March 1995.

93 Noordin Sopiee quote from "The Asian Way", *Asiaweek*, 2 March 1994.
Muzaffar and Rhee quotes from interviews by the author.

93 Kishore Mahbubani's call to the West reported in David I. Hitchcock, op.cit.

93–4 Mahbubani's article "Go East, Young Man" appeared in the *Far Eastern Economic Review*, 19 May 1994.

94 Modern vs Western quote from David I. Hitchcock, op.cit.

96 Muzaffar quotes from an interview by the author.

96–7 Anwar Ibrahim quotes appeared in "Mahathir Strikes Chord Among Japanese", *Nikkei Weekly*, 12 December 1994, and "Press

Freedom is an Asian Value", *The Asian Wall Street Journal*, 10 December 1994.

97   Lee Yuen Tseh quote from an interview by the author.

97–9   Tu's statements from "Confucianism is No Ban to Asian Democracy", *The Asian Wall Street Journal*, 23 May 1995, and "China Looks to Confucius as Marxist Theory Fades", *The Asian Wall Street Journal Weekly*, 10 October 1994. Fukuyama's quotes from 23 May 1995 issue.

99   Confucian values in Singapore education reported in "Confucianism, New Fashion for Old Wisdom", *The Economist*, 21 January 1995.

99–100   De Bary quotes reported in "China Looks to Confucius as Marxist Theory Fades", *The Asian Wall Street Journal*, 10 October 1994.

         International Confucian Association quote reported in "Confucian Works Still Inspire", *China Daily*, 6 October 1994.

101   Koh quote and information from "Reports of America's Sorry Demise May Just Be a Bit Exaggerated", *International Herald Tribune*, 8–9 October 1994.

102   Mahathir quote from "Rediscovering Islam", *Wings of Gold*, March 1995.

         Megatrends 2000, John Naisbitt and Patricia Aburdene, William Morrow and Co. Inc., New York, 1990.

         Mosque destruction and haircuts reported in "Time-Traveling in Asia", *The World & I*, April 1995.

103–4   Family statistics from various sources, including David Hitchcock, op.cit., and "Asian Family Values are Under Attack", *Window*, 23 September 1994. Lu quotes from the *Window* article.

105   Beijing survey reported in "Modern Family Values Evolving in Beijing", *China Daily*, 23 January 1995.

         PDA in Japan reported in "Japanese Lovebirds Kiss off Tradition", *The Asian Wall Street Journal Weekly*, 14 November 1994.

105–6   Nobue Nakamura, Ken Lyle and Misao Kawaii quotes, and Tokyo Dome event reported in "Dirty dancing: Japan 'OLs' Take it Off", *Los Angeles Times*, 15 December 1993.

         Wahid Supriyadi, Lam Peng Er and Marzuki Darusman quotes from interviews by the author.

Atiya Singh quote from *Bangkok Post*, 13 February 1995.

107   JJ's quotes reported in "Shanghai Dances to a Different Tune", *Business Times* (Singapore), 17–18 September 1994.

108   Chen and Yan information from "20 Years of Asian Growth", a section which appeared in the 24 November 1994 issue of *Far Eastern Economic Review*.
      Qufu and Kong Qingz data and Lou quotes from "Entrepreneurial Zeal in Name of Confucius", *The Asian Wall Street Journal*, 15 March 1995.

109   Values education information from "Teaching Asia to Stay Asian", *The Economist*, 8 October 1994; "Confucianism, New Fashion for Old Wisdom", *The Economist*, 21 January 1995; and "The Classics are Back", *Asiaweek*, 21 June 1996.

110   Almonte quote from the *Manila Times*, 9 April 1995.
      Liak Teng Kiat quote from "Life of the Party", *Far Eastern Economic Review*, 29 December 1994/5 January 1995.

111   Kim Dae Jung quotes appeared in "Is Culture Destiny", *Foreign Affairs*, November/December 1994.

111–12 Aung San Suu Kyi quotes from "Listen: The Culture of Democracy and Human Rights is Universal", *International Herald Tribune*, 7 December 1994.

112–13 Lee quote, studies on the economic benefits of democracy and *The Economist* quote from "Democracy and Growth, Why Voting is Good for You", in the 27 August 1994 issue.
      Mahathir quote from "How Free a Choice?", *Asiaweek*, 21 April 1995.

113   Lingle article data and suits reported in "Singapore, Contemptible", *The Economist*, 21 January 1995; and "Singapore's Philosophers", *The Wall Street Journal*, 19 October 1994.

113–14 Chan Heng Wing quote from "Singapore Makes Clear in Letter its Tolerance of Criticism is Limited", *The Asian Wall Street Journal Weekly*, 2 January 1995.

114   Louis Cha quote from "Free Press Can Triumph Over China's Influence", *South China Morning Post*, 23 April 1994.

115   Cheong Yip Seng quote from "Speaking of Asian Values", *Asiaweek*, 14 December 1994.
      Asiaweek voting quote from "How Free a Choice?", *Asiaweek*, 21

April 1995.

Chuan Leekpai quote from "Democracy in Asia", *USA Today*, 16 December 1994.

115–16 Commission for a New Asia statement reported in "The Asian Way", *Asiaweek*, 2 March 1994.

116 Koh quote from an interview by the author.

Kim Dae Jung quote from "Is Culture Destiny", *Foreign Affairs*, November/December 1994.

Thomas quote from "The Universality of Human Rights", *New Straits Times*, 26 January 1995.

117 Li Peng quote appeared in "Inching Forward on Rights", *Far Eastern Economic Review*, 7 April 1994.

Religion and rights quotes from Kim Dae Jung's article "On Asian Democracy", which appeared in the 28 April 1995 issue of *Asiaweek*.

Walter Truett Anderson quote from *Megatrends 2000*, op.cit., p. 153.

118 Human rights code reported in "Regional Briefing", *Far Eastern Economic Review*, 6 April 1995.

Trade unionist and Leipziger quotes reported in "Business First, Freedom Second", *Time*, 21 November 1994.

118–19 Statistics and quotes on Christianity from various sources, including "The Pope Sees 'Harvest of Faith' from Fields of Asia", *Washington Times*, 30 January 1995; "The Great Awakening", *Asiaweek*, 17 August 1994; and "Blessed are the Rich", *The Economist*, 10 December 1994.

119–20 New Age spiritualism in Japan reported in "Japanese Embrace New Age Lifestyles", *Nikkei Weekly*, 17 October 1994.

Crowell visit to China described in "The Great Awakening", *Asiaweek*, 17 August 1994.

120–21 *Far Eastern Economic Review* quotes on Buddhism, Luang Poh Koon, Yantra Ammarro Bhikku and Phra Dhammakaya information reported in the 4 May 1995 issue.

122–3 *The Economist* quotes from a Special Report on Islam that appeared in the 4 August 1994 issue.

Far Eastern Economic Review and Khalid Ahmed quotes reported in "March of the Militants", in the 9 March 1995 issue.

123 Mohammed Sadli quote reported in "In Other Words", *Far*

Eastern Economic Review, 9 March 1995.

124 World Bank age statistics, retirement schemes information and quote reported in "Honor Thy Father", *Far Eastern Economic Review*, 2 March 1995.

125 Lai quote from an interview by the author.

126 Nordin Sopiee and Yung Wei quotes from interviews by the author.

127 Fukuyama quote from *The End of History and the Last Man*, Avon Books, New York, 1992, p. 324.

Chapter 4: From Government-controlled → Market-driven

129 *The Asian Wall Street Journal* quotes on China's Communists and party membership reported in "China's Communists Seek a New Role", in the 20 December 1994 issue.

130 Huynh Thanh Chung quote from "Rising from the Ashes", *Business Week*, 23 May 1994.

131 General information on Vietnam from "Vietnam: Determined to be a Tiger but in Need of Help", *International Herald Tribune*, 21 October 1994.
     Business Week quote on companies in Vietnam from "Destination Vietnam", 14 February 1994 issue.

132 World Bank information from "Vietnam: Determined to be a Tiger but in Need of Help", *International Herald Tribune*, 21 October 1994.

133 Ge Bulei quote from "Soldiers of Fortune: China's PLA", *The Asian Wall Street Journal*, 25 May 1994. Vietnam military information from "In Peacetime, Vietnam's army turns to business", *New York Times*, 21 July 1996.

134 Yuan Mu description from "State Business", *Far Eastern Economic Review*, 23 February 1995.

135–6 Khoo Eng Choo, Sachs, *Far Eastern Economic Review* and Anwar Ibrahim quote from "Privatization Pioneer" in the 19 January 1995 issue.

136–7 Sick man of Asia information, including company investment, from "Shaking Manila out of its Slumber", *Business Week*, 31 October 1994.

137   Gongzalez quotes from "Taking off from Clark", *Asiaweek*, 6 July 1994. Subic Bay information from various sources including "The Selling of Subic", *Asiaweek*, 19 July 1996.

Koo quote from "Hong Kong East?", *Forbes*, 2 August 1993.

138   Leber quote from "Shaking Manila out of its Slumber", *Business Week*, 31 October 1994.

Business Times (Singapore) quote on India's growth from "India's 'Big Ship' Economy: Plenty of Room to Grow", in the 25 October 1994 issue.

139   *Far Eastern Economic Review* quote on India's capital stock from "Spinning Out of Control", in the 9 March 1995 issue.

139–40 George statement and *Far Eastern Economic Review* quote from "The India Boom?" in the 19 January 1995 issue.

141–41 Mahathir quote reported in "Co-operate for Global Commonwealth", *New Straits Times*, 14 November 1994. Freris statements from "Re-inventing the Asian Mircale", *Asiaweek*, 13 January 1995.

141   Asian investment from "The Pacific Century", *Forbes*, 15 July 1996.

Jennings quote from a speech given in Brussels, 16 September 1994.

142   Daewoo data from "Koreans Give Vietnam a Lift", *Washington Post*, 9 February 1996.

Proton quote reported in "Re-inventing the Asian Miracle", *Asiaweek*, 13 January 1995.

Il-suk quote from "Samsung and NEC Make Virtue of Necessity", *Financial Times*, 14 February 1995.

144   Japanese data from "Into China", *The Economist*, 16 March 1996; "Exporting a Surplus", *Far Eastern Economic Review*, 4 July 1996; and "The Pacific Century", *Forbes*, 15 July 1996.

Courtis quote from "Japan Inc. Alters Tactics to Target Asian Consumers", *The Asian Wall Street Journal*, 17 May 1994.

145–6   Data on foreign workers from "The Lure of Asia" and "Merry Go Round", both from the 3 February issue of *Far Eastern Economic Review*; "Give and Take", in the 25 May 1995 issue; "Welcome Exchange" in the 29 February 1996 issue; and "Asia's Labour Pains", *The Economist*, 26 August 1995.

147–8   Ramos quotes from "Cross-Border 'Growth Triangles' Promote

Prosperity in East Asia", *International Herald Tribune*, 30 November 1994.

148–9 *Asia Inc.* growth triangle information and Sopiee quote from "The Overdue Triumph of the Trade", in the April 1994 issue.

149 Jennings quote from a speech given in Brussels, 16 September 1994.

150 *The Asian Wall Street Journal* on the Great Wall from "The Not so Great Wall", in the 18 April 1994 issue.

151 Infrastructure projects in Asia reported in "Building the New Asia", *Business Week*, 28 November 1994.
Reed estimate from "The Race for the Investment Dollar", *South China Morning Post*, 5 November 1994.

153 Gokongwei and *The Asian Wall Street Journal* quote from "The Race is On", in the 18 April 1994 issue.

154 *Financial Times* quote on Pakistan's hub power project reported in "Public and Private Meet at the Hub", in the 31 October 1994 issue.

155 Multinational firms competing in Asia reported in "Building the New Asia", *Business Week*, 28 November 1994.
Fernstrom quote from "How to Pay for Super Projects", *Asian Business*, November 1994.
List of emerging regional players described in "The Race is On", *The Asian Wall Street Journal*, 18 April 1994.

157 *Asiamoney* quote from "Asia's Golden Age of Growth", November 1994 issue.
Asian Business quote on Asia's capital markets from "Here Comes the Money", in the May 1994 issue.

158 Asia's stock markets come of age information and *The Economist* quote on Asian markets from "A Survey of Asian Finance", a special report in the 12 November 1994 issue.

160 Dragon bond quote from "Here Comes the Money", *Asian Business*, May 1995. Additional information from "A Survey of Asian Finance", a special report in *The Economist*, 12 November 1994.

161 Vietnam's banking sector quote from "Foreign Help Wanted", *Far Eastern Economic Review*, 6 October 1994.

163 Param Curaraswamy quote from an interview by the author.
Corruption in China and Western diplomat quotes from "Hands

in Every Pocket", *Newsweek*, 28 March 1994.

Corruption in India information from "India's Biggest Turn-Off: Political Corruption", *Business Times* (Singapore), 9 March 1995.

164   Goh Chok Tong statement from "Pay Raise Plan Gets a Rise Out of Public", *Los Angeles Times*, 5 December 1994.

167   Asia's wealthiest from "The Pacific Century", *Forbes*, 15 July 1996.

Chapter 5: From Villages → Supercities

169   Urban animal projection from "Urbanization, Human Security and Survival", a document for the United Nation's Development Program "Asia Pacific 2000" by Anwar Fazal.

169–70 Many population figures are from "Asia's Choking Cities", an excellent article on the Asian population situation which appeared in *Newsweek*, 9 May 1994.

170–71 Rice miller quote from "Seeds of Despair", *Far Eastern Economic Review*, 3 April 1993.

171   Hong Kong information and Pryor quote reported in "The Lessons of Hong Kong", *Newsweek*, 9 May 1994.

171–2 Singapore model description, and George Yeo Yong Boon and Lee quotes from "Selling Success", *Asiaweek*, 13 July 1994.

174   Zhang Xinsheng statement from "In the City of Suzhou", *Washington Times*, 8 July 1994.

175   Government plans to move 440 million people reported in "Birth of the Instant City", *The Economist*, 10 September 1994.

176   Alice City project described in "Megacities, Mega-Solutions", *Asian Business*, February 1994.

Information on Malaysia's new capital city from "Malaysia's edifice complex", *The Economist*, 2 September 1995.

176–8 Information on migrants from various sources, including "China's Millions on the Move", *Newsweek*, 7 March 1994.

New York Times and Blum quotes from "China Migrants: Economic Engine, Social Burden", in the 29 June 1994 issue. *People's Daily* and Cai Haishan quote reported in "China's Millions on the Move", *Newsweek*, 7 March 1994. Fan Gang quotes from both articles.

178–9 Liu Binyan quote from "Peasants in Search of Urban Prosperity", *International Herald Tribune*, 30 May 1994.

The Economist quotes on Vietnam and poverty statistics from "The Call of the City", in the 4 March 1995 issue.

World Bank conclusions reported in "Countryside 'is key to Vietnam's development'", *Financial Times*, 24 February 1995.

180 Suchart Suksom quote from "Separate & Unequal", *Far Eastern Economic Review*, 14 April 1994.

Indonesian rural reforms and poverty, Asikin Mohamad and BRI quotes from "Rural Poverty Waning in SE Asia", *Washington Times*, 15 July 1994.

181 *Business Times* quote from "The Changing Face of Indonesian Agriculture", 10 March 1995.

181–2 Ifugao rice terraces and *Bangkok Post* quotes from "Progress Takes Toll on Eighth Wonder of the World", 16 March 1995 issue.

182 Chinese farmland statistics reported in "Farmland Decreases Drastically", *China Daily*, 10 February 1995.

182–3 Xishan farmer, *The Asian Wall Street Journal* and grain expert quotes from "As Industry Devours Land, China's Grain Imports Soar", in the 13 March 1995 issue.

184 *Bangkok Post* and Dr Ubonrat Siriyuvasak quotes appeared in "Where Angels Fear to Tread", in the 21 March 1995 issue.

The Economist quote on urban housing from "China Discovers All Mod Cons", in the 20 August 1994.

185 Beijing urban real estate prices from "No Place Like Home", *Far Eastern Economic Review*, 28 July 1994.

Bangkok Post on Land Reclamation Act and mother from Laem Chabang on "sacrifice for development" quotes from "Under Siege", which appeared in the 5 March 1995 issue.

186 Kastorius Sinaga quotes from "Land-Love Strong Among Villagers", *Jakarta Post*, 15 March 1995.

The Economist quote on Tianjin resident from "China Discovers All Mod Cons", in the 20 August 1994 issue.

187 Asia's emerging supercities list, and Denise Yue quote from "Asia's Supercities", *Business Week*, 24 April 1995.

World's tallest buildings reported in "The Great Asian Steeple Chase", *New York Times*, 25 June 1995.

188 Thai Farmers' Bank report from *Shipping Times* (Malaysia), 11 August 1995.

Chapter 6: From Labor-intensive ➜ *High Technology*

191   Sri Lanka telephone description from "Asian Telecommunications Guide", a supplement to *Asiamoney*, October 1994.

193–5 Feng quote from "New Strategies, New Industries as Taiwan Goes Global"; the ten strategic industries, subsidies given, and *International Herald Tribune* quote from "A Leading Source of Capital"; additional information on Taiwan from previous articles and "Economic Success Set to Continue"; all from a special advertising section in the *International Herald Tribune*, 10 October 1994.

196–7 Hsieh, Wu Tao-yuan and Yau You-wen quotes from "High Tech Taiwanese Come Home", *New York Times*, 19 July 1994. Quotes from Dr Lee from an interview by the author.

Hsieh sales estimate and little Singapore quote reported in "Now for Its Next Miracle", *Asia Inc.*, November 1994.

198   *Business Week* statement on PhD recipients and quotes about Asians returning home from "Have Skills, Will Travel—Homeward", *Business Week* special 21st Century Capitalism edition, 19 December 1994.

199–200 *Asian Business* quotes on Singapore and Korea from "Asia Chases R&D Successes", in the April 1994 issue.

200–1 Pradeep Singh and G. Jagannath Raju descriptions from *Business Week* article cited directly above.

Dewang Mehta, Vittal and Yourdon quotes appeared in "Competitive Advantages Through Indian Software Services", a special advertising supplement to *Forbes ASAP*, 5 December 1994.

201–4 Facilities in Singapore, *Business Week* quotes, Indian engineers, education centers and income information from "High Tech Jobs All Over the Map", *Business Week* special 21 Century Capitalism edition, December 1994.

204   Made in China quote from "China High-Tech Spree Pays Dividends", *Nikkei Weekly*, 7 November 1994.

205   *Business Week* quotes on Taiwan from "Very Well Made in Taiwan", a special advertising section in the 28 November 1994 issue.

206   *Business Week* quote on South Korea from "South korea, the New Titan of Technology", a special advertising section in the 28

November 1994 issue.

Political and Economic Risk Consultancy Ltd. and World Bank quotes appeared in "Go-Go Growth Points Up Shortage of Skilled Labor", *Los Angeles Times,* 29 November 1994.

207 *Far Eastern Economic Review* quote and information on graduates from "Failing Grade", in the 29 September 1994 issue.

208 Carkeek quote from "Acute Skilled-Labor Gap Exacts a Price in Thailand", *The Asian Wall Street Journal Weekly,* 19 September 1994.

209 Transmission system and Padilla quotes, AT&T sales, and information on high-tech purchase reported in "End of Export Curbs Spurs Technology Sales to China", *The Asian Wall Street Journal,* 2 January 1995. *The Asian Wall Street Journal* quote on transfer of brainpower appeared in "Telecom Firms Vie to Bring Latest Technology to China", in the 1 April 1994 issue.

210 Asia gets wired section from various sources, including "Asian Telecommunications Guide", a supplement to *Asiamoney,* October 1994; "Switched on", *Far Eastern Economic Review,* 24 November 1994; and "Telecommunications in Asia", *Far Eastern Economic Review,* 7 April 1994.

211 Kan quote from "Paving the Highway", *Asiaweek,* 14 September 1994.

Telephone and call data from "The Technology Revolution", *Asiaweek,* 15 December 1995; and *World Press Review,* March 1996.

212 *The Economist* information on Chinese market satellite needs reported in "The Long March Back to China", in the 5 November 1994 issue.

213 Skeldon quote and reverse flow estimates from *Asia Inc.,* August 1995.

Chapter 7: From Male Dominance → Emergence of Women

218 Solo quote from "Japan Discovers Woman power", *Fortune,* 19 June 1989.

219 Chinese statistics on family size and decision makers reported in "More Young Couples in Shaghai Go for One Child", *Straits*

Times, 17 May 1994; and "China, No-Child Families", *World Press Review*, May 1994.

Business Times (Singapore) quote on career women in Asia quote from "Women's Liberation, Asian-Style", in the 3 August 1994 issue.

220–21 Soin quotes from "Women's Groups Here Not 'Aping the West Blindly'", *Straits Times*, 14 March 1995.

221   Charatsri quote from "Alone in a Man's World", *Far Eastern Economic Review*, 12 January 1995.

Climaco quote from "Champion of the Working Woman", *New Straits Times*.

222   Studies on the need for managers in Indonesia reported in "Women in Management", *International Studies of Management & Organization*, Winter 1993–94.

222–3 Women in the service sector from *The Asian Economic Commentary*, Merrill Lynch, November 1994.

Korea and Japanese service sector women percentages from *Women of Japan and Korea: Community and Change*, edited by Joyce Geld and Marian Lief Palley, Temple University Press, 1994.

Male executive comment reported in "Leaping the Gender Gap in Asia", *Business Times* (Singapore), 8 November 1993.

223   Statistics on women managers reported in the Winter 1993–94 issue of *International Studies of Management & Organization*, "Competitive Frontiers, Asian Women in Management"; and *Competitive Frontiers, Women Managers in a Global Economy*, Blackwell Publishers, Oxford, 1994; both edited by Nancy J. Adler and Dafna N. Izzraelli.

224   Chin quote from "The Toothpaste and Bungalow Portfolio", *Forbes*, 14 March 1994.

Information on women financial experts from "Where to Put Your Money?", *Far Eastern Economic Review*, 19 October 1995.

226   Dr Chow data from an article in the 16 November 1993 issue of the *South China Morning Post*.

Zhang quote from "Successful Stories of Women CEOs", *China Daily*, 23 August 1994.

228   *China Wakes* by Nicholas D. Kristof and Sheryl WuDunn, Nicholas Brealey Publishing, London, 1994.

Meo quote from "Network of Chinese Rim Pacific", *Los Angeles*

Times, 22 July 1990.

229   Statistics on women entrepreneurs from various sources, including "Japanese Working Women Strike Back", *Fortune*, 31 May 1993; *International Studies of Management & Organization*, Winter 1993–94; *Competitive Frontiers, Women Managers in a Global Economy*, Blackwell; "The Woman Entrepreneur's Recipe for Success", *Business Times* (Singapore), 31 October 1994; and "Women's Economic Role Grows", *China Daily*, 11 June 1994; and *Women: Looking Beyond 2000*, United Nations, New York, 1995.

230   Chanut quote from "Iron Butterflies", *Fortune*, 7 October 1991. Kadir quote from "Housewife who Built Empire from Nothing", *Financial Times*, 9 June 1994.

231   Chiang quote reported in "The Woman Entrepreneur's Recipe for Success", *Business Times* (Singapore), 31 October 1994.
Khatijah Ahmad quote from "Into the Big Time", *Asiaweek*, 14 December 1994.

232   Ma quote from "The First Lady of Hong Kong", *Bazaar*, April 1994.
Mori description from "Doyenne of Fashion", *Far Eastern Economic Review*, 21 July 1994.
Tilaar quote from "Beauty Secrets", *Far Eastern Economic Review*, 24 November 1994.

234–5 D. Rounnag Jahn quote from "Asian Women Hear a Call to Politics", *China Daily*, 25 June 1994.
Women in office from "Women Rising", *Asiaweek*, 1 September 1995.

235   Hong Kong women in politics from "A Woman's Place", *Far Eastern Economic Review*, 12 January 1995.
Doi quote from "Outspoken Doi Tackles New Goals", *Nikkei Weekly*, 28 November 1994.
Asiaweek quote on the Philippines and political descriptions from "Women Power", *Asiaweek*, 9 June 1995.

236   Supatra Masdit quote from "Helping Women into Politics", *Newsweek*, 30 May 1994.
Kumaratunga quote from "Sri Lanka Swears in Woman President", *Boston Globe*, 13 November 1994.

237–8 Zia quote from "A Woman Leader for a Land that Defies Islamic

Stereotypes", *New York Times*, 17 October 1993.

Wu quotes from "Winning Ways of Madam Wu", *South China Morning Post*, 6 July 1995.

239 Quotes and material on population demographics from "Disappearing Girls", *Asiaweek*, 3 March 1995.

240 Charatsri quote from "Alone in a Man's World", *Far Eastern Economic Review*, 12 January 1995.

Viravaidya quote from "Flesh-Trade Options", *Far Eastern Economic Review*, 14 April 1994.

Chakrapand quote from "Thai Women Can Be Educated to Reject Prostitution", *The Asian Wall Street Journal Weekly*, 31 October 1994.

Amihan Abueva information from "Suffer the Little Children", *Newsweek*, 25 July 1994.

242–3 Meng quote from an interview with the author.

Statistics regarding women and education from *International Studies of Management & Organization*, Winter 1993–94; and *Competitive Frontiers, Women Managers in a Global Economy*, Blackwell.

244 Kartini Day described in *International Studies of Management & Organization*, Winter 1993–94.

245–6 *Asiaweek* quote on Muslim and Islamic communities from "Women's Rights" in the 17 November 1993 issue.

Quote on rural China and India from "Narrowing the Gender Gap", *Asiaweek*, 17 March 1995.

248 Liou Fey Ying quote translated from Global Views' Executive Women's Special, 1992.

Chapter 8: From West → East

252 Lee and Tsang Yok Sing quotes from "China's Cloud Over Hong Kong: Is '97 here?", *New York Times*, 5 July 1995.

Anson Chan's quote from "Keeping the Faith", *Sunday Morning Post*, 23 April 1995.

253 House quote from "Why Hong Kong Must Remain in Hong Kong", *The Asian Wall Street Journal*, 7 June 1995.

255 Keating quote and Australian data from "Australia's Place in Asia", *Asiaweek*, 31 March 1995.

257 Hunt quote from "America is Short-Sighted on Asia", *The Wall Street Journal*, 6 July 1995.

258 Rhee quote from an interview by the author.

259 US census data reported in "Southeast Asians Highly Dependent on Welfare in U.S.", *New York Times*, 19 May 1994.
Lai quote from a converrsation with the author.

260–1 Ow Yang Hsuan observation made in conversation with the author. World Bank data reported in "Asia's Welfare", *Far Eastern Economic Review*, 23 June 1994.
Transpacific and Aoyama quotes, and survey on Asians in business from "Hot and in Demand", in the November 1994 issue.

261–2 Profiles appeared in "Masters of the Deal", *Transpacific*, November 1993. Asian film maker information from "Hot and in Demand", *Transpacific*, November 1994.
Some Asian numbers from "The Pacific Century", *Forbes*, 15 July 1996.

262–3 *American Demographics* and Yu quotes, and data on Asian-Americans in the suburbs from "Asians in the Suburbs", *American Demographics*, May 1994.

264 Lam quotes, list of Silicon Valley companies started by Asian-Americans, and Asian organizations from "Asian Immigrants New Leaders in Silicon Valley", *New York Times*, 14 January 1992.

265–6 Section on Yaohan Plaza and Kono statement drawn from "An Asian in the Great Midwest", *American Demographics*, May 1994.

267–8 Issey Miyake quotes and information on designers, Feng and Tam quotes all from "Asian Designers Go West", *The Asian Wall Street Journal*, 15 July 1994.

270 Mahbubani quotes from "The Pacific Way", *Foreign Affairs*, January/February 1995.

271–2 List of forty-something leaders and *Asiaweek* quotes from "Generation 2000" in the 5 October 1994 issue.

272–3 Anwar Ibrahim quotes from "Anwar, We Need a Truely Just Order", *The Star*, 7 October 1994.

274 Wong quote from an interview by the author.

277 Ho and *Asiaweek* quotes from "Learn the Language that Has Economic Value", *Asiaweek*, 15 December 1993.

278 Sun quote from "Will China Play by the Rules?", *Business Ethics*, May/June 1995.

Index

With thanks to...

My deepest gratitude to the following friends for their contribution to *Megatrends Asia*.

Singapore

Professor Tommy Koh

Mr Alan Chan

Professor Chen Charng Ning

Mr Chew Kah Guan

Mrs Chin Ean Wah

Assoc Prof Chin Kin Wah

Mr Chong Huai Seng

Mr Leslie Fong

Mrs Theresa Foo

Mr Goh Kian Chee

Mr Richard Hoon

Mr Vikram Khanna

Mr Koh Buck Song

Assoc Prof Koh Tai Ann

Mr Peter Kong

Mr Kua Phek Long

Mr Kwa Chong Seng

Dr Lee Suan Yew

Mr Lee Teong Sang

Dr Catherine Lim

Mr Lim Wen Chyi

Ms Gretchen Liu

Mr Lim Jim Koon

Mr Low Beng Tin

Mr Stuart Merrilees

Mr Harpreet Singh Nehal

Mr Ng Gek Nga

Mr Ng Seng Leong

Mr Sutjahjo Ngaserin

Mr Gophinath Pillai

BG Tan Yong Soon

Mr Gordon Seow

Dr Kanwaljit Soin

Mr Tan Cheng Gay

Mr Tan Hup Thye

Mr Tan Kwi Kin

Mr Wilson Tan

Dr Teh Kok Peng

Mr Tong Chong Heong

Assoc Prof Wee Chow Hou

Mr Alfred H K Wong

Mr Wong Meng Quang

Mr Steve S V Wong

Mr Y Y Wong

Mdm Yeong Yoon Ying

Mr Zainul Abidin Rasheed

Mr Arun Mahizhuan

Mr Ooi Giok Ling

Mr Yap Mui Teng

Mr Gwee Wee Chen

Prof Dr Chan Heng Chee

Jakarta

Dr Djisman S Simandjuntak

Professor M Sadli

Professor Haryati Soebadio

Mr Wijarso

Dr R B Suhartono

Lt Gen Poerbo Soewondo

Maj Gen Pandji Soesilo

Dr Johan Syahperi Saleh

Colonel Mulya Wibisono

Colonel Sardan Marbun

Mr Marzuki Darusman

Mr Djoko Sudjatmiko

Ambassador A B Loebis

Mr Wahid Supriadi

Maj Gen Soebiyakto

Mr Jakob Oetama

Ms Toeti Adhitama

Ms Annie Bertha Simamora

Professor Magnis Suseno

Ms Pia Alisjahbana

Ms Myra Sidharta

Prof Suhadi Mangkusuwondo

Dr Mudji Sutrisno

Mr Sofjan Wanandi

Dr Willem B Wanandi

Ms Shanti L Poesposoetjipto

Mr Steve Sondakh

Ms Clara Joewono

Mr Djohan Effendi

Mr Soendaroe Rachmad

Mr Neil Martin

Ms Natalia Soebagijo

Shanghai

Wang Dao Ham	Dr Tang Yun wei	Prof Cheng En Fu
Prof Wei Guo Zhang	Michael Sun	Jin Shun Fa
Yue Yao-Xing		

Suzhou

Chen Hao	Zhao Qiubo	Wang Shi Qing

Kuala Lumpur

Y Bhg Tan Sri Zainal Abidin Sulong	YB Mr Chua Jui Meng	Dr Rozali Mohamed Ali
Tuan Haji Ramli Othman	Dr Stephen Leong	Prof Dr Ariffin Bey
Y Bhg Tan Sri Ramon Navaratnam	Y Bhg Tan Sri Geh Ik Cheong	Dr Chandra Muzaffar
Mr Abdul Rahman Adnan	Mr Abu Bakar Hj Abdul Karim	Dr Chong Kwong Yuan
Mr A Navamukundan	Dr Peter Shephard	Mr Rustam Sani
Prof Shamsul Amri Baharuddin	Mr Anwar Fazal	Dr Tan Tat Wai

Hong Kong

Mr L Gordon Crovitz	Ms Anna Wu	Mr Ronnie Chan
Mr Jimmy Lai	Mr Alan Smith	Mr John Hung
Prof Wang Gung Wu	Prof Ming K Chan	Mr Martin Lee, QC
Mr Daniel Ng Yat-Chiu	Mr Barry Wain	Mr Richard C M Wong
Mr Winston W Y Siu	Mr Luis P Lorenzo, Jr	Mr Willy P Y Shee
Mr Patrick Chong	Ma Vivian Yuchengo (Locsin)	Mr Anurut Vong vanij
Mr Jose Antonio U Gongzalez	Mr Edmund Cheng	Mr Chuck Theisen
Emily Lau	Paul Cheng	Peter Clark

Taiwan

Ms Dianne Ying	Mr Huang-Hsiung Huang	Mr S C Ho
Mr Wen C Ko	Mr Yuan-Tseh Lee	Mr Y C Lo
Mr Casper Shih	Mr Yen-Shiang Shih	Mr Shen-Nan Tong
Mr Hsung-Hsiung Tsai	Mr Yung Wei	Mr Yoshisuke Iinuma
Mr Yoshikazu Ishizuka	Mr Thomas F Jordan	Mr Mikio Kato
Ms Yuri Konno	Mr Moritaka Moriuchi	Ms Akiko Murai
Mr Kiyoshi Nakamura	Mr Toshishige Namai	Dr A A Sultan
Ms Merle Aiko Okawara		

Manila

Ms Gloria L Tan Climaco
Mr Felipe Alfonso
Mr Jaime Augusto Zobel de Ayala
Dr Ma Luisa Doronila

Mr Washington SyCip
Mr Emil Javier
Ms Cynthia Rose Bautista
Dr Florangel Braid

Mr Peter Garrucho
Mr Jose L Chuisia, Jr
De Ledivina Carino

Seoul

Mr Dong-Se CHA
Mr Kyung-Won KIM
Mr Suk-Chae LEE
Mr Sang-Woo RHEE
Mr Soo-Gil YOUNG

Mr Dae-Whan CHANG
Mr Kwang-Doo KIM
Mr Bong-Sung OUM
Mr Byung-Nak SONG

Mr Dong-Sung CHO
Mr Bon-Ho KOO
Mr Ung-Suh PARK
Mr Sang-Mok SUH

Bangkok

Prof Charas Suwanwela MD
Khunying Supatra Masdit
Prof Dr Vicharn Panich
Prof Dr Phaichitr Uathavikul
Prof Dr Jetana NarkVachara
Mrs Vasana Mututanont

Dr Krasae Chanawongse
Dr Chai-Anan Samudavanija
Mr Phayap Phyormyont
Prof Dr Yongyuth Yuthavong
Mr Staporn Kavitanon
Prof Nitaya Suwanwela MD

Dr Supachai Panitchpakdi
Prof Dr Sippanondha Ketudat
Khunying Thongtip Ratanarat
Mr Staporn Jinachitra
Mrs Chutaporn Lambasara
Assoc Prof Dr Salag Dhabanandana

Assoc Prof Dr Praneee Kullavanijaya Assoc Prof Dr Amara Pongsapich

Bombay

Mr Prakash Hebalkar
Mr Parvez Damania
Dr Kirit Parikh
Mr Darryl D'Monte
Mr Pratap Padode

Mr Kishore Chaukar
Mr Kiron Kasbekar
Mr Shrikant Inamdar
Mr M R Pai
Mr Prakash Idnani

Mr Nadir Godrej
Ms Nazneen Karmali
Prof Suhas Sukhatme
Ms Meena Menon
Mr Albert Lewis

Nanjing

Chen De Ming
Prof Colin Chiu
Prof Yu Shoyi
Hu Si
Wu Rui-Lin
Prof Wu Keming

Prof Lin-Yue Lu
Prof Marielle C C Teo
Prof Zheng Ming Yuan
Prof Shuming Zhao
Huang Ziao Ping
Prof Wang Zhiguo

Prof Chen Yi
Hingrong Lian
Charles G Rogalske
Prof Yang Xiu
Prof Zhang Yongtao
Zhang Jian Feng